Fahri Karakaya, PhD
Erdener Kaynak, PhD
Editors

How to Utilize New Information Technology in the Global Marketplace: A Basic Guide

Pre-publication REVIEWS, COMMENTARIES, EVALUATIONS . . .

"The significant issues of internationalization of business and the utilization of information technology are blended together in a relevant, practical, and easy-to-follow presentation. This book is a worthy supplement to any course in international business."

Mahmoud M. Yasin, PhD
Associate Professor
of Management,
East Tennessee State University

More pre-publication
REVIEWS, COMMENTARIES, EVALUATIONS . . .

"The editors should be congratulated for producing a volume with a good deal of merit. My overall impression is that a concise, well-written source is now available to instructors considering new information technologies for teaching international business subject matter. The papers selected for inclusion in this volume offer the instructor better insights into the use of computers–from data retrieval techniques and databases to simulations and an expert system. If international business instructors are considering the use of computer-related tools for their class, this volume offers a series of evaluations of the latest computer information techniques and tools with an eye to their utility as teaching tools.

The main strength of this volume is that all the chapters are written from a user's perspective–the authors have class-tested each of their reported techniques and computer software. Each chapter is well worth reading. I believe the editors have done an excellent job of selecting such a variety of topics."

Ronald S. Rubin, PhD
Professor of Marketing,
University of Central Florida

"Increased global competition coupled with the revolutionary pace of technological innovation make this collection particularly relevant. Its timeliness is greatly enhanced by the curricular reexamination and overhaul underway in many business schools. Future managers will need to work in global environments using information technologies.

Proliferation of computer databases such as Disclosure/Worldscope, National Trade Data Bank, the World Trade, and others require that both students and faculty as well as managers become familiar with, and adapt to using these sources. Such training needs to begin at the college level if graduates are to have an edge, giving their employers a better chance to compete successfully. Managers who know how to use these tools will have the edge sought by the new cross-sectional corporation."

Michael V. Laric, PhD
Associate Dean and Professor
of Marketing
Robert G. Merrick School of Business

More pre-publication
REVIEWS, COMMENTARIES, EVALUATIONS . . .

"**M**ost international business textbooks on the market today neglect the wealth of information sources available to the student. Consequently, the student may be fairly well prepared theoretically, but have little ability to solve applied international business problems.

What I liked most about this book was the overview chapters of various international databases available to the student and how these databases could be used to solve specific case problems. Furthermore, the hands-on approach to these chapters makes the prospect of teaching international business much more enjoyable for the instructor. Last, by developing a proficiency with 'technological' tools, students acquire a skill that is easily transferable to other college courses and to their eventual business careers."

Linda Ann Riley, PhD
Director, Center for Economic Development Research;
Associate Professor,
Department of Marketing,
New Mexico State University

"**H**ow to Utilize New Information Technology in the Global Marketplace: A Basic Guide* should make excellent supplemental reading material to introduce students to the interactive worlds of computer software and international business.

The text is an outstanding tool for educators who are seeking to incorporate computer software applications in the classroom. Through a collection of several research papers, it provides students as well as educators with an abundance of knowledge and resources pertaining to computer software applications in the field of international business and management."

Kamlesh T. Mehta, DBA
Director of Center
for Global Business Studies,
St. Mary's University

International Business Press
An Imprint of The Haworth Press, Inc.

How to Utilize New Information Technology in the Global Marketplace
A Basic Guide

INTERNATIONAL BUSINESS PRESS
Erdener Kaynak, PhD
Executive Editor

New, Recent, and Forthcoming Titles:

International Business Handbook edited by V. H. (Manek) Kirpalani

Sociopolitical Aspects of International Marketing edited by Erdener Kaynak

How to Manage for International Competitiveness edited by Abbas J. Ali

International Business Expansion into Less-Developed Countries: The International Finance Corporation and Its Operations by James C. Baker

Product-Country Images: Impact and Role in International Marketing edited by Nicolas Papadopoulos and Louise A. Heslop

Multinational Strategic Alliances edited by Refik Culpan

Market Evolution in Developing Countries: The Unfolding of the Indian Market by Subhash C. Jain

A Guide to Successful Business Relations with the Chinese: Opening the Great Wall's Gate by Huang Quanyu, Richard Andrulis, and Chen Tong

Industrial Products: A Guide to the International Marketing Economics Model by Hans Jansson

Euromarketing: Effective Strategies for International Trade and Export edited by Erdener Kaynak and Pervez N. Ghauri

Globalization of Consumer Markets: Structures and Strategies edited by Salah S. Hassan and Erdener Kaynak

International Negotiating: A Primer for American Business Professionals by Michael Kublin

How to Utilize New Information Technology in the Global Marketplace: A Basic Guide edited by Fahri Karakaya and Erdener Kaynak

The Global Business: Four Key Marketing Strategies edited by Erdener Kaynak

How to Utilize New Information Technology in the Global Marketplace

A Basic Guide

Fahri Karakaya, PhD
Erdener Kaynak, PhD
Editors

International Business Press
An Imprint of The Haworth Press, Inc.
New York • London • Norwood (Australia)

658.4058
H847

Published by

International Business Press, an imprint of The Haworth Press, Inc., 10 Alice Street, Binghamton, NY 13904-1580

Library of Congress Cataloging-in-Publication Data

How to utilize new information technology in the global marketplace: a basic guide
    Karakaya, Erdener Kaynak (editors).
       p.   cm.
    Includes bibliographical references and index.
    ISBN 1-56024-900-5 (acid free paper).
    1. Business–Data processing. 2. International business enterprises–Data processing. 3. Information technology. 4. Information resources management. 5. Information storage and retrieval systems–Business. 6. Expert systems. I. Karakaya, Fahri. II. Kaynak, Erdener.
    HF5548.2.U78 1994
  658.4'038'011–dc20   94-17914
                                                                  CIP

CONTENTS

Chapter 9. Electronic On-Line Data Retrieval
in International Business   **191**
    Fred Miller
    Linda Gillespie Miller

Chapter 10. International Accounting
in the Information Age   **219**
    Beryl Barkman

ABOUT THE EDITORS

Fahri Karakaya, PhD, is Professor of Marketing and Director of the MBA program at the University of Massachusetts, Dartmouth. He has conducted numerous consulting projects in the areas of market entry and marketing research, and operates the Market Research and Data Analysis Group, a marketing research firm in Westport, Massachusetts. The author of the book *Barriers to Entry and Market Entry Decisions: A Guide to Marketing Executives*, Dr. Karakaya has published in the *Journal of Marketing* and other refereed journals and has made numerous presentations in national conferences. His many research interests include strategic marketing, marketing research techniques, consumer behavior, and computers and marketing education. He was chair of the 1991 American Marketing Association Microcomputers in Marketing Education National Conference. Dr. Karakaya is a member of the American Marketing Association, the Academy of Marketing Science, the Academy of Management, and the International Management Development Association.

Erdener Kaynak, PhD, is Professor of Marketing at the School of Business Administration at the Pennsylvania State University at Harrisburg. He has extensive teaching, research, consulting, and advising experiences on five continents, in over thirty countries. A prolific author, Dr. Kaynak has published 18 books and over 150 articles in refereed scholarly and professional journals on international marketing and cross-national/cultural consumer behavior in a number of languages. One of his books was translated into Chinese and another one into Japanese. He has served on the Board of Governors of the Academy of Marketing Science and currently serves in the capacity of Director and Executive Vice-President of International Management Development Association (IMDA). Dr. Kaynak also serves on a dozen or so U.S. and European-based marketing and international business journal review boards and is Executive Editor for International Business Press (IBP) as well as being Senior Editor (International Business) for The Haworth Press, Inc., where he serves as Editor of *Journal of Global Marketing, Journal of International Consumer Marketing, Journal of*

Teaching in International Business, Journal of International Food and Agribusiness Marketing, and *Journal of Euromarketing.* As a Guest Editor, he has prepared special issues for a number of leading U.S. and European journals. He was also the organizer and Chair or Co-chair of seven major international conferences. Dr. Kaynak is also listed in *Who's Who in America* and *Who's Who in Advertising.*

CONTRIBUTORS

Abdel M. Agami, PhD, Professor of Accounting, Old Dominion University, Norfolk, VA

Beryl Barkman, PhD, Associate Professor, University of Massachusetts, North Dartmouth, MA

S. Tamer Cavusgil, PhD, Professor of Marketing, Michigan State University, East Lansing, MI

John William Clarry, PhD, Assistant Professor of Business Administration, Upsala College, East Orange, NJ

Lucette B. Comer, PhD, Associate Professor of Marketing, Florida International University, Miami, FL

Cüneyt Evirgen, PhD, Assistant Professor of Marketing, Michigan State University, East Lansing, MI

Snorri Gislason, MBA, The University of West Florida, Pensacola, FL

Richard K. Harper, PhD, Assistant Professor of Economics, The University of West Florida, FL

Gary P. Kearns, MBA, Senior Vice President, Shawmut Bank, Boston, MA

Fred Miller, PhD, Professor of Marketing, Murray State University, Murray, KY

Linda Gillespie Miller, MACT, Systems Analyst, University of Kentucky, Murray, KY

Michel Mitri, PhD, Systems Analyst, Michigan State University, East Lansing, MI

J.A.F. Nicholls, PhD, Associate Professor of Marketing, Florida International University, Miami, FL

Kate Jones-Randall, MSLIS, Business and Economics Librarian, University of Massachusetts, North Dartmouth, MA

Edward W. Schmitt, PhD, Associate Professor of Marketing, Villanova University, Villanova, PA

Richard Sjolander, PhD, Associate Professor of Marketing, The University of West Florida, Pensacola, FL

K. Venkataraman, MBA, Systems Specialist, Ford New Holland, New Holland, PA

Preface

This book is intended for use in international business/management, international marketing, and international accounting courses as a supplemental textbook. In addition, the material covered in this book can be utilized as a training tool for business executives who have an interest in international business. Examples using step-by-step instructions are included to teach the use of various computer software packages and databases without the complexities of using a computer.

Fahri Karakaya
Erdener Kaynak

Chapter 1

Recent Developments in International Business Education and Practice

Fahri Karakaya
Erdener Kaynak

INTRODUCTION

International business education and practice have shown dramatic changes during the last decade because of more emphasis placed on global trade by the U.S. and other governments, and because of innovations taking place in computer information technology. Academicians and practitioners have been working together to develop new computer software programs. Recent developments in the areas of expert systems, computer databases, and simulation games have added different dimensions to the international trade practice and to the international business curriculum at business schools around the world.

In recent years, lower prices of hardware and software, and availability of qualified user support personnel have facilitated and accelerated the utilization of new information technology at colleges, universities, government agencies, and in business organizations. Although there is very little research concerning the extent of the use of expert systems, international databases, and simulation by businesses, the majority of businesses seek assistance from the U.S. Department of Commerce Databases. Also, a survey conducted by Berman and McNeeley (1990) showed that in over 95% of corporate marketing departments, microcomputers were used by nonclerical marketing personnel.

COMPUTER UTILIZATION IN U.S. BUSINESS SCHOOLS

According to the Ninth Annual UCLA Survey of Business School Computer Usage (Frand and Britt 1992), 171 schools re-

1

ported having a total of 35,530 microcomputers with an average of 223 per school. Figure 1 shows the average system per school and average percentage growth from 1985 to 1992. The average system per school had almost tripled from 1986 to 1992. However, as expected, the average growth rate had slowed down from 64% in 1986 to just 4% in 1992.

EXPECTATIONS FROM BUSINESS SCHOOLS

A study of 127 U.S. firms with international operations showed that most firms preferred international managers with overseas experience. However, most undergraduate and graduate students do not have overseas experience nor are they in a position to gain international business experience before graduating. Courses such as international business finance, international accounting, international marketing, international law, and academic or special executive development training programs serve as close substitutes for overseas experience (Reynolds and Rice 1988). In recent years, there have also been efforts on the part of some U.S. business schools to introduce culturally focused and culturally enhanced courses into the business curriculum with an eye towards making the future graduates more fine tuned with international market realities. Business curriculum internationalization efforts supported by the American Assembly of Collegiate Schools of Business (AACSB) are developments in the right direction.

Lane (1992) reflects on the tasks facing educators. These tasks include: (1) teaching students to think globally; (2) exposing students to international dimensions of business and management, and (3) developing students that can perform effectively as managers in a global economy. Finney and Von Glinow (1988) claim that neither academic nor organizational approaches are preparing U.S. managers adequately for successful careers as international managers. These researchers propose joint programs undertaken by organizations and business schools. Interestingly, however, in internationalization of the business curriculum, most business programs in the U.S. have added an international marketing course as a quick fix (Larson 1991). A course in international marketing, which only deals with marketing issues, is not enough to prepare students for

FIGURE 1. Microcomputer Availability and Annual Growth Rate at Business Schools*

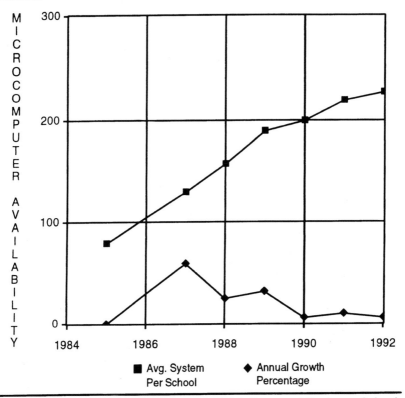

■ Avg. System Per School ◆ Annual Growth Percentage

*Data Obtained from the Ninth Annual UCLA Survey of Business School Computer Usage

doing business in an international arena. Of course, there is no business course that can match the business experience gained in a foreign country, but computer based instructional technologies may provide the training needed in an economically feasible and timely manner in the student's home country (Cornwell and Bruce 1991).

Although many business schools have integrated a variety of computer use into their business programs, the number of schools employing computers in their international business courses is expected to be relatively small. The same is also true for international businesses.

Ellen, Bearden, and Sharma (1991) report that users are not motivated to adopt to many technological innovations introduced by firms. This is mainly because of "resistance to change." According to Schein (1985), people do not resist to new technology, but to the possible changes that the new technology may bring. To be globally and domestically competitive, utilization of new technologies by businesses is a must. Similarly, in order to be effectively prepared for future jobs, business students need to know how to access international business databases and learn how to run international business companies by utilizing the existing databases, simulation and expert systems in their business educations. This kind of process, of course, necessitates instructors of business courses to change first and to be a change agent also.

SPECIAL OVERSEAS BUSINESS EDUCATION PROGRAMS

In addition to utilizing computer technology in international business courses, some colleges and universities have changed their traditional ways of teaching international business. Some universities conduct student exchange programs and overseas field trips. According to Vertesi (1992), there are two basic organizational structures which predominate study abroad and exchange programs in business schools around the world. The first and most commonly used model in North America is a highly centralized Study Abroad Office. In most cases, these type of programs are funded by the central administrations. In a decentralized model, on the other hand, the business schools control their own exchange programs. Thus, the resources are allocated locally to some sort of Faculty Study Abroad Office. Short overseas programs, such as the two-week summer course in Reims, France, offered by Northeastern University, expose graduate students to experiential learning in an overseas environment (Sarathy 1990). Texas Christian University's study abroad program in Cologne, Germany is another successful example of such programs (Boatler 1990). University of Massachusetts Dartmouth has a two-week field trip abroad, designed to study how overseas businesses operate. Recent trips for the university's students included Great Britain, France, and Russia.

University of British Columbia has had experience with an island program in international studies. In this program, students travel in a group from their home university to a foreign country to study. Local students from the foreign nation are not mixed into the classes. The classes are taught in the students' regular language of study, and faculty are from the home university. These programs are a less stressful experience for students, although at the cost of less cultural interaction (Tretheway 1992). Other universities and colleges also have similar programs in both graduate and undergraduate international business education. Northern State University in South Dakota began a new international business major within the school of business in 1989. According to Hendon (1989), the objectives of the program are to (1) prepare students to understand America's trading partners, and (2) teach the technical knowledge needed in the international business environment.

Boston University's International Graduate Management Programs had grown from 111 students in 1980 to 1,400 in 1990. This university's foreign sites include London, Brussels, Rome, and Israel. The university has formed alliances with local institutions that provide market access, facilities, knowledge of local business and political practices, and contacts with faculty and representatives from other institutions (Pendergast 1991).

SOURCES OF SECONDARY DATA IN INTERNATIONAL BUSINESS

There are a variety of government and other agencies that provide data on international markets. Malhotra (1992) gives a good listing of these sources and some of the services they offer.[1] In the U.S., these sources include the following:

1. U.S. Department of Commerce;
2. Agency for International Development;
3. Small Business Administration;
4. Export-Import Bank of the United States;
5. Department of Agriculture;
6. Department of State;
7. Department of Labor, and
8. Port Authority of New York and New Jersey.

In addition to a number of publications and computerized databases, the U.S. Department of Commerce also offers services such as a foreign buyer program, matchmaker events, trade missions, an export contact list, and custom statistical service for exporters. A number of international organizations located in the U.S. are also good sources of international secondary data. For example, United Nations, World Bank, and other international agencies have micro-economic data for the countries around the world. The major international organizations are listed below:

1. United Nations;
2. Organization for Economic Cooperation and Development;
3. International Monetary Fund;
4. World Bank;
5. International Chambers of Commerce;
6. Business International;
7. Euromonitor;
8. World-Casts;
9. Industry Data;
10. Commission of the European Communities to the United States, and
11. Japanese External Trade and Research Organization (JETRO).

Firms can also seek information from organizations located in foreign countries. Foreign governments, trade associations, and marketing research firms are good sources of secondary data. For some countries (i.e., mostly underdeveloped and developing countries), however, it may be necessary to obtain data from more than a single source because inconsistencies exist among different reporting agencies.

UTILIZING COMPUTERS IN INTERNATIONAL BUSINESS

Most businesses utilize computers for the purpose of analyzing marketing research data. Gathering information about prospective customers in international markets can be expensive and time consuming without the help of computers. Making sound managerial decisions is possible without actually going into foreign markets. New software packages in expert systems and simulation are utilized as aids in decision making. Expert systems and simulation softwares can also be employed in executive training and development. The subsequent chapters of this book illustrate how organizations and students of international business can utilize computers. A brief discussion of databases and other developments are presented here.

Computer Databases

A variety of international database packages are currently available on the market. Some of these databases are easily accessible and at a very reasonable price. In fact, several of them are free to those who wish to use the federal government collections at most university or college libraries. The most widely available databases and data retrieval services include the following: (1) National Trade Data Bank; (2) Disclosure/Worldscope; (3) World Trade Exporter; (4) World Trader; (5) PC Globe/MacGlobe; (6) Lotus One Source CD/Corporate: International Public Companies, and (7) DIALOG Business Connection.

National Trade Data Bank: This is probably the most popular database that is utilized in international business courses. It is available from the U.S. Department of Commerce and updated monthly. Universities and colleges with federal government collections already have this database. It contains approximately 100,000 documents from the CIA, Federal Reserve System, Export Import Bank, and Overseas Private Investment Corporation.

Disclosure/Worldscope: This database has data on 6,000 companies from 24 countries. It is similar to the Lotus database available in many university libraries. SIC codes and industry names can be used for searching and identifying new markets. It contains data on sales, income and growth rates, foreign assets, return on assets, and asset turnover.

Word Trade Exporter: The World Trade Exporter provides a link to over 850 external databases. It is designed to aid small and medium-sized U.S. businesses. It has 160 trade topics, a trade directory, a trade bibliography, and a notepad used for editing and notetaking purposes.

World Trader: The World Trader profiles 125 countries and supplies regional maps. In addition, it lists 2,500 international trade shows and analyzes trade data by country.

PC Globe/MacGlobe: This database contains geographical, demographical, political, climate, currency conversion, and economic information on 190 countries. It also has an atlas with geographic databases.

Lotus One Source CD/Corporate: International Public Companies: This software is one of five databases under the CD/Corporate brand name. This and another database called CD/Investment International Equities have an international focus. CD/Corporate: International Public Companies (CD/CIPC) utilizes data from *Extel Financial Card Services,* an on-line financial information service for international companies. It contains data on 9,404 companies. Company annual reports, profit and loss statements, historical financial data, and information on corporate backgrounds are included in the database.

CD/CIPC allows users to perform investment analysis, analysis of mergers and acquisitions, financial historical analysis of companies and industries, and analysis of competitors. Users can download text and data into Lotus 1-2-3 spreadsheet and other software programs, including word processing packages such as WordPerfect, MS-Word, and others. Thus, one can transfer mailing lists for special direct mail promotion or transform data into spreadsheets and statistical software packages for statistical analysis.

Electronic Data Retrieval (CD-ROM and On-Line Data Retrieval): An example of this type of service is the well-known "DIALOG Business Connection." Using this service can be costly to novice consumers, since they have to pay for time logged onto the system. Some examples of the databases that exist in the DIALOG Business Connection include Dun and Bradstreet International, Business International, Infomat International Business, and PTS International Forecasts.

Computer Simulation

The ability to obtain information by skillful observation is a talent needed by managers. "This skill is essentially the ability to learn how to learn; gathering information in real time, reformulating problem definitions, drawing tentative conclusions, taking initial action, and feeding the results of those actions back into the process." (Lane 1992, p. 135). Students and managers can learn these techniques by utilizing computer simulation. In fact, Senge (1990, p. 313) calls the computer simulation the "technology of learning organization" and claims that personal computers are making it possible to integrate learning about complex team interactions with learning about complex business interactions. The addition of equivocality and dynamic complexity are essential ingredients to making the computer simulation more realistic. These additions can be thought of as international management's equivalent of wind tunnels or practice fields (Lane 1992).

Currently there are only two simulation packages, "Export to Win!" and "The Management of Strategy in the Global Market Place," for use in international business or international marketing. The Export to Win! simulation software is marketed by Southwest Publishing Company, well-known and widely used in international business courses. Thus, firms can experiment with the computer simulations and enter hypothetical foreign markets to gain experience.

The Management of Strategy in the Global Market Place is a new simulation software and is described in detail in Chapter 5. There are advantages of utilizing an international business simulation software in teaching students or in training business executives. The first and foremost advantage is that they allow users to learn about international business practices and strategy development without the risk of losing actual dollars if firms were to venture in international markets. Simulations represent the "real world" to a great extent and provide insights that are difficult to gain in traditional international business or marketing courses. Also, users learn and develop managerial skills from the feedback provided by the simulation software.

Expert Systems

"The Country Consultant©" is the only expert systems software available for use in international marketing courses. Presently, this software is in the developmental stage and it has been used as a teaching tool. It includes 39 markets, 98 industries, and 11 entry modes into international markets. It is mainly an application of artificial intelligence to international marketing. This software includes processed marketing information in the form of expert knowledge. The Country Consultant© is designed to assist marketing executives and marketing students in making informed market entry decisions into international markets.

DISCUSSION AND CONCLUSIONS

As the number of available international databases, simulation games, and expert systems increases, and they are made known to international business executives and faculty teaching in this discipline, the number of users will also increase. In utilizing the information technology in international business or in business curriculums, it is necessary for executive trainers and faculty members to commit themselves to spend time learning these developments. In addition, adequate user support is needed to assist faculty and students in college or university environments.

The databases mentioned in this chapter and others can be used to assign student term projects intended to gather data on foreign countries, foreign competition, and methods of exporting overseas. It is necessary, however, to caution the users of the databases about database accuracy! As pointed out by Mahmoud and Rice (1988), there are some practices followed by database suppliers that could produce unreliable information. Therefore, users of databases may sometimes have to cross-validate the gathered information by utilizing more than a single database.

Instructors of international business courses can utilize computer simulation games and expert systems in an attempt to meet the needs of businesses and better train students for the real world. Again, user support is needed to assist faculty and students in integrating the simulation games or expert systems packages, especially when faculty and students first begin to use them. Using the computer simulation games, expert systems, or even the databases requires a considerable amount of time investment on behalf of the faculty and executive trainers or consultants. However, once learned, the computer assisted teaching tools are worth the investment.

END OF CHAPTER QUESTIONS

1. What are some possible sources of international secondary data?

2. Overall, in what areas can managers involved in international business utilize computers today?
3. Explain the difference(s) between microcomputer-based databases and the electronic data retrieval (on-line data retrieval)?
4. How could the use of expert systems be helpful to managers in marketing their products in international markets?

NOTES

1. This section draws heavily on Naresh Malhotra (1992), "Designing an International Marketing Research Course: Framework and Content," *Journal of Teaching in International Business.* 3(3): 1-27.

REFERENCES

Berman, Barry and Brian J. McNeeley. (1990). A Comparison of Microcomputer Usage Between Corporate Marketing Personnel and Undergraduate Marketing Students at AACSB-Accredited Schools, *American Marketing Association Educators' Proceedings*, 163-167.

Boatler, Robert. (1990). Study Abroad: Impact on Student Worldmindedness, *Journal of Teaching in International Business*, 2 (2), 17-23.

Cornwell, Bettina T. and Tonna R. Bruce. (1991). Strategic Perspectives for International Education Providers, *Journal of Teaching in International Business*, 3 (2), 41-51.

Ellen, Pam S., William O. Bearden, and Subhash Sharma. (1991). Resistance to Technological Innovations: An Examination of the Role of Self-Efficacy and Performance, *Journal of the Academy of Marketing Science*, 19 (4), 297-307.

Finney, Michael and Mary Ann Von Glinow. (1988). Integrating Academic and Organizational Approaches to Developing the International Manager, *Journal of Management Development*, 7 (2), 16-27.

Frand, Jason L. and Julia A. Britt. (1992). *Ninth Annual UCLA Survey of Business School Computer Usage*, Los Angeles: The John E. Anderson Graduate School of Management at UCLA.

Hendon, Donald W. (1989). *International Business Studies*, Washington, DC: American Association of State Colleges and Universities; Aberdeen, SD: Northern State University.

Lane, Henry W. (1992). Methods For Learning Involved in Internationalizing Management Education: Experimenting with Silent Meetings, Microcultures, and Microworlds, in *Global Perspective: Internationalizing Management Education*, A. M. Rugman and W. T. Stanburg (eds.), Vancouver: University of British Columbia, 345-352.

Larson, Clifford E. (1991). Globalization of Business Curriculum and International Marketing: Symbiotic or Antithetic, *Journal of Teaching in International Business*, 3 (2), 19-27.

Mahmoud, Essam and Gillian Rice. (1988). Database Accuracy: Results From a Survey of Database Vendors, *Information and Management*, 15, 243-250.

Malhotra, Naresh. (1992). Designing an International Marketing Research Course: Framework and Content, *Journal of Teaching in International Business*, 3 (3), 1-27

Pendergast, William R. (1991). Ten Years of International Programs, *Journal of Teaching in International Business*, 3 (2), 75-81.

Reynolds, John I. and George H. Rice. (1988). American Education for International Business, *Management International Review*, 28 (3), 48-57.

Sarathy, Ravi. (1990). Internationalizing MBA Education: The Role of Short Overseas Programs, *Journal of Teaching in International Business*, 1 (3-4), 101-118.

Schein, Edgar H. (1985). *Organizational Culture and Leadership*, San Francisco: Jossey-Bass.

Senge, Peter M. (1990). *The Fifth Discipline: The Art & Practice of the Learning Organization*, New York: Doubleday.

Tretheway, Michael W. (1992). Island Programs: The UBC Experience with a Summer Program in France, in *Global Perspective: Internationalizing Management Education,* A. M. Rugman and W. T. Stanburg (eds.), Vancouver: University of British Columbia, 345-352.

Vertesi, Catherine. (1992). Role and Methods of Student Exchanges in Internationalizing Management Education, in *Global Perspective: Internationalizing Management Education*, A. M. Rugman and W. T. Stanburg (eds.), Vancouver: University of British Columbia, 331-44.

Chapter 2

Utilizing Expert Systems in International Marketing

Fahri Karakaya
Erdener Kaynak
K. Venkataraman

INTRODUCTION

One of the most significant economic developments since World War II is the increasing internationalization of business. Henry Ford built a near 100 percent American-made automobile in 1919. The only foreign element in the Model T was rubber from Malaysia. However, things began to change in the 1960s. Henry Ford II directed all Ford activities to consider the selection of sources of supply not only in its own country but also sources located in other countries. Today, world cars, assembled from all over the world and sold all over the world are a fact. Ford Festiva was designed in the United States, engineered by Mazda in Japan, and is being built by Kia in Korea principally for the American market. Although business has been conducted across national boundaries for centuries, during the last decade or so business dealings have escalated on a global scale. Today, foreign earnings account for more than 50 percent of total earnings in GM, DEC, Johnson & Johnson, NCR, and Gillette Corporations. Coke derives 70 percent of its earnings from abroad (Forbes 1988). Leading corporations around the world have increasingly turned their attention to international business in order to maintain a competitive edge in today's dynamic and volatile global market (Jain 1987). The international dimensions of business have become an everyday fact of life for corporations, consumers, and government in virtually every country. As the world becomes a global marketplace, a tremendous transformation in international business and marketing activities is taking place, creating international markets in which the old approaches, strategies, and tactics are no longer adequate. New approaches and concepts, and new ways of doing things are needed for businesses to effectively compete in the international environment, and new techniques are needed to aid businesses in their international marketing decision making.

In general, the basic nature of marketing does not change from domestic to international marketing, but marketing outside national boundaries does create certain opportunities and poses some special problems. International marketing, unlike domestic marketing, requires operating simultaneously in more than one kind of environment, coordinating these operations, and using the experience gained in one country for marketing decisions in another country. International marketers must not only be sensitive to different global marketing environments, but must also be able to balance marketing moves worldwide in order to seek optimum results for the company.

The decisions faced by international marketers are very complex. These decisions have to do with the task of comparing the marketing systems in those countries which the company is interested in with the methods of marketing applicable in the home country, so that short-term and long-term marketing strategies relevant to the international environment can be developed (Kaynak 1985, p. 8). For example, the first decision in international marketing, called the commitment decision, requires a company to identify relevant external and internal factors and assign weights and scores to each factor. Identification of relevant factors can be done in a semi-structured fashion by starting with a super-set of external and internal factors and eliminating the ones not directly applicable to the company. Assigning weights and scores to each factor usually requires judgement and can be considered unstructured. Other decisions in international marketing are taken by using a combination of structured, semi-structured and unstructured techniques. In general, a part of each decision is based on the analysis and interpretation of an enormous quantity of international data using quantitative techniques. The other part of each decision is qualitative and it is based on the experience of the firm in similar international situations and the subjective judgement of international marketers.

Computers have been used as a tool for making business decisions for almost three decades. Marketing information systems have been in use in corporations for more than a decade. Their use, however, has predominantly been in quantitative business decisions. When heuristic or "rule of thumb" problem solving was needed rather than formal analytic techniques and when decisions made were based on incomplete and uncertain information, traditional computer information systems could be of very little help. A new generation of computer information systems known as "Expert Systems," coupled with the traditional marketing information system offer a unique potential in international marketing where marketing strategies are based on complex and constantly changing global market conditions.

OBJECTIVES

The objectives of this chapter are to:

1. Examine how expert systems are useful in international marketing decision areas,
2. Provide guidelines for the use of expert systems in international marketing decisions, and
3. Show country, industry, and company applications where expert systems can be successfully used in international marketing.

In light of this general framework, the specific purposes of this chapter are to develop a set of evaluative criteria for the use of expert systems, examine the nature of decisions in major international marketing decision areas, and evaluate each decision area against the set of criteria to determine if expert systems are suitable for that decision area. The following major international marketing decision areas are examined:

1. *Commitment decision:* Deciding whether to remain a domestic marketer or to go abroad
2. *Region/country/market selection decision:* Deciding which region and/or country to enter

3. *Mode of market entry decision:* Deciding how to enter and stay in a foreign market
4. *Marketing mix (operations) decision:* Deciding on the marketing programs and strategies
5. *Organizational decision:* How to organize and coordinate company activities in foreign markets

The technology required (computer hardware and software) to build expert systems exists today. In fact, expert systems are currently in use in medicine, finance and financial services, manufacturing and engineering, and automotive maintenance. Construction of expert systems for international marketing is particularly difficult because international marketing decisions are dominated by the influence of highly subjective and perceptual factors, and the decisions are taken under great environmental uncertainties. You will see an application of expert systems in international marketing in the next chapter. This software called "The Country Consultant" was recently developed at Michigan State University by a team of researchers.

COMMITMENT DECISION

The *commitment decision* involves answering the following question (Kaynak 1991, p. 19): "Given the firm's home market position and resource base, are foreign market opportunities attractive enough to mobilize an international marketing effort?" A firm's decision to go international is a strategic decision because it reflects a major change in the scope of its product-market and organization-environment relationships. This strategic decision about the expansion of business environments is dependent on the following factors: (1) managerial perceptions of the future business outlook; (2) the firm's relevant environment, and (3) its corporate goals and objectives. Therefore, the *commitment decision* is one of the most crucial decisions a company makes in internationalizing its operation. An erroneous commitment decision could drive the company into bankruptcy.

A company needs to perform internal and external analysis for making a commitment decision (also referred to as SWOT analysis–Strength, Weakness, Opportunity, and Threat analysis). The internal analysis involves (1) analyzing the firm's resources; (2) evaluating the firm's competencies and weaknesses, and (3) considering the firm's corporate missions and objectives. The external analysis involves the assessment of international environment for market opportunities and problems. The firm needs to make this decision in the face of an overabundance of information from both internal and external sources due to improved computer technology and, more often than not, ambiguous organizational goals and objectives for global marketing.

A meaningful distinction can be made between two opposing decision-making modes in the commitment decision. These two styles are (1) a formal and structured strategic planning mode, and (2) a disjointed, adaptive, and incremental decision making-mode that leads to the constant doubting of the commitment decision at more advanced stages of international marketing (Cavusgil 1985). In this chapter, we emphasize the need for a formal structured strategic planning process at the commitment decision stage.

A multi-factor matrix model is suggested as a starting point in the commitment decision process. The firm should first list *all factors relevant to the commitment decision* process. The next step is to *classify the factors* as external and internal. It is important to *identify both strengths and weaknesses* in the internal factors list, and to *identify both opportunities and threats* in the external factors list. The company should then proceed to *give appropriate weights* to each factor. It should then *compare the company's position* on each factor with the major competitors' positions for the same factor by assigning scores. A score can be negative if the factor is a weakness or a threat. Sample score tables for external and internal factors are shown in Tables 1 and 2. Cumulative scores for a company and three hypothetical competitors are shown in Table 3.

Table 3 should give the company an idea of where it would stand in relation to its competition in the international arena. The company can adjust factors, weights, and scores in Tables 1 and 2 in an iterative manner until it feels comfortable that all appropriate factors have been considered.

When we consider the amount of information to be processed in the commitment decision, the multi-factor matrix model offers an excellent vehicle to put the different factors in a form that is easy to

TABLE 1. External Factors (Industry Attractiveness) Score for Commitment Decision

Industry Attractiveness Items	Weight	X Rating	= Value
Overall Market Share	0.20	4.00	0.80
Annual Market Growth Rate	0.20	5.00	1.00
Historical Profit Margin	0.15	4.00	0.60
Competitive Industry	0.15	2.00	0.30
Technological Requirements	0.15	3.00	0.45
Inflationary Vulnerability	0.05	3.00	0.15
Energy Requirements	0.05	2.00	0.10
Environmental Impact	0.05	1.00	0.05
Social/Political/Legal	Must be acceptable		
Industry Attractiveness Score =			3.45

implement, communicate, and understand. The model allows a firm to fit any number of criteria depending on the situation. However, the model fails to accommodate interaction among the factors considered and the impact it may have on the outcome of the decision. It also attempts to boil down business strategy to the interplay of a small number of rather arbitrary dimensions which may ignore important specific aspects of the business planning environment. When we consider the significance of the commitment decision, the result of which may make or break the firm, it is necessary to complement this decision model with some other tool, such as the expert system.

The expert system would attempt to ensure that all relevant factors have been identified and proper scores assigned to each factor, based on the firm's past experience and the past experience of other firms in the same industry. In applying the decision criteria (Table 4), we can see that the commitment decision score is 38.5 (4+2+5+3+4.5+5+4+5+3+3 = 38.5) out of 50 points.

The expert system goes on to ask literally hundreds of questions in areas such as (1) past experience of the firm, (2) international

TABLE 2. Internal Factors (Business Strength) Score Table for Commitment Decision

Business Strength Items	Weight	X Rating	= Value
Market Share	0.10	4.00	0.40
Share Growth	0.15	4.00	0.60
Product Quality	0.10	4.00	0.40
Brand Reputation	0.10	5.00	0.50
Distribution Network	0.05	4.00	0.20
Promotional Effectiveness	0.05	5.00	0.25
Productive Capacity	0.05	3.00	0.15
Productive Efficiency	0.05	2.00	0.10
Unit Costs	0.15	3.00	0.45
Material Supplies	0.05	5.00	0.25
R & D Performance	0.10	4.00	0.40
Managerial Personnel	0.05	4.00	0.20
Business Strength Score =			3.9

TABLE 3. Multi-Factor Matrix Cumulative Score Table for Commitment Decision

Identifier	External Score	Internal Score
Company	3.45	3.90
Competitor A	1.45	1.60
Competitor B	4.15	2.20
Competitor C	4.65	4.50

marketing organization, (3) production aspects, (4) financial aspects, (5) product assessment, and (6) external environment assessment. At any time, the user can ask what (elaborate) or why (explain). The expert system then comes up with observations and specific recommendations.

TABLE 4. Suitability of Expert System for Commitment Decision

	Decision Criteria	Characteristic Score
1	Domain of the decision	Narrow Broad 5 -- **4** ---------- 1
2	Need for interdisciplinary knowledge	No Yes 5 ----------**2** -- 1
3	Nature of key relationships in the domain	Logical Computational **5** -------------- 1
4	Decision area knowledge-intensive or data-intensive	Knowledge Data intensive intensive 5 ------**3** ------ 1
5	Structure of the decision domain	Semi Structured/ structured unstructured 5 -- **4.5** -------- 1
6	Is knowledge in decision domain incomplete?	Yes No **5** -------------- 1
7	Is heuristic ("rule of thumb") or formal analytical technique used in decision?	Heuristics Analytical 5 -- **4** ---------- 1
8	Are there recognized marketing experts that take decisions demonstrably better than amateurs?	Yes No **5** ------------- 1
9	Are experts able to explain their thought process to nonexperts?	Yes No 5 ------**3** ------ 1
10	Decision making requires a direct interface between managers and the computer system	Yes No 5 ------**3** ------ 1

REGION/COUNTRY/MARKET SELECTION DECISION

Decisions related to foreign market entry, expansion, and conversion require a systematic framework of analysis. The region/country selection decision involves three steps: (1) assessment of region/country risk, (2) assessment of strategic attractiveness, and (3) region/country grouping. Step (3) is optional but highly recommended if the company plans simultaneous entry into multiple regions/countries/markets. A model for a region/country/market selection decision is shown in Figure 1. This is a modified version of a conventional model in which an expert system is used in the different selection stages: preliminary screening, company-market matching, estimating industry market potential, and forecasting company sales potential. The stages in which expert systems can be used are indicated by double-lined boxes.

Assessment of Region/Country/Market Risk

There are over 150 countries in the world; of these, the majority would like the employment generated, technology and know-how transferred, and the tax revenues earned as a result of foreign investment, and may appear to offer entry markets. Many countries go out of their way to attract foreign investment by offering lures ranging from tax exemptions to low-waged, amply skilled labor. These inducements, valid as they may be in certain individual cases, have repeatedly led to hasty foreign market entry (Jain 1987, p. 190-193). International business involves a wide variety of inherent risks. Export markets, carefully developed and nurtured, may suddenly collapse because of inherent changes in target markets, imposition of exchange controls, or protectionist trade policy measures. Imports of raw materials, components and parts, or capital equipment may face restricted supplies or major increases in cost due to shifting conditions–economic or political–in principal supplier countries. International lending may face restrictions on repayment of interest and principal, rescheduling or outright default (Walter 1988, p. 7-19).

Risk assessment can be done objectively and fairly inexpensively. A company rarely needs to do first-hand research in all countries. A number of well-known general surveys can provide companies with general political risk summaries or studies of specific countries. The markets surviving region/country/market risk are then assessed for strategic attractiveness. Countries/regions should be examined for attractiveness from three broad perspectives: (1) marketing potential, (2) manufacturing potential, and (3) manufacturing and marketing potential. A battery of criteria should be redeveloped to fit the specific requirements of the corporation. Basically, the criteria should focus on the following five factors:

1. Future demand and economic potential of the country in question;
2. Distribution of purchasing power by population groups or market segments;
3. Region/country/market specific technical product standards;
4. "Spillover" from the national market (via standards, regulations, norms, or economic ties) to other markets (for example, the U.S. National Electric Manufacturers' Association standards are widely applicable in Latin America, and British Standards apply in most of the Commonwealth countries), and
5. Access to vital resources (qualified labor force, raw materials sources, suppliers).

Each factor is assigned a score from 1 to 10. Each criterion is assigned a value of 1 to 5 that signifies the importance of the criterion. This results in an index number for each region/country/market indicating its overall attractiveness.

Region/country/market selection decision can be systematic and quantitative. Independent agencies and consultants provide political risk assessment. World Bank, various U.N. agencies, and the U.S. Department of Commerce provide comprehensive and accurate statistics in hundreds of areas for almost all countries/regions in the world. The most difficult part of the region/country/market selection decision is to identify the criteria and factors by which to conduct region/country/market comparative analysis. Applying the decision criteria (Table 5) to relevant factors in the identification phase of region/country/market selection decision, we can see that it scores 37 out of 50. An expert system can help in two ways in this decision area:

1. Help the company identify relevant factors based on company objectives and the type of business the company is in so that the selection process does not become unnecessarily costly and the results are fully relevant to the company.
2. Consolidate inputs to each factor, analyze and summarize them into an index of overall region/country/market attractiveness index.

FIGURE 1. Region/Country/Market Selection Decision Model (Double-lined boxes indicate expert system use in that decision)

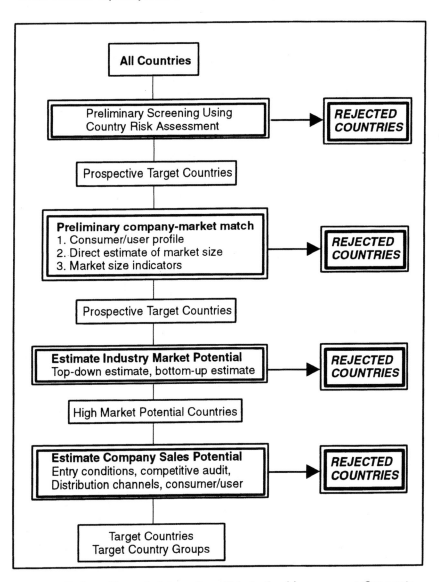

Source: Erdener Kaynak, *International/Marketing Management: Concepts, Techniques and Cases*, mimeographed, Hummelstown, 1991, p. 88.

The major benefits of using an expert system for region/country/market selection decisions are its ability to direct the company locus on relevant factors, blend quantitative and qualitative criteria, and provide an explanation at every stage of factor selection and analysis.

MODE OF MARKET ENTRY DECISION

When a company makes the commitment to go international, it must choose a market entry strategy. This decision should reflect an

TABLE 5. Suitability of Expert System for Region/Country/Market Selection Decision

	Decision Criteria	Characteristic Score	
1	Domain of the decision	Narrow	Broad
		5 -- 4 ----------- 1	
2	Need for interdisciplinary knowledge	No	Yes
		5 -- 4 ----------- 1	
3	Nature of key relationships in the domain	Logical	Computational
		5 -------------- 1	
4	Decision area knowledge-intensive or data-intensive	Knowledge intensive	Data intensive
		5 ------ 3 ------ 1	
5	Structure of the decision domain	Semi structured	Structured/ unstructured
		5 ----------- 2 -- 1	
6	Is knowledge in decision domain incomplete?	Yes	No
		5 -- 4 ----------- 1	
7	Is heuristic ("rule of thumb") or formal technique used in decision?	Heuristics	Analytical
		5 ------ 3 ------ 1	
8	Are there recognized marketing experts that take decisions demonstrably better than amateurs?	Yes	No
		5 -------------- 1	
9	Are experts able to explain their thought process to nonexperts?	Yes	No
		5 -- 4 ----------- 1	
10	Decision making requires a direct interface between managers and the computer system	Yes	No
		5 ------ 3 ------ 1	

analysis of market potential, company capabilities, and the degree of marketing involvement and commitment management is prepared to make. A company's approach to foreign marketing can require minimal investment and be limited to infrequent exporting with little thought given to market development. Or, a company can make large investments of capital and management effort to capture and maintain a permanent, specific share of world markets. Even though companies begin with modest export involvement, experience and expansion into a larger number of foreign markets increases the number of entry strategies used. There are a variety of foreign market entry strategies from which to choose. They include the following (Kotler 1988):

1. indirect exporting
2. direct exporting
3. licensing
4. joint ventures
5. direct investment

Each entry strategy has particular advantages and shortcomings depending on company strengths and weaknesses, the degree of commitment the company is willing or able to make, and market characteristics (Catoera 1990, p. 338-339). Mode of entry or operations decisions are affected by and interact with the region/country/market selection decision and commitment decision. Each mode has its general advantages and disadvantages. But companies must move from the general to the specific. They must decide on an entry mode for a particular product and for a particular country or region. Given the number of alternatives, this usually becomes a monumental task.

A company's overall foreign-market entry strategy is an aggregation of several individual product/market strategies. Companies need to design an entry strategy for each product and each foreign market. Differences among foreign markets make highly risky the assumption that a particular entry strategy would draw the same response across different products or different country markets. In deciding on the most appropriate entry mode for a particular product and a target foreign country, managers need to consider several, often conflicting, external forces in the target country as well as several factors internal to the company. Target country factors include market factors (such as sales potential, competition, and distribution channels), production factors (such as the quality, quantity, availability, and cost of inputs for local production), and political, economic, and sociocultural factors (such as government policies toward international trade and investment, geographic distance, attributes of the economy, and the cultural distance between home and target-country societies).

How managers respond to external country factors in choosing an entry mode depends on factors internal to the company. They include product factors (such as technological intensity and the need for adaptation, pre-and post-purchase services, and the degree of differentiation), and resource/commitment factors (such as resources in management, capital, technology, and functional skills, and the willingness to commit them to foreign markets).

The diversity of forces and the need to assess their strengths and future directions combine to make the mode of entry decision a complex process with many traders among alternative entry modes. This level of complexity often leads to a compromise, and companies follow one of the two decision rules: (1) the naive rule or (2) the pragmatic rule (Root 1988, p. 2-21).

The naive rule is to use the same entry mode, such as agent distributor exporting, for all target countries. Because country markets and entry conditions are heterogeneous, the naive rule leads companies to forsake promising markets that cannot be penetrated with their single entry mode or to end up in markets with an inappropriate mode.

The pragmatic rule is to find an entry mode that "works." In most instances, companies start assessing export entry, and only if such entry is infeasible do they go on to assess another mode. This rule avoids the two pitfalls of the naive rule, and it also saves management time and effort. But it fails to lead companies to the most appropriate mode. A workable mode is not necessarily the right mode.

An expert system can facilitate systematic comparison of entry moves with respect to a particular product and target country and allow managers to follow a strategy rule that recognizes the right entry mode as a key element in a company's foreign market entry strategy. Applying the decision criteria (Table 6), we can see that the mode of entry decision scores 39 out of 50. An expert system could be of use in this decision area.

An expert system also makes the planning process iterative. For instance, an evaluation of alternative entry modes may bring about a revision of market objectives or even start a search for a new target region/country/market. The expert system works as follows:

1. Recall user inputs to the commitment decision. This provides the system information on company internal factors such as resource availability and willingness of management to commit the resources to international activities;
2. Recall user inputs to strategic attractiveness during the region/country/market selection as target region/country/market;
3. Seek high level product factor information from the user (such as need for adaptation, technological intensity, etc.), and
4. Match company internal strengths and weaknesses to attributes of each country and suggest mode of entry for each region/country/market.

The process would work best if the expert system were used in the first two decision areas of international marketing, but it can also be used independently for the mode of market entry decision area. If used independently for this decision area, the user will be required to answer many questions about the company and each region/country/market in which the company seeks to enter.

MARKETING MIX (OPERATIONAL) DECISION

Marketing mix or decision variables are the set of marketing tools that companies use to pursue their marketing objectives in the target market. One can see that a marketing mix is selected from a great number of possibilities. If product quality could take on one of two values, and product price is constrained to lie between $500 and $1,500 (to the nearest $100), and advertising and distribution expenditures are constrained to lie between $10,000 and $50,000 (to the nearest $10,000), then 550 ($2 \times 11 \times 5 \times 5$) marketing mix combinations are possible. In addition, companies that contemplate operations in one or more foreign markets must decide how much to

TABLE 6. Suitability of Expert System for Mode of Entry Decision

	Decision Criteria	Characteristic Score
1	Domain of the decision	Narrow Broad 5 -- 4 ---------- 1
2	Need for interdisciplinary knowledge	No Yes 5 ---------- 2 -- 1
3	Nature of key relationships in the domain	Logical Computational 5 -------------- 1
4	Decision area knowledge-intensive or data-intensive	Knowledge Data intensive intensive 5 -- 4 ---------- 1
5	Structure of the decision domain	Semi Structured/ structured unstructured 5 -- 4 ---------- 1
6	Is knowledge in decision domain incomplete?	Yes No 5 -- 4 ---------- 1
7	Is heuristic ("rule of thumb") or formal analytical technique used in decision?	Heuristics Analytical 5 -- 4 ---------- 1
8	Are there recognized marketing experts that take decisions demonstrably better than amateurs?	Yes No 5 -------------- 1
9	Are experts able to explain their thought process to nonexperts?	Yes No 5 -- 4 ---------- 1
10	Decision making requires a direct interface between managers and the computer system	Yes No 5 ------ 3 ------ 1

adapt their marketing mix to local conditions. At one extreme are companies that use a standardized marketing mix worldwide. Standardization of the product, advertising, distribution channels, and other elements of the marketing mix promises the lowest costs because no major changes have been introduced. At the other extreme is the idea of customized marketing mix, where the producer adjusts the marketing mix elements to each target market, bearing more costs, but hoping for a larger market share and return. Between these two extremes, many possibilities exist (Kotler 1988,

p. 393-399). Here we will examine potential adaptations that firms might make to their product, price, distribution, and promotion as they enter foreign markets, and to what extent expert systems can be of help in this decision area.

To evaluate the suitability of expert systems, we need to apply the decision criteria (Table 7) for each of the marketing mix elements. Applying it to one of the elements, say price, we can come up with a score of 35 out of 50. We can also come up with similar scores for each of the marketing mix variables.

At first glance, expert systems may look well suited for the selection of each of the variables. There are good sets of rules governing product and price decisions, and a reasonably sound set of rules with many host country constraints governing products and distribution. A company may be tempted to code these rules in a knowledge base and use the expert systems for international marketing mix decisions. As noted before, however, a very important limitation of expert systems is that they work best if confined to a narrow domain because building and maintaining a large-knowledge base is very difficult. Defining the domain is extremely important because expert systems have fragile behavior at the boundaries. A system does not give the right answer if a problem is not confined entirely to a specific domain. Decisions based on broad, interdisciplinary knowledge are not suitable for expert systems at the current level of their technology. Marketing mix variables are not independent of each other. There are interrelationships and synergic effects among marketing mix variables. An expert system used independently for the selection of each element, working in one domain at a time, at best, would be able to choose the "most appropriate" product strategy, pricing strategy, promotion strategy, and distribution strategy independent of each other. But this would lead to optimal individual decisions and a suboptimal or even a disastrous overall decision.

This does not preclude the use of expert systems in this decision area, but the way in which they are used should be modified. In *commitment decision*, region/country/market selection decision, and mode of entry decision, we provided the expert system with internal and external information, provided a finite set of alternatives (like passive entry mode, semiactive entry mode, and active

TABLE 7. Suitability of Expert Systems for Price Decision

	Decision Criteria	Characteristic Score	
1	Domain of the decision	Narrow 5 --------------	Broad 1
2	Need for interdisciplinary knowledge	No 5 --------------	Yes 1
3	Nature of key relationships in the domain	Logical 5 ----------- 2 --	Computational 1
4	Decision area knowledge-intensive or data-intensive	Knowledge intensive 5 ------ 3 ------	Data intensive 1
5	Structure of the decision domain	Semi structured 5 -- 4 ----------	Structured/ unstructured 1
6	Is knowledge in decision domain incomplete?	Yes 5 -- 4 ----------	No 1
7	Is heuristic ("rule of thumb") or formal analytical technique used in decision?	Heuristics 5 -- 4 ----------	Analytical 1
8	Are there recognized marketing experts that take decisions demonstrably better than amateurs?	Yes 5 --------------	No 1
9	Are experts able to explain their thought process to nonexperts?	Yes 5 -- 4 ----------	No 1
10	Decision making requires a direct interface between managers and the computer system	Yes 5 ------ 3 ------	No 1

entry mode for the mode of entry decision) and asked the expert system for the best choice among the alternatives. We asked the expert system to do goal oriented reasoning. The approach for marketing mix decision needs to be different. As we saw, if we provide a set of finite alternatives for each element in the marketing mix and ask the expert system to pick the best alternative for each element, we would end up with a suboptimal marketing mix decision. To avoid this, we must provide internal and external information, a set of values for the marketing mix variables, and ask the expert system to analyze and "grade" the choice of marketing mix variables. Based on the "grade," and comments from the system, we would iteratively adjust values for the mix elements for optimal "grade." The specific sequence of steps will be:

1. For each region/country/market, select the best preliminary values for marketing mix variables. This is done in the conventional manner, using meetings and discussions with key experts in the company. This involves deciding on product extension or adaptation, ethnocentric or geocentric pricing, intensive or exclusive distribution, and so on;
2. Provide the values for the mix and internal and external information to the expert system;
3. Based on the "grade" and comments from the expert system, adjust the mix variables in a meaningful manner. Adjustment in any variable must be feasible and practical for that region/country/market. Obtain the best "grade" possible;
4. Repeat steps 1 through 3 for each country, and
5. Based on results for each country, decide (again in the conventional manner, using meetings) if standardization of any of the mix elements is practical.

The advantage of this approach is that the company becomes aware of the optimal marketing mix for each region/country/market, though it may decide to compromise and standardize some of the elements for cost reasons. If the company standardizes, it can provide new values for marketing mix elements and see how effective standardization will be.

ORGANIZATIONAL DECISION

Choosing an ideal organizational structure that fits the international marketing strategy and how it responds to international market demands is an important and complex issue. Simultaneous pressures for greater integration and greater diversity create strain in structuring the organization. Essentially, there are six different organizational structures available for international companies: (1) international division structure, (2) geographic/regional structure, (3) product structure,

(4) matrix structure, (5) functional structure, and (6) hybrid structure (see Jain 1987, p. 655-669).

The goal of designing an organizational structure in international markets is to enable the company to respond to differences in international environments and at the same time enable the firm to extend valuable corporate knowledge, experience, and know-how from the home market to the entire corporate system. The choice of an appropriate form of organizational structure for an international firm should be determined based on several criteria:

1. *Diversity of Product Lines:* Most firms with a high degree of product diversity decentralize on a product basis, rather than on an area basis. Firms producing a few similar products will not decentralize on a product basis, because of the high degree of interdependence among these products.
2. *Size of Firm and Evolution of Corporate Organizational Structure:* Firms that derive a substantial portion of business from foreign operations usually drop the international division structure in favor of a product or geographic structure, which facilitates growth.
3. *Location of Subsidiaries and Their Characteristics:* A company that emphasizes local and regional variations will lean toward the geographic structure because specific geographic variation must be specifically catered to.
4. *Economic Blocs:* Companies operating within a regional economic bloc usually integrate their subsidiaries within the bloc area to deal better with trade barriers and oversee these operations by establishing special regional organizational units.
5. *Quality of Management:* The decentralization of authority to the local level can become a problem because the quality of management may vary from country to country. However, authoritative committees either at the corporate or regional level with majority control can be used to offset this potential problem.
6. *Management's Orientation:* The orientation of a company's management toward different aspects of doing business is a factor that affects the choice of an organization's structure. These aspects include considerations such as management's

attitudes toward foreigners and overseas environments, management's willingness to take risks and seek growth in unfamiliar circumstances, and management's ability to make compromises to accommodate foreign perspectives.

The ultimate decision of a firm's international organizational structure is based on specific factors unique to the company's operating environment. But, methods of organizing and managing international activities have matured enough to put them in the form of following basic rules, as shown in Table 8. However, one must be cautious that changes in external environment together with new complexities that arise from corporate responses to these changes would necessitate modification and enhancement of the rule set.

Applying the decision criteria (Table 9), we can see that the organization decision scores 41 out of 50 and is well suited for expert systems. However, the following caution must be exercised. As the international operating environment becomes more complex, there is great temptation for companies to try to look for ideal organizational structure solutions or to imitate the organizational characteristics and strategic postures of their successful competitors. U.S. multinational managers are being told to "rein-in far-flung subsidiaries, standardize global products, and pull the decision-making power back to the home office" like the Japanese companies have done for years. But the appropriate response to the developing international organization cannot be captured in a formula. While the company's tasks are shaped by its external environment, its ability to perform those tasks is constrained by its "administrative heritage"–the company's existing configuration of assets, its traditional distribution of responsibility, and its historic norms, values, and management style. This internal organizational ability cannot be changed overnight. We advocate the use of expert systems in this decision area, but caution that management must be careful about the speed of implementation of the expert system's recommendation.

CURRENT APPLICATIONS AND A LOOK TO THE FUTURE

The expert systems literature is replete with examples of commercially successful expert systems in many areas, both in public

TABLE 8. Suitability of Basic Organizational Structures to Corporate Concerns

	Area of Corporate Concern	Inter-na-tional	Prod-uct	Geo-graph-ic	Matrix	Func-tional	Hybrid
1	Rapid Growth	Med	High	Med	High	Med	Med
2	Diversity of Products	Low	High	Low	High	Low	High
3	High Technology	Med	High	Low	High	High	Low
4	Few Experienced Managers	High	Med	Low	Low	High	Med
5	Close Corporate Control	Med	High	Low	High	High	Low
6	Close Government Relations	Med	Low	High	Med	Med	Med
7	Product Considerations Should Dominate	Low	High	Low	Med	Low	Med
8	Geographic Considerations Should Dominate	Med	Low	High	Med	Low	High
9	Functional Considerations Should Dominate	Low	Med	Low	High	Med	Med
10	Relative Cost	Med	Med	Low	High	Med	High

Source: J. William Widing, Jr., Reorganizing Your Worldwide Business, *Harvard Business Review.* May-June 1973, p. 159.

domain and used locally within firms (Chorafas 1981, p. 203-223). These areas include accounting and auditing (EASY, ICOR, Exper-Tax), agriculture, banking, computer configuration and trouble-shooting (X/CON, IDT), finance and financial services, laws, pro-cedures, and administration, manufacturing, medicine (Mycin, Dendral, ESMP), mining (Prospector), and speech recognition (Hearsay-II). However, relatively little information is available in the literature about the use of expert systems in international mar-keting. A limited number of academically sponsored experimental expert systems are being developed in some international business areas such as international negotiations, transfer pricing, quality management, taxation, and strategic planning. These expert systems show promise of commercial viability. Of the academically spon-sored and commercially available expert systems, three are note-worthy. This chapter will review these three current applications,

TABLE 9. Suitability of Expert System for Organization Decision

	Decision Criteria	Characteristic Score
1	Domain of the decision	Narrow Broad 5 -- 4 ---------- 1
2	Need for interdisciplinary knowledge	No Yes 5 -- 4 ---------- 1
3	Nature of key relationships in the domain	Logical Computational 5 -------------- 1
4	Decision area knowledge-intensive or data-intensive	Knowledge Data intensive intensive 5 -- 4 ---------- 1
5	Structure of the decision domain	Semi Structured/ structured unstructured 5 -- 4 ---------- 1
6	Is knowledge in decision domain incomplete?	Yes No 5 -- 4 ---------- 1
7	Is heuristic ("rule of thumb") or formal analytical technique used in decision?	Heuristics Analytical 5 -- 4 ---------- 1
8	Are there recognized marketing experts that take decisions demonstrably better than amateurs?	Yes No 5 -------------- 1
9	Are experts able to explain their thought process to nonexperts?	Yes No 5 -- 4 ---------- 1
10	Decision making requires a direct interface between managers and the computer system	Yes No 5 ------ 3 ------ 1

and consider the future of expert systems in international marketing. A comprehensive expert system, The Country Consultant©, will not be discussed here since the next chapter is fully devoted to this software.

Current Expert Systems Applications

NEGOTEX: An Expert System Application to International Negotiation

NEGOTEX (Rangaswamy et al. 1989) is an expert system that provides guidelines to individuals and teams preparing for international marketing negotiations. The prototype was developed and tested by a team of developers as a research project in The Wharton School of Business, University of Pennsylvania. The developers state that negotiations play a key role in the formation of exchange relationships in international marketing. In preparing for a negotiation, a manager needs expertise to combine and process many related facts and concepts in order to identify an effective negotiation strategy. Good negotiators rely on experience, knowledge, and intuition to develop comprehensive negotiation strategies. Marketing managers engaged in international contract negotiations may not always have such expertise. An expert system can aid in training novices and in preparing more experienced managers for international negotiations.

The international negotiation domain is a suitable context for exploring expert systems for marketing applications. It has the typical feature of a semi-structured domain generally considered appropriate for the application of expert system methodology. A large number of contextual as well as self- and opponent-based factors determine negotiation outcomes. Practitioners and researchers often use several qualitative "rules of thumb" for deciding on effective negotiation strategies. Conventional modeling techniques generally are inadequate for representing these heuristics, especially when the various factors interact in complex patterns. The knowledge could be modeled better by means of expert system methodology.

The objective of NEGOTEX is to stimulate a user's thinking by providing some expert tips in a systematic and organized way for the user's particular situation. It does this by asking the user a series of questions regarding the context of negotiation, their philosophical approach to negotiating, and the nature of the other party to the negotiation. NEGOTEX then makes recommendations concerning several aspects of the negotiation, such as preparing for the negotiation, team composition, communication approaches, and behavioral response. The knowledge base was developed using a range of knowledge sources including academic and practitioner publications. To enhance the value of the system to the user, the developers have added three explanatory features: (1) WHAT, to give users a detailed definition of terminology used in the system's questions and recommendations, (2) HOW, to report in detail how the system arrived at certain recommendations, and (3) WHAT IF, to enable users to test the sensitivity of the system's recommendations to changes in input scenarios.

TRANSFER: An Expert System Approach to Transfer Pricing

TRANSFER (Kirsch et al. 1991) is a PC-based expert system for transfer price decision making in both domestic and international transfer of goods and services among different divisions or subsidiaries of a corporation. The system was developed at Bowling Green State University, Ohio. The developers state that in situations where the output of one division or subsidiary is used as an input by one or more of the firm's other divisions or subsidiaries, the firm is confronted with the complex problem of establishing the price at which the product or service will be transferred between the divisions or subsidiaries. The area is made more complex when the transfers are across country borders. Since transfer prices are critical in determining subsidiary profits or divisional performance, systemization of the decision process should prove beneficial to the firm. However, transfer pricing decision rules are somewhat fuzzy and experts use rules of thumb to arrive at transfer prices.

TRANSFER is conceptually grounded upon an accounting decision tree. The decision tree seeks to graphically represent various transfer pricing scenarios based upon the path through the tree. TRANSFER is based on the premise that if the goal structure, market structure, and costing systems of a firm are known, it should be possible to arrive at the optimal transfer price by applying a set of optimization rules. The system asks the user a number of questions to determine the goal structure, market structure, and costing systems of the firm, type of transfer, firm organization, external market, and the like. It contains a knowledge base populated with IF-THEN rules derived from interviewing a "transfer pricing expert" with over 25 years of experience. The software provides a workable solution to the complex and difficult problem of charting a path through a many-branched decision tree to arrive at the desirable transfer price.

The developers of this software also state that after the development of TRANSFER, they became aware of a large expert system under development in Exxon. The Exxon system would link several databases and computer transfer prices based on company policy. The Exxon system appeared to be company and industry specific, whereas TRANSFER presents a generalized approach to transfer pricing policy making, and to the determination of the appropriate transfer pricing strategy in a variety of corporate structures and environments.

Business Insight

Business Insight (Business Resources Software 1991) is a PC-based expert system designed to help a firm in defining and analyzing its strategic plans. It gathers information from the user using a dialogue technique, formulates or analyzes strategic plans and points out inconsistencies in implementation plans. It appears to be most useful in formulating strategies for new product introduction and in evaluating marketing mix strategies. It has a knowledge base that contains theories and insights suggested by management experts such as Michael Porter and Philip Kotler. The system is very useful in determining the effectiveness of the marketing mix and can be utilized to arrive at optimal values for variables in the international marketing mix.

The Business Insight is useful in analyzing a marketing mix decision and in comparing a number of marketing mix decisions to come up with the optimal one. The system handles both quantitative and qualitative information and has the ability to accept marketing mix information to a considerable degree of detail. Its scoring technique is easy to comprehend even by inexperienced expert systems users. One should note that it does not seem suitable for other international marketing decisions such as the *commitment decision, country selection decision, mode of market entry decision,* and *organization decision.*

FUTURE DIRECTIONS IN THE USE OF EXPERT SYSTEMS IN INTERNATIONAL MARKETING

Expert systems are expected to show a nearly doubled market base by 1995 (Wang, Porter, and Cunningham 1991). The future of expert system technology lies not in encoding limited, specialized expertise as the majority of current systems do. The brightest future for this technology involves supplementing and integrating human decision makers in enriched communication and information environments. Such systems will be noted for their advanced data distribution capabilities, user interfaces, and adaptability. Expert systems are also forecasted to experience substantial gains in software complexity. Future expert systems will utilize databases, additional cooperative agents, networking and administrative procedures, and sophisticated user interface management systems.

Global trade will long remain the mainstay of the economies of most countries in the world. Despite the "America First" parochialism employed by politicians in economically troubled times, more and more American companies are getting involved in international trade in order to be competitive in the global marketplace. The formation of the European Community, the unification of Germany, the breakup of the former Soviet Union, the collapse of communism, and the end of the cold war era all present firms with market opportunities which were unimaginable only a few years ago. In the future, successful international companies will be the ones that react in a positive and constructive way to changes and developments taking place in the global environment. To develop and maintain their competitive edge, firms will be required to make more decisions in international marketing areas and they will be making these decisions more frequently.

Though the use of expert systems in international marketing is still in its infancy, demand for expert systems is likely to grow as more firms internationalize. Looking far ahead, one can visualize the international marketeers of the future that have taken the use of expert systems for granted. One can envision expert systems evolving to such an advanced stage that they

- are capable of linking to governmental and private demographic and country databases, eliminating the need for international marketing users to input the information,
- can access and make use of econometric and statistical models to provide international marketing users the combined power of modeling and judgemental reasoning,

- can link to simulation models in intelligent decision support systems, again to provide international marketing users the power of simulation in combination with judgemental reasoning,
- contain expert knowledge of all international marketing domains, so they are capable of handling decisions that overlap more than one domain.

High cost and relatively long-development time are the two major obstacles in the development of expert systems today. Lengthy questionnaires needed by many expert systems to gather input from users is an obstacle to the use of expert systems. A number of relatively new technologies show promise to overcome these two obstacles so more firms will be able to afford and use expert systems (Brown 1991, p. 3-18). Some new frontiers in information technology that will help accelerate the development of expert systems and encourage their use in international marketing decisions are described below:

1. *Powerful and Inexpensive Expert System Shells:* These will enable the developers to have a "head start" by providing an empty knowledge base with the knowledge representation mechanism, inference engine, and the user interface. The knowledge base will then be populated with rules by the knowledge engineer.

2. *Parallel Processing Computers:* Current machines process all their data in a serial fashion, so the speed of their computation is limited by the slowest of their processing elements. Parallel architecture is beginning to evolve. These machines will be capable of processing data concurrently, increasing the processing speed manyfold.

3. *Intelligent Questionnaires:* Many expert systems use automated versions of paper questionnaires to gather input from the users. Traditional questionnaires can exceed 200 pages to gather a firm's relevant internal and external information. Automated intelligent questionnaires determine the relevant questions based upon the answers to previous questions and ask only those relevant questions, thus speeding the process considerably. Intelligent questionnaires also perform consistency checking reducing the need to go back to the user for clarifications.

4. *Hypertext:* When hypertext is available for selected words in a question or comment and a user does not understand a term that is highlighted, an explanation can be requested directly. The simple application of the hypertext concept promises to make systems significantly easier to use and, therefore, more effective.

5. *Client Systems:* Work has begun on expert systems for continuous audit of on-line systems. In addition to performing tests of controls, these expert system will compare current transaction profiles with historical profiles, analyze the type and frequency of data accesses by user, and identify and attempt to explain the causes of unusual variances.

6. *CD-ROMs:* A CD-ROM: may contain the firm's past experiences, and the relevant company policies in an international environment. This reduces the load on the knowledge base and helps accelerate the development of knowledge bases by providing standard company rules (policies) in a CD-ROM.

7. *On-Line Databases:* Advances in telecommunications enable a firm to acquire information about other companies in the same industry from on-line databases. As the use of on-line databases becomes more common, so will their integration into expert systems.

8. *Integration Tools:* Advances in hardware, software, operating systems, and interface technology will enable expert systems to communicate with databases on mainframes and software such as spreadsheets, modeling and statistical packages, and text processing, making them an extension of expert systems.

9. *Voice, Image, and Text Processing:* Expert systems would be able to recognize input in the form of voice, diagrams, or text, thereby enhancing their ability to gather more expert rules for their knowledge bases. Some experts find it impossible to explain their domain of expertise verbally. Image processing will enable expert systems to interpret technical diagrams and use the information in arriving at their recommendations.

CONCLUSIONS

This chapter presents an argument for the use of expert systems in international marketing. The argument is based on the belief that the globalization of markets is at hand and international marketers will be called upon to make decisions more often than before, that existing technology is inadequate to aid in such decisions, and that expert systems are well suited to aid judgemental decisions in international marketing. To keep pace with global competition, firms must provide high quality products and services to the marketplace. This translates to the design of products that are easier to manufacture, faster to enter the market, and are more reliable and safer to operate and maintain than many products of yesterday. The best managers realize that this can only be achieved by an organization-wide commitment to quality and cost consciousness. Some effective ways to achieve cost competitiveness are global sourcing, global financing, global manufacturing, and strategic alliances with firms abroad. These require a firm to consider international operations and be able to make the right international decisions. Expert systems help firms to choose the right international parameters. The decision tables used to evaluate the suitability of expert systems in different international marketing decisions indicate that expert systems are suited for all major international marketing decisions.

Expert systems have added a new dimension to the use of computers. Through the use of expert systems, computer power can now be applied to decisions that require people to use their judgemental reasoning. Expert systems are particularly suited in international marketing, where good decisions call for both quantitative and qualitative judgemental reasoning. Firms need to design and carry out sound strategies to enter and sustain foreign markets. The use of expert systems in international marketing decision areas will significantly improve the quality of strategic, tactical, and operational level decisions in international marketing, and will be essential to allow companies to remain competitive in the global economy of the 1990s and beyond.

REFERENCES

Brown, Carol E. (1991). Expert Systems in Public Accounting: Current Practice and Future Directions, *Expert Systems with Applications,* 3(1), 3-18.
Business Resources Software (1991). Reproduced from the demonstration diskette of an expert system, Business Insight by Business Resources Software, Inc. 2013 Wells Branch Parkway #305, Austin, TX 78728. Tel: 1-800-423-1228.

Catoera, Philip R. (1990). *International Marketing*. Seventh Edition, Homewood, IL: Richard D. Irwin Inc., 338-339.

Cavusgil, S. Tamer. (1985). Decision Making in Global Marketing. *Global Perspective In Marketing*, edited by Erdener Kaynak, New York: Praeger Publishers, 173-182.

Chorafas, Dimitris N. (1987). *Applying Expert Systems In Business*. New York: McGraw-Hill Book Company, 203-223.

Davis, Stanley M. (1988). Organizational Design, *Handbook of International Management*, edited by Ingo Walter, New York: John Wiley & Sons, 12-14.

Forbes (1988). The 100 Largest U.S. Multinationals, (July 25), 248-250.

Jain, Subhas C. (1987). *International Marketing Management*. Second Edition, Boston: PWS-Kent Publishing Company.

Kaynak, Erdener. (1985). Globalization in International Markets, *Global Perspectives In Marketing*, edited by Erdener Kaynak, New York: Praeger Publishers.

Kaynak, Erdener. (1991). *International Marketing Management: Concepts, Techniques and Cases*. Mimeographed, Hummelstown, PA, 5.

Kirsch, Robert J., Strouble, Dennis D., Johnson, Wayne A., and Stan G. August (1991). Transfer: An Expert System Approach to Transfer Pricing, *Expert Systems with Applications*, edited by Jay Liebowitz, 3(4) 481-487.

Kotler, Philip. (1988). *Marketing Management*, Sixth Edition, Englewood Cliffs, NJ: Prentice Hall, 71-72, 393-399.

Rangaswamy, Arvind, Eliasberg, Jehoshua, Burke, Raymond R., and Jerry Wind. (1989). Developing Marketing Expert Systems: An Application in International Negotiations, *Journal of Marketing*, (October) 24-39.

Root, Franklin R. (1988). Entering International Markets, *Handbook of International Management*, edited by Ingo Walter, New York, John Wiley & Sons, 2-1 to 20-21.

Walter, Ingo. (1988). Country-Risk Assessment, *Handbook of International Management*, edited by Ingo Walter, New York, John Wiley & Sons, 7-3 to 7-19.

Wang, Lin, Porter, Alan L., and Scott Cunningham. (1991). Expert Systems: Present and Future, *Expert Systems with Applications*, 3(4), 383-396.

Chapter 3

Using Expert Systems in International Business: The Case of an Intelligent Knowledge Base– The Country Consultant©

Cüneyt Evirgen
Michel Mitri
S. Tamer Cavusgil

INTRODUCTION

Evaluation and assessment of foreign market attractiveness is one of the most important steps in selecting markets to enter. Poor assessment may lead to poor decisions and investments which may lead to irrecoverable losses for the companies. Hence, it is crucial to know what to look for in evaluating foreign market attractiveness and to correctly identify the information categories relevant to foreign market selection for entry. Such knowledge of the important criteria to use in foreign market assessment is also necessary for evaluating ongoing foreign operations and for decisions regarding their future. In evaluating or assessing the attractiveness of a foreign market, it is necessary to consider the complete picture of information requirements rather than concentrating on specific dimensions with a myopic approach.

This chapter describes the use of a computer program called The Country Consultant©,[1] an "intelligent" knowledge base designed to aid international marketing professionals in dealing with market evaluation and selection issues.

The Country Consultant© is one of the expert system applications in international business being developed by a team of researchers at the International Business Centers (IBC) of Michigan State University (MSU).[2] This decision support tool is an "intelligent" knowledge base that contains information on foreign markets. Its "intelligence" stems from its capability to infer evaluative judgements on foreign market characteristics based on other information stored in its database when direct information is not available. In addition, it contains processed judgemental information about various characteristics of foreign markets.

The term "intelligent database" refers to a class of database structures and querying methods that employ techniques from artificial intelligence (AI). These AI techniques are employed to deal with uncertainty and incompleteness in the content of the database. Thus, intelligent databases commonly *infer* responses to queries for which there is no explicit data. The Country Consultant© is, by this definition, an intelligent database. Its inference method is briefly described later in this chapter. However, since it contains processed information just as an expert's knowledge rather than simple data, it is in effect an intelligent knowledge base.

As information becomes more complex and decision-making time frames grow shorter, the need to merge AI with database technologies will continue to grow. The Country Consultant© brings these technologies together in an attempt to aid the decision-making process in international marketing. In this way, it serves as a valuable tool supporting the counseling and advisory tasks at IBC.

THE COUNTRY CONSULTANT©

The Country Consultant© is a continuously-updated intelligent knowledge base of market research information pertaining to several countries throughout the world. This system allows the user to extract, in a structured way, information on issues such as economic climate, commercial environment, market access issues, cultural variables, and political and legal factors. Topics covered may be general or industry-specific.

The Country Consultant© is an innovative product of ongoing research in AI applications in international marketing. The tool provides market information for key trading partners of the United States. The program does not contain statistical or demographic data in a raw form. Rather, it incorporates judgements and guidelines pertaining to various aspects of the countries in question. It is also organized by specific industries and entry modes.

In other words, The Country Consultant© contains processed information in the form of qualitative, judgemental knowledge. The ultimate purpose of this knowledge is to aid the end-user (presumably someone without an in-depth understanding of the target markets) to make intelligent decisions pertaining to selection of the best countries to enter for marketing their products and/or services.

Moreover, such an "intelligent" system whose "intelligence" arises from its inferencing capabilities when explicit information is scarce or not available (just as an expert would do) is highly likely to be beneficial for anyone (including both academicians, market researchers, and managers or executives) who needs reliable, relevant, and timely information on foreign markets. In addition, it uses an indexing schema that accounts for the various information models cited in the literature.

Dimensions of International Business Knowledge

Information in The Country Consultant© is catalogued according to four *concept types*. These concept types include: *markets* (i.e., countries, geographic regions, and trading blocs); *industries* (i.e., classifications of manufactured goods and services); *entry modes* (i.e., strategies for foreign market entry); and market *features* (i.e., characteristics or attributes of the market that impact the decisions of the international marketer).

A *feature* is an attribute of a country which helps to categorize the information available on that country. Examples of features include economic environment, commercial environment, intellectual property protection, tariffs, etc. In other words, features range from macro categories such as commercial environment to very micro categories such as patent protection. All these attributes help to narrow down the information found through market research and determine where it fits in The Country Consultant©. *Industries* are product/service classifications which are used by The Country Consultant©. Again, industries are categorized at different levels of aggregation, such as consumer goods or medical goods or pharmaceuticals. *Entry mode* refers to the way by which companies interested in entering foreign markets may choose to follow, such as export or foreign direct investment. Finally, *market* is the country that is being analyzed. The four concepts are independent of each other and each includes a number of subcategories arranged along a hierarchical structure with the exception of the market concept.

For example, one can look for information on intellectual property protection (a feature) of the computer software industry (an industry) in India (a market). Similarly, one can find information on non-tariff barriers (a feature) of pharmaceuticals (an industry) in Thailand (a market) for exporting (an entry mode). Any combination of a particular feature, industry, entry mode, and market, as in the previous example, will be referred to as a *concept combination* from now on. Any concept combination can be utilized to search for desired information.

Records in the knowledge base are of two types, judgements and guidelines. *Judgements* are evaluative statements about a particular concept combination, stating that the situation is good or bad, getting better or worse. *Guidelines*, on the other hand, contain nonjudgemental information such as descriptive data or how-to guides. Each judgement and each guideline in the database is tied to one and only one specific concept combination.

In addition to performing the function of extracting judgemental and descriptive information, The Country Consultant© includes an *artificial intelligence* facility that allows it to query the database or make "best guesses" on the combination of these concepts based on other, related information. There is also the capability to compare and contrast features and industries of various countries, as well as gathering statistics of all the records in the database. Finally, for advanced users, there is the capability to alter the structure of the knowledge base by revising the features, industries, entry modes, and markets, and by altering the semantic relationships that exist between these concepts. The overall structure of The Country Consultant©, as well as the flow of information, are presented in Figure 1.

It is also important to explain the criteria used in identifying the categories included under the concepts and the hierarchies developed. The categories included under the feature concept and their

Figure 1. Structural Components and Information Flow of The Country Consultant©

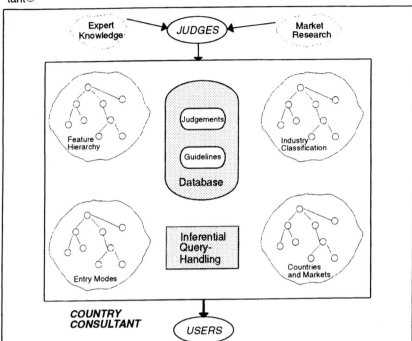

Judge enters information based on expert knowledge and market research findings. User queries the system for information, which triggers inferencing process. Semantic networks aid in knowledge organization and inferencing.

hierarchical ordering are identified through a thorough review of the theoretical and empirical studies reported in the literature and through consulting experts in the field. Figure 2 shows the main information categories included in the feature concept in The Country Consultant© and how they are related to the information categories suggested in the literature.

The categories included under the industry concept are a variation of the industry classifications used by the U.S. Department of Commerce. Various forms of entry to foreign markets are included under the entry mode concept. Finally, there are the markets, the countries with which the U.S. has international business relations.

The features, industries, and entry modes can be accessed in either

Figure 2. Relation of Features Used in The Country Consultant© to the Information Categories Suggested in the Academic Literature

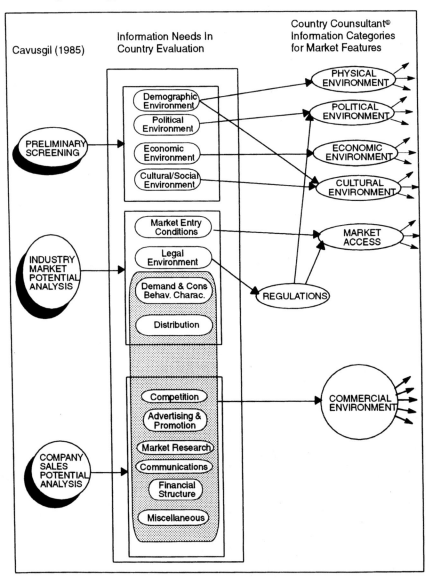

alphabetical or parent-child (hierarchical) order. In a parent-child relation, each concept type is divided into a macro (parent) and a micro (child) concept. For example, in the parent-child listing of the feature concept, commercial environment is a macro feature, or "parent" under which features such as demand, competition, or distribution infrastructure are micro features, or its "children." Likewise, distribution infrastructure is further subdivided into rail, communication, sea, air, and road infrastructures. For these latter features, distribution infrastructure will act as a macro feature. Parent-child relationships play an important role in the inference process in The Country Consultant©.

Entries to The Country Consultant© are made in the form of either *judgements* or *guidelines* for particular concept combinations. Each judgement or guideline is tied or related to a particular concept combination. Judgements are evaluative in nature, i.e., they provide evaluative information for the concept combination they are related to. Hence, the data used in arriving at the judgement must be concrete enough to derive a conclusion about the particular concept combination. A judgement includes the current state (excellent, good, fair, poor, or terrible) and its foreseen future direction (rapidly improving, improving, stable, deteriorating, or rapidly deteriorating).

Guidelines, on the other hand, provide descriptive information which would assist in conducting business in a foreign country, but which is not necessarily evaluative in nature. For example, they may contain a how-to guide or just some statistical information.

Information can be searched in The Country Consultant© by specifying a concept combination. The system responds to such a query by finding the related judgement and guideline both of which are easily and immediately accessible to the user. If no judgement exists in The Country Consultant© that is related to the chosen concept combination, the system can *infer* a judgement, using artificial intelligence techniques, based on judgements available for other "closely" related concept combinations. The definition of "close" is at the user's discretion since s/he can define the *inference strategy* to be followed. The different query options will be described later.

How The Country Consultant© Infers Evaluation

Obviously, a database with a large number of industry classes, markets, features, and entry modes will have a very large possible number of judgements. Currently the breakdown of conceptual primitives in the database is as follows: 57 market features; 98 industry categories; 11 entry modes; and 39 markets. This results in 2,396,394 $(57 \times 98 \times 11 \times 39)$ possible judgements in the database. Of course, it is not feasible for experts to enter all of these judgements. This is especially true because we are forcing judgements to be well-researched, and well-supported. Therefore, The Country Consultant© should be able to infer what a judgement should be upon request, even if that judgement has not been explicitly entered by an expert, based on the explicit judgements that are "conceptually close" to it.

Additionally, with such a large knowledge base, it is important to maintain the integrity of its content. Judgements should be consistent with each other. Thus, The Country Consultant© should be able to "second-guess" judges. Inferring what a judgement should be based on conceptually close judgements helps in this regard.

Hence, in addition to serving as a repository of processed, judgemental knowledge, The Country Consultant© also has the facility to respond intelligently to queries made by the user. If it cannot find a judgement that specifically meets the user's query, it can infer a likely value for that judgement by searching the knowledge base for conceptually similar judgements. Moreover, it can provide a "second guess" for the evaluation of a concept combination if a judgement has already been entered.

Validation of Information in The Country Consultant©

The validation process for The Country Consultant© is sequential and dynamic in nature. It consists of three stages for internal and external validation of the system.

The first stage focuses on initial screening and structural development of The Country Consultant©. Here information entered by students and researchers is screened for qualitative errors and concept combinations. The second stage focuses on expert opinion-qualitative testing where The Country Consultant© is put through a rigorous in-house testing process. In this phase, internal consistency of information and its reliability is tested. The third stage consists of validation coupled with expert opinion.

STEP-BY-STEP INSTRUCTIONS
FOR QUERYING THE COUNTRY CONSULTANT©

There are four ways of querying The Country Consultant©:[3] (1) querying for multiple records, (2) single-record query, (3) through inference, and (4) through data statistics. Each one of these options is described below with examples.

1. Querying the Database for Multiple Records

The first screen the user will see when s/he runs The Country Consultant© will be the main screen which is presented in Figure 3. Once you press F7 (Query) from the main screen, you will be given the option to enter the specific query for database records to retrieve. This query consists of specifying the type or records wanted (judgement, guideline, or both); the judgements you want to concentrate on (excellent, good, fair, poor, terrible); the features, industries entry modes, and/or markets desired; and the range of dates desired. Entering a database query consists of the following steps:

1. The Country Consultant© asks you to select JUDGEMENT, GUIDELINES, or both. To select one or more of these, press ENTER with the cursor positioned there. You will see a mark appear at the left of that entry. (LDClick with the mouse will do the same.) Once finished selecting, press the F8 key to continue.
2. If you had picked JUDGEMENT, you will be presented with the possible judgements to focus on. You may pick one or more, or none, then press F8 to continue. If you select none, then all judgement types will be included in the search . . . there will be no constraint imposed.
3. Next, you will be presented with an alphabetized list of features to select. Again, you may choose any or none. If you select one or more, the search will be constrained to searching only for records pertaining to the selected features.
4. Next, you will be presented with an alphabetized list of industries to select. Again, you may choose any or none. If you select one or more, the search will be constrained to searching only for records pertaining to the selected industries.
5. Next, you will be presented with an alphabetized list of entry

modes to select. Again, you may choose any or none. If you select one or more, the search will be constrained to searching only for records pertaining to the selected entry modes.

6. Next, you will be presented with an alphabetized list of markets to select. Again, you may choose any or none. If you select one or more, the search will be constrained to searching only for records pertaining to the selected markets.

7. Finally, you have the option to specify the range of dates desired. Records that are retrieved will have been entered (or last modified) within the desired range of dates.

Note: in the query, you *must* constrain the search somewhat, either by specifying certain features, industries, entry modes, or markets. Figures 4 through 10 show the screens and menus that appear throughout the querying process.

After you have completed your query, The Country Consultant© will search for all records that match your request. If any are found, these will be listed for you. Each item in the list will show the

Figure 3

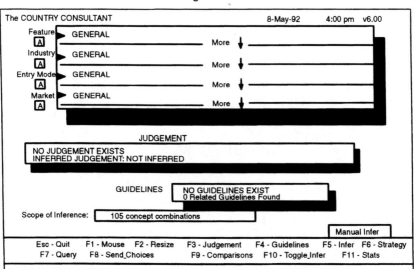

The main screen of The Country Consultant©

judgement (or guideline), market, feature, industry, and entry mode, as shown in Figure 11.

At this point, you have the following options, based on pressing a function key or a mouse button:

Esc–Quit. Takes you back to the Main Screen.

RClick–This will display the text of the item over which the cursor is currently placed (see Figure 12).

Enter or LDClick–This selects an item from the list. A mark will appear to the left of this item indicating that it was selected.

F7–Print Choices. This will print out each judgement and guideline that is currently selected (i.e., all those that were marked via Enter or LDClick).

F8–Edit Choices. This takes you to the Judgement Edit Screen or Guideline Edit Screen for all selected items. In this way, you can edit records from the Database Query Screen.

2. Single-Record Query from Main Screen

The user is able to search for a specific *concept combination* (feature, industry, entry mode, and market) directly from the main screen, by using the appropriate windows. This is done using the FEATURE, INDUSTRY, ENTRY MODE, and/or MARKET windows on the main screen, as illustrated in the following pages.

First, you will notice that these windows, although each is only one line deep, actually consist of menus of several items from which to select. For example, the features window consists of almost 100 possible features. You can see this by putting the cursor in the FEATURE window (by LClick with the mouse), then paging up and down in the window (pressing the PgUp and PgDn key). You will notice the word "More" at the bottom of the FEATURE window. This indicates that there are more items that can be seen.

Another way to see multiple features is to resize the FEATURE window. To do this, place the cursor in this window, then press the F2 (resize) function key. You will see that the FEATURE window has been enlarged, showing many items from the list of features. Note that these items are shown in alphabetical order, with the exception that GENERAL is at the top (see Figure 13).

Figure 4

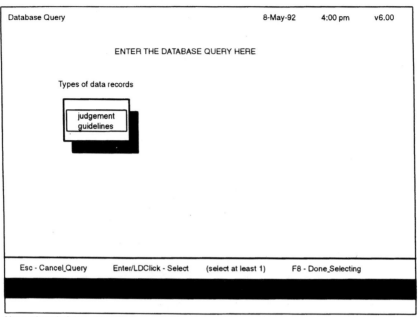

Database Query	8-May-92	4:00 pm	v6.00

ENTER THE DATABASE QUERY HERE

Types of data records

judgement
guidelines

Esc - Cancel Query   Enter/LDClick - Select   (select at least 1)   F8 - Done Selecting

User selects judgements, guidelines or both.

To select a feature, you can page down to the desired feature, and press ENTER or LDClick. Alternatively, you can type in the first few letters of the desired feature. You will notice that as you type these letters, the desired feature will become visible. Finally, when selected, the feature will have a mark on its left. The same method can be used to select an industry, entry mode, and/or a market from their associated windows.

Once you have made your selections, press the F8 key to "send your choice." Then, The Country Consultant© will attempt to find a judgement and guideline that matches the desired concept combination. If a judgement was found, this will be reflected in the top line of the JUDGEMENT window of the main screen. Likewise, if a guideline was found, it will be shown in the GUIDELINES window.

For example, Figure 14 shows the judgement that was found when the user selected "Intellectual Property Protection" as the

Figure 5

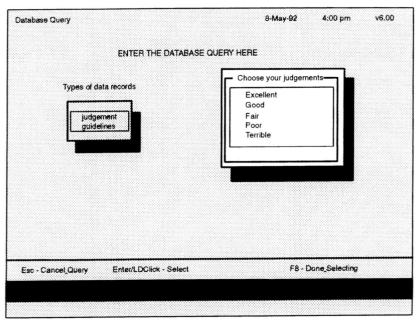

User can now specify which judgement types to search.

feature and "Canada" as the market (industry and entry mode were left at "GENERAL"). As can be seen, a judgement was found for this concept combination, but no guidelines were found. According to the judgement, which had been entered in October 1991, the intellectual property climate in Canada is good.

If you want to see the reasons for this judgement, you can do an RClick with the cursor placed at the first line of the JUDGEMENT window. When you do this, another window will pop up showing the text justifying this judgement (see Figure 15). In this example, the text was extracted from the Overseas Business Report, provided by the U.S. Department of Commerce.

3. Inference

Because of all the possible features, industries, entry modes, and markets covered in The Country Consultant©, there will frequently

Figure 6

Database Query   8-May-92   4:00 pm   v6.00

ENTER THE DATABASE QUERY HERE

Types of data records   ┌─ Choose your judgements ─┐

judgement   Good
guidelines   Fair
                                          Poor

┌─ Features ───┐
│ GENERAL   │
│ Air Infrastructure   │
│ Antitrust Legislation   │
│ Balance of Payments/Foreign Debt   │
│ Banking   │
│ Barriers   │
│ Best Prospects List   │
│ Business Customs   │
│ Business Incentives   │
└──────────────────────────── More ↓ ─────────────────────────────────────┘

Esc - Cancel Query   Enter/LDClick - Select   F8 - Done Selecting

Now, the user can select the desired features. If none are selected, the system will not constrain the search on features. . . all features will be included in the search.

be concept combinations for which no record (judgement or guideline) exists. In such a case, The Country Consultant© can make an "educated guess" about the judgement or guideline via a technique called *inference*. Inference is a process whereby The Country Consultant© searches for records pertaining to related concepts in order to estimate the judgement that was queried. The related concepts are identified through the hierarchical relationships among each concept type. The hierarchy for each concept type can be viewed through the main screen as shown in Figure 16.

This section describes how the user can invoke inference in CC. The inference process is invoked from the main screen. There are three elements involved in inference:

(1) Setting the desired feature, industry, entry mode, and market. This is done via the *single-record query* described above.
(2) Setting the *inference strategy*, or alternatively, using the de-

fault inference strategy. The inference strategy determines the *inference scope*, which bounds the conceptual distance that can be searched.

(3) Invoking inference, either via manual inference invocation or via auto-inference.

An Example: Inferring the Copyright Protection Climate for Computer Software in the European Community.

In this example, we show how The Country Consultant© makes a "best guess" about a user's query for which there are no explicit judgements or guidelines in the database. The sample query pertains to the copyright protection climate for software in the European Community (see Figure 17). As indicated by the first line of the JUDGEMENT window, there is no explicit information about

Figure 7

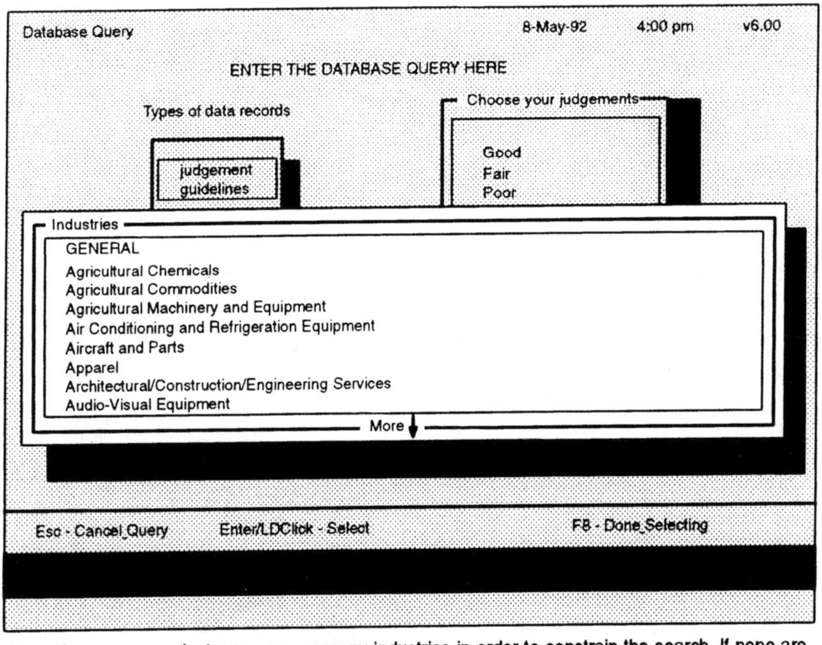

Now, the user can select zero, one, or many industries in order to constrain the search. If none are selected, the search will not be constrained to any industries, otherwise the search will be constrained to only those industries selected.

Figure 8

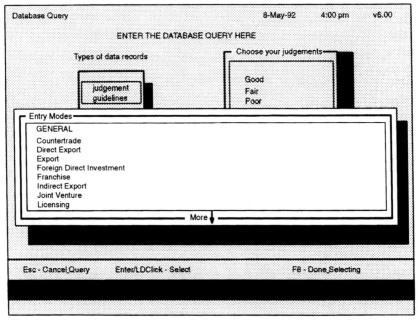

Now, the user can select zero, one, or several entry modes for constraining the search.

this topic in the database. Also, notice that no inference has been performed yet, as indicated in the second line of the JUDGEMENT window.

Likewise, in the GUIDELINES window, the top line indicates that there is no guideline for the current concept combination, and the second line shows that no inference has been performed.

The Scope of Inference

Although no inference has been made as of yet, you can see which concepts will be searched when you initiate an inference. On the main screen, the *scope of inference* window indicates how many concept combinations will be generated for the search, 96 in this case. If you do LDClick in this window, another window will pop up indicating the specific features, industries, entry modes, and markets that will be included in the search (see Figure 18).

Figure 9

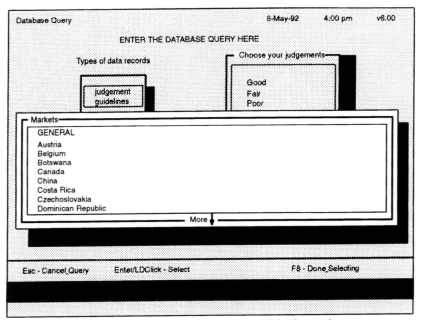

Now, the user can select zero, one, or several markets for constraining the search.

In this case there are two features, six industries, one entry mode, and eight markets involved in the search. If you multiply these numbers together, you will arrive at the 96 concept combinations shown in the scope of inference window. Thus, all combinations of these concepts will be included in the search.

Setting the Inference Strategy

If you want to see how this scope of inference was determined, you can display the inference strategy. In addition, you can change it, which results in a different scope. To see the inference strategy from the main screen, press the F6 key. A window will pop up which shows, for each concept type, the number of steps up the *parent-link* and down the *child-link* that can be searched (see Figure 19). The number of steps will affect the scope of inference by setting a boundary on the search. In addition, for each concept type,

Figure 10

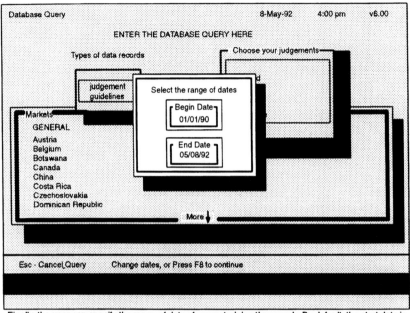

Finally, the user can specify the range of dates for constraining the search. By default, the start date is 1/1/90 and the end date is today's date. If satisfied, just press F8, otherwise change the date(s) you want and then press F8.

the *attenuation factor* is shown. The attenuation factor affects the weighting assigned to judgements that are found in the search. The user can choose to use this (default) inference strategy, or enter his or her own. To change any steps or attenuation entry, place the cursor there and replace the number. Then press F8 to save the inference strategy. This will cause the next inference to use your own inference strategy.

You will be asked whether to make this change permanent. If you say yes, then this inference strategy will be used whenever that feature, industry, entry mode, and market appears again in a query. Otherwise, it will only be used for the current query's inference.

Be cautious about the steps you indicate in your inference strategy. The number of concept combinations can grow exponentially with each additional step included in the search process. Obviously, this can have a significant impact on the search time, as well as

Figure 11

| Database Query | | | 8-May-92 | 4:00 pm | v6.00 |

The following records match the database query you requested

J/G	Market	Feature	Industry	Entry Mode
Good	Canada	Copyrights	GENERAL	GENERAL
Excellent	Germany	Copyrights	GENERAL	GENERAL
Fair	Mexico	Copyrights	GENERAL	GENERAL
Poor	Italy	Intellectual P	GENERAL	GENERAL
Good	Dominican Re	Intellectual P	GENERAL	GENERAL
Good	Canada	Intellectual P	GENERAL	GENERAL
Poor	Honduras	Intellectual P	GENERAL	GENERAL
Poor	Netherlands	Intellectual P	Computer Software	GENERAL
Excellent	Germany	Patent Prote	GENERAL	GENERAL
Good	Ireland	Patent Prote	GENERAL	GENERAL
Poor	Canada	Patent Prote	Drugs and Pharma	GENERAL

More ↓

| Esc - Quit | Enter - Choose | RClick - Explain_J_or_G | F7 - Print_Choices | F8 - Edit_Choices |

This list results from querying the database for records pertaining to intellectual property protection and copyrights for various Western countries.

leading to a large number of irrelevant judgements and/or guide-lines. As a general rule, your scope of inference should not exceed a few hundred concept combinations.

Initiating the Inference Process

To initiate the inference process, press the F5 (Infer) key from the main screen. A screen will appear indicating that The Country Consultant© is inferring, and will continually show you how many of the combinations have been searched and how many judgements and guidelines have been found. At the end of the search, the main screen will reappear. If judgements or guidelines were found, this will be indicated in the second line of the judgement or guidelines window, respectively, as shown in Figure 20.

Figure 12

Database Query			8-May-92	4:00 pm	v6.00

The following records match the database query you requested

J/G	Market	Feature	Industry	Entry Mode
Good	Canada	Copyrights	GENERAL	GENERAL

Illegal copying of software has been one of the major problems
of the Dutch and European software trade. A joint effort by the
Dutch legal authorities, local software importers, and producers
has reduced the problem somewhat. In January 1993, all
members of the E.C. are expected to have laws against
the illegal copying of software in effect.

(Country Marketing Plan, 1990).

Esc -

Here, the user does RClick on the "Netherlands is poor in protecting computer software property" item. An explanation of this item pops up as a result of the RClick. The user can press Esc to return to the list after reading the text.

At this point, you can see which related judgements were found that caused this inference to take place. To do so, position the mouse cursor over the second line of the judgement window and press LDClick.

A window will pop up which shows the judgements, as shown in Figure 21. The value of each judgement, and its feature, market, industry, and entry mode will be displayed. At this point, the user can see the text for any judgement desired by doing RClick at the desired judgement.

Alternatively, the user can select judgements to print or edit pressing Enter or LDClick (to select), then pressing F7 or F8 keys (for print or edit, respectively). (Note: this concept of using Enter or LDClick to select entries, then pressing a function key to edit or

Figure 13

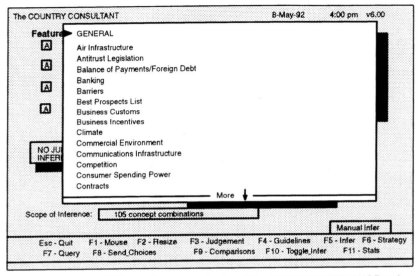

You can resize the FEATURE box. The same can be done for the INDUSTRY, ENTRY MODE, and MARKET boxes.

Figure 14

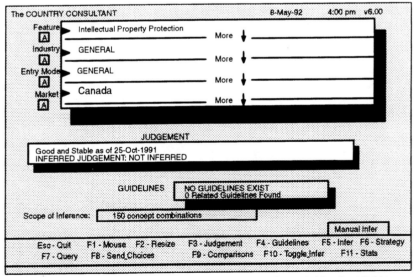

A query of intellectual property protection for Canada results in a judgement of Good and Stable.

Figure 15

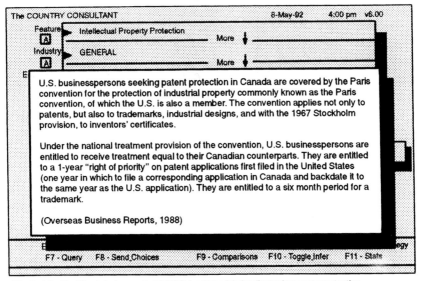

The text that justifies a judgement of GOOD for Canada's intellectual property protection.

print the selections, is available at many points throughout The Country Consultant©.)

4. Using Database Statistics

The Country Consultant© allows the user to gather statistics of judgement and guidelines records that it contains. These statistics show a distribution of judgements from excellent through terrible for any concept (feature, industry, entry mode, or market) you wish to see. In addition, it allows you to select queries similar to those used in the Database Query option described above.

To use the database statistics option from the main screen, press the F11 (Stats) key. You will first be asked whether you want to gather statistics for the entire database or just a portion of the database, as shown in Figure 22. If you select only parts of the database, you are taken through the query process, as described in Section 1. Otherwise, The Country Consultant© immediately begins to gather statistics for the entire database. If your database is very large, this could take a few minutes to do.

Figure 16

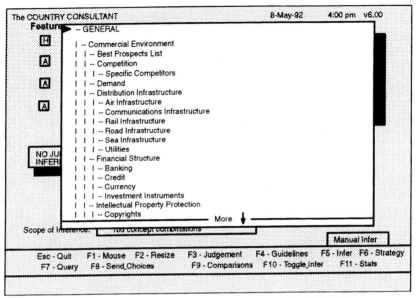

By doing LDClick on the "A" beside the feature window, and then pressing F2 (Resize), the user can see the features in hierarchical order.

After the statistics are gathered, you are shown a screen which displays the numbers of excellent, good, fair, poor, and terrible judgements, as well as guidelines, for all concepts involved in the query. This gives you a "birds-eye" view of the current state of the database.

The database statistics screen shows four scrollable windows, one each showing features, industries, entry modes, and markets (see Figure 23). You can page down and up each of these windows to see additional concepts and their associated statistics. Alternatively, you can resize a desired window by putting the cursor in that window and pressing the F2 (Resize) key (see Figure 24).

Each window shows the number of excellent, good, fair, poor, and terrible judgements, and the number of guidelines for each of its associated concepts. Also note that there is a one- or two-letter code to the left of each concept. For example, in the expanded feature window of Figure 24, note the letters "SG" to the left of the word "Copyrights." This code indicates that the distribution of judgements are "skewed good," or that there are more good judge-

Figure 17

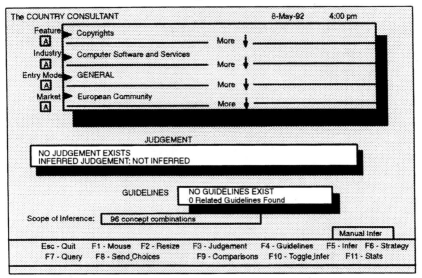

The JUDGEMENT box indicates that there is no judgement in the database pertaining to the user's query. Likewise, the GUIDELINES box shows no guidelines in the database.

ments than bad judgements pertaining to copyrights in the database. The possible codes are listed below, with their associated meanings:

SG–Skewed Good. Better judgements predominate.

SB–Skewed Bad. Worse judgements predominate.

U–Uniform. Judgements are distributed evenly.

N–Normal. Average judgements seem to predominate, approaching a normal curve.

BM–Bimodal. Both extremes tend to predominate over the average.

These codes indicate a very approximate idea of how the judgements are distributed from excellent through terrible for the associated concept.

The user can obtain more detailed information about the judgements and guidelines. For example, suppose you want to see the good judgements for patent protection. As you can see from Figure 24, there are three such judgements. By doing LDClick with the cursor over the number 3 (under Good, to the right of Patent Protection), you will see

Figure 18

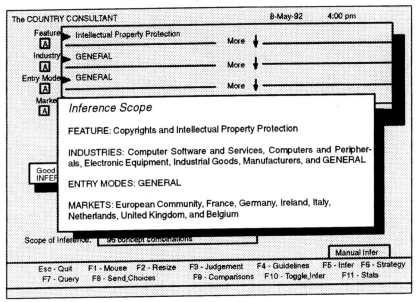

When you LDClick in the Scope of Inference window, all concepts involved in the search are shown.

the judgements in question via a new window that pops up. Figure 25 illustrates this.

From this new window, you have several options. Doing RClick with the cursor over one of the entries in this window will cause another window to pop up showing the text behind the judgement, as shown in Figure 26. (This is similar as in the inference and database-query modes.) Alternatively, LDClick to select F7 or F8 allows you to print or edit selected judgements.

ADVANTAGES AND DISADVANTAGES OF USING THE COUNTRY CONSULTANT©

The Country Consultant© has certain features that qualifies it as an intelligent knowledge base that can assist managers in arriving at informed decisions about foreign markets and international marketing operations.

Figure 19

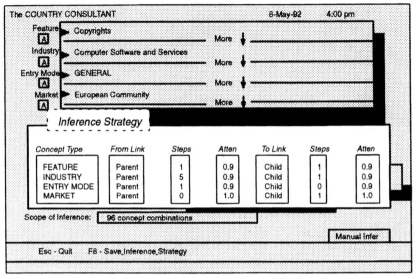

The Inference Strategy box allows you to view and alter the inference strategy in terms of scope (via parent- and child- steps) and in terms of weighting (via parent- and child- attenuations).

First, The Country Consultant© is not just a database storing raw data, but it provides expert information. Judgements by experts in international business are incorporated into the database which actually make it an industry, country, and entrymode specific knowledge base. In fact, raw data are rarely presented–only in cases to represent trends or in guidelines. Thus, the user can either use the information presented in decision making directly or use it to compare with his/her own or others' judgements and evaluations.

Second, by presenting information rather than data on foreign markets, The Country Consultant© is expected to fill a gap in international business, i.e., the unavailability of processed information about foreign markets. Raw data are not of much use unless they are sorted, analyzed, and processed into a meaningful form. The Country Consultant© provides ready-to-use information by compiling the relevant data and information presented in published documents or reports and supplementing this with expert consultation.

Figure 20

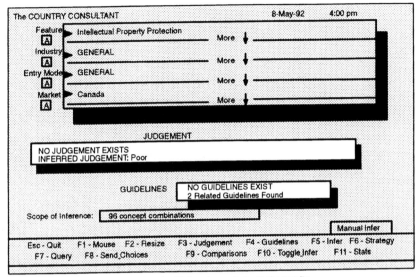

After the inference, the judgement and guidelines boxes indicate the results.

Third, The Country Consultant© software is designed to have the inference capacity, i.e., making a judgement when the database does not have a judgement or guideline that exactly meets the user's query. In such a case, it can infer a judgement based on available judgements about conceptually related or similar fields. Thus, even if the database is incomplete (as it almost certainly will be), it can still give reasonable answers to queries for which it may not contain explicit data.

Fourth, the information categories included in The Country Consultant© are identified through a thorough review of the theoretical or empirical studies reported in the literature and through consulting experts in the field. The Country Consultant© will be helpful to the decision maker at each stage of the sequential process for analyzing foreign markets, i.e., preliminary screening, industry market potential analysis, and company sales potential analysis.

Fifth, The Country Consultant© is designed to be flexible enough to adjust to the dynamic nature of international business and to suit the needs of every company/user interested in going interna-

Figure 21

The COUNTRY CONSULTANT			8-May-92	4:00 pm
Inference Based On: Protection				
Poor	Netherlands	Intellectual P	GENERAL	GENERAL
Poor	Italy	Intellectual P	GENERAL	GENERAL
Poor	Italy	Intellectual P	Computer Softw	GENERAL
Poor	Italy	Copyrights	GENERAL	GENERAL
Excellent	Germany	Copyrights	GENERAL	GENERAL
Poor	Netherlands	Copyrights	Computer Softw	GENERAL

JUDGEMENT
NO JUDGEMENT EXISTS
INFERRED JUDGEMENT: Poor

GUIDELINES   NO GUIDELINES EXIST
2 Related Guidelines Found

Scope of Inference: 96 concept combinations

Manual Infer

Esc - Main_Screen   Enter - LDClick-Select   RClick-Show_Explanation
F7 - Print_Selected_Judgements   F8 - Edit_Selected_Judgements

If the user does LDClick with the cursor on the second line of the Judgement box, another box pops up displaying all the related judgements found via inference.

tional or selecting a foreign market. The structure of The Country Consultant© is not rigid and it can easily be expanded to include other information categories if the need arises due to the specific needs of users. Moreover, the database can and should be updated periodically or if there are abrupt changes in the country. The user can always judge the timeliness of the information by checking the precise date when the judgement was made. It is most critical that the database of the tool must be updated since the information provided will be valuable and relevant only if it is up-to-date.

Sixth, the source of information and/or data used by the expert in coming to a conclusion is also described for each judgement or suggestion made which will enable the user to see how the judgement is supported. Thus, the user can always double-check if he/she desires to do so or consult the sources for more detailed information.

Seventh, The Country Consultant© will allow the managers to utilize their time more efficiently by presenting the information they need in a user-friendly software form. This takes the burden of

Figure 22

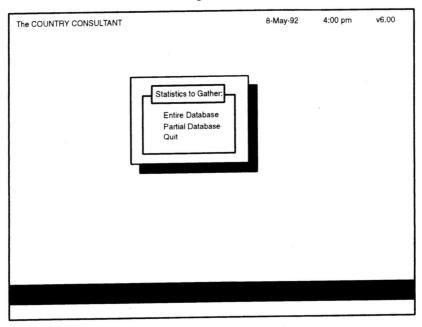

You can gather statistics for the entire database or just a partial database.

going through and analyzing a bulk of documents and reports away from the manager. Moreover, the managers can check the country reports prepared by subordinates or other departments by comparing them with the information in The Country Consultant©.

Eighth, The Country Consultant© gives information about best prospects which are those industries within a country that are most attractive for exports. These industries are given in rank order of attractiveness which will aid the companies in identifying the most prospective industries and concentrating their efforts. This type of information will also be helpful for companies who are either diversified or interested in diversifying into other industries.

Ninth, the user can get information on any level of aggregation desired. He/she may query the database to look for general trends in the country as a whole or in specific industries. It is possible to query judgements for very specific market features such as political

Figure 23

Database Statistics			8-May-92	4:00 pm		v6.00

FEATURE	EXCE	GOOD	FAIR	POOR	TERR	GUIDE
SG Copyrights	1	2	1	2	0	4
SB Intellectual Property Protection	0	2	0	7	0	2
N Patent Protection	1	3	3	2	1	8

More ↓

INDUSTRY	EXCE	GOOD	FAIR	POOR	TERR	GUIDE
SG GENERAL	2	7	2	7	0	23
U Agricultural Chemicals	0	0	0	0	0	0
U Agricultural Commodities	0	0	0	0	0	0

More ↓

ENTRY MODE	EXCE	GOOD	FAIR	POOR	TERR	GUIDE
SB GENERAL	2	8	4	12	1	25
U Countertrade	0	0	0	0	0	0
U Export	0	0	0	0	0	0

More ↓

MARKET	EXCE	GOOD	FAIR	POOR	TERR	GUIDE
SB GENERAL	0	0	0	2	0	0
SG Austria	0	2	1	0	0	1
U Belgium	0	0	0	0	0	0

More ↓

TOTAL JUDGEMENTS: 27   TOTAL GUIDELINES: 26

Esc - Quit	F2 - Resize_ Window	F7 - Print_ Stats

The Database Statistics Screen.

stability, business customs, product standards, tariff levels, etc. For example, The Country Consultant© can provide information even for very specific queries such as the labeling standards for exporting pharmaceuticals to the country. The level of specificity or aggregation is controlled by the user which is another distinguished feature of The Country Consultant©.

Finally, The Country Consultant© is also a very useful pedagogical tool that would contribute to the students' learning when it is used in the classroom. In fact, the tool has been used in some undergraduate and graduate classes at Michigan State University

Figure 24

Database Statistics		8-May-92	4:00 pm		v6.00

	FEATURE	EXCE	GOOD	FAIR	POOR	TERR	GUIDE
SG	Copyrights	1	2	1	2	0	4
SB	Intellectual Property Protection	0	2	0	7	0	2
N	Patent Protection	1	3	3	2	1	8
U	Royalties	0	0	0	0	0	5
BM	Trademarks	0	1	0	1	0	7
SB	TOTALS	2	8	4	12	1	26

Esc - Quit	F2 - Resize_ Window	F7 - Print_ Stats

The Database Statistics Screen with the FEATURES window resized.

successfully and the students' experience with The Country Consultant© has contributed to their learning of international marketing in various ways. The feature hierarchy in The Country Consultant© presents a cohesive and integrated framework for information requirements in foreign market evaluation. Through working with The Country Consultant©, the students have been able to learn about the information categories and their subcategories that are important in evaluating foreign markets. The tool has also helped them to learn how to conduct research in international marketing. After having gone through their experience with The Country Consultant©, the students had a better understanding of desk research in international marketing and how to go about doing that type of research.

Figure 25

Database Statistics			8-May-92	4:00 pm	v6.00

FEATURE	EXCE	GOOD	FAIR	POOR	TERR GUIDE
SG Copyrights	1	2	1	2	0	4
SB Intellectual Property Protection	0	2	0	7	0	2
N Patent Protection	1	3	3	2	1	8
U Royalties	0	0	0	0	0	5
BM Trademarks	0	1	0	1	0	7

Stats Records:

Good	Ireland	Patent Protect	GENERAL	GENERAL
Good	Netherlands	Patent Protect	GENERAL	GENERAL
Good	France	Patent Protect	Drugs and Phar	GENERAL

Esc - Main_Screen	Enter/LDClick-Select	RClick-Show_ Explanation
F7 - Print_Selected_Judgements	F8 - Edit_Selected_Judgements	

By doing LDClick on the number "3" under "good" for patent protection, a window pops up showing the three "good" judgements.

The possible disadvantages of The Country Consultant© can be described in two different contexts. First, if it is used to extract knowledge, the issues relate to the reliability and validity of the information provided. These issues are dealt with through an extensive dynamic validation process developed in-house which we have discussed elsewhere in the literature. However, the process requires continuous maintenance and thus, is very labor intensive. Second, the structure of the tool can be used to build one's own knowledge base. The issue, then is to make sure that extreme care is given to the market research process. In addition to these, The Country Consultant© is a very sophisticated tool that requires the user to get familiar with it before s/he can use it efficiently. However, this is the case for most types of software and the eventual benefits that will be obtained by using the tool will more than outweigh any costs associated with it.

Figure 26

Database Statistics   8-May-92   4:00 pm   v6.00

FEATURE	EXCE	GOOD	FAIR	POOR	TERR	GUIDE
SG Copyrights	1	2	1	2	0	4
SB Intellectual Property Protection	0	2	0	7	0	2
N Patent Protection	1	3	3	2	1	8
U Royalties	0	0	0	0	0	5
BM Trademarks	0	1	0	1	0	7

Judgement

The Netherlands belongs to the World Intellectual Property Organization (WIPO), is a signatory of the Paris Convention for the Protection of Industrial Property, and conforms to accepted international practices for protection of technology and trademarks. Patents for foreign inventions are granted retroactively to the date of original filing in the home country, provided the application is made through a patent lawyer. Patents are valid for 20 years. Since the Netherlands and the U.S. are both parties to the Patent Corporation Treaty of 1970, patent rights to the Netherlands may be obtained at the time of filing in the U.S. if the PCT application is used.

(Country Market Plan, 1990)

Esc - Main Screen   Enter/LDClick-Select   RClick-Show_ Explanation
F7 - Print Selected Judgements   F8 - Edit Selected Judgements

Doing RClick over the "Netherlands good patent protection" judgement causes the explanation text to pop up.

TECHNICAL REQUIREMENTS FOR USING THE COUNTRY CONSULTANT©

The Country Consultant© software is designed for personal computers using the DOS operating system. It requires 3 MB of memory space to run. The amount of hard disk space needed will depend on the amount of information that is stored. Currently, we have about 3,000 judgements/guidelines and about 20 MB of hard disk space used to store it. Additionally, operation of the tool is made easier if a mouse is attached to the computer.

SUGGESTIONS FOR TERM PROJECTS

The main benefit of using The Country Consultant© in the classroom is to provide an alternative method of teaching students how to do research in the area of international marketing. An advantage of using the database is that it imposes a structure on the student's research activity that is not normally found in other class projects such as term papers. Because the information in The Country Consultant© is categorized according to market feature, industry classification, and entry mode, this provides a framework for students to use in their research effort. In short, imposing such a structure helps to focus the student by giving him or her an idea of what it is s/he is looking for. In short, The Country Consultant© can be used as a pedagogical tool for teaching business students techniques of international market research.

In one type of project, the students (individually or in teams of two) can be assigned to gather secondary information about a country pertaining to the various features, industry classifications, and entry modes of The Country Consultant©. Students would be expected to gather this information from government documents (such as U.S. Department of Commerce Country Market Plans), trade journals and periodicals (such as *Business International,* Price Waterhouse, or Dun and Bradstreet reports), academic literature, or any other timely and reliable sources they could find.

In addition to gathering information about the market, the students would also be asked to thoroughly analyze the information. Specifically, they would need to classify it according to the appropriate feature, industry, and entry mode. This involves extracting paragraphs, sentences, or phrases from the literature, then segregating and categorizing these text fragments. This is perhaps the most challenging and time-consuming aspect of the assignment. It requires the student to do a sort of *content analysis* of the text, and to really understand what the text is saying.

Finally, after collecting, disaggregating, classifying, and assigning judgements to the market research information, students would be asked to enter the information directly into The Country Consultant©. Thus, these students will get hands-on experience in using the software.

Another type of assignment can be to focus on an industry. That is students (individually or in teams of two) would be assigned an industry, and would study this industry across several markets. Other than the change in focus, data collection and analysis processes of the students, the evaluation process would be the same as in the above example.

The students would be evaluated according to several criteria. The quantity of judgements and guidelines entered for the country would be one indicator. They would also be graded based on the comprehensiveness of the information they entered. In other words, were they covering many bases or just concentrating on a few features of the market? The accuracy of information classification would also be a major indicator. The number and quality of the sources used would be another criteria.

END OF CHAPTER QUESTIONS

1. What is an intelligent database?
2. What are the main problems in international market research?
3. How is The Country Consultant© structured? What are its main components? What is the difference between a judgement and a guideline?
4. What is meant by inference?
5. How can the database of The Country Consultant© be queried? What are the differences between different query methods?
6. How can The Country Consultant© be used:
   a. by companies?
   b. in the classroom?
7. What are issues of concern with The Country Consultant©?

NOTES

1. The Country Consultant© software is copyrighted by Michigan State University.
2. IBC is comprised of two units. The Center for International Business Education and Research (CIBER) is a national resource center funded by the U.S.

Department of Education. Development of Country Consultant© and other expert systems is taking place at CIBER as part of its research activities. The Michigan International Business Development Center (MI-IBDC) provides counseling and assistance in internationalization and export planning to small and medium-sized companies in Michigan.

3. In the following descriptions, RClick refers to a single right click on the mouse, RDclick refers to a double right click on the mouse, LClick refers to a single left click on the mouse, LDclick refers to a double left click on the mouse.

Chapter 4

International Business Simulation I: Using Export to Win!

Richard K. Harper
Richard Sjolander
Snorri Gislason

INTRODUCTION

Export to Win! is an excellent tool to introduce the user to various factors involved in exporting. The program is applicable for use in both classroom and professional settings. Export to Win! is user friendly. People with no experience in exporting can run through the simulation without a problem. Of course, their performance will improve with experience. It is also interesting for people with limited to moderately extensive experience in exporting. Export to Win! introduces the user to several options for dealing with many of the problems typically faced by an exporter. Professional exporters might, therefore, be introduced to an alternative solution to a problem they have encountered.

OBJECTIVES

The stated goal of this simulation is "to serve as an aid in learning to export successfully on an international scale, thereby increasing market share and profits . . ." (Export to Win!). The participants' task is to generate at least $6 million in export revenues by the end of five years through export sales. With the knowledge of exporting that can be gained through about four hours of working with the simulation, that sales volume is easily attainable. Someone with experience in international business might reach this goal in one or two hours, as they would not need to spend as much time learning about the various options available to the firm. From there on the user can choose different options and try to further increase sales.

The learning objectives of the simulation, as stated on one of the first screens viewed each time the program is opened, are:

- to learn that exporting makes good business sense;
- to learn to research and put together a market plan by locating and selecting markets; and
- to discover how the right mix of promoting and pricing, along with strategies of adapting and expanding product lines will allow a company to market on a global basis.

The simulation provides an entertaining, as well as, informative method for the user to learn the basics of exporting. It can be used as a stand-alone product without an instructor, or in a more structured learning environment to gain an understanding of many of the terms that are typically foreign to the experience and training of domestic business types. Concepts such as the hedging of transactions risks have stumped business students for generations. When introduced as a natural part of the exchange process in Export to Win! students grasp the concept quickly.

WHEN SHOULD YOU USE EXPORT TO WIN!?

In the Classroom

Export to Win! is a smart idea when you have an international business term paper to do. Probably the most common assignment that instructors give in college-level international business courses is a term project in which students themselves become international businesspeople. Students are asked to assume a corporate identity, either real or created, and told to conquer a foreign market. Typically, you are asked to pick a product or service and then define what is unique about doing business in a foreign environment. You probably will have to find information on characteristics of the population, such as age distribution, income, or cultural characteristics that might be relevant to sales of your product.

In Business

Obviously, in selling your product, you need to first establish whether a potential market exists for your product. Here, you need information on who the potential customers are and how to reach them. This is where you put all those marketing research classes to work! You will also want to use the resources available in the National Trade Data Base (also reviewed in this book), such as the *ABC's of Exporting,* or the articles published in *Business America.* Additionally, you might want to contact the local export specialist at the Department of Commerce, International Trade Administration.

What you will also need to know, and what makes your international business project very different from other marketing research you may have done, is how to go about the business of taking your business international. Export to Win! is especially helpful with the nuts and bolts of going international. What should your contractual arrangements be with your potential business partner in a foreign market? What are the different pricing strategies which you might use for your product, and where could you find numerical examples?

Do you ship the product CIF, FOB, FAS, or CI, and what exactly do these terms mean? What are the different methods commonly used in the payment of international transactions? It is in answering these and dozens of other basic procedural questions that Export to Win! is especially helpful (see Figure 1). It provides the guidance necessary to quickly understand what is involved in overseas expansion.

How It Works

The Export to Win! simulation, or game, walks you through a generic international marketing process as export manager of XE-BEC, requiring you to answer international business questions at

FIGURE 1

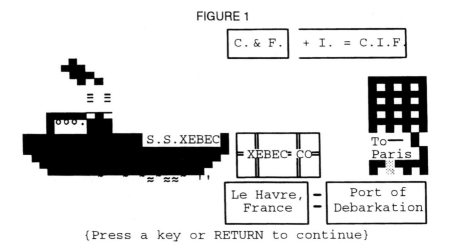

{Press a key or RETURN to continue}

each step of the way. Because it is done as a game, you will end up paying a lot of attention to the process XEBEC uses to go international as you try to beat the game. This process is just as applicable to a real world product as it is to XEBEC's systems. You develop intuition and start assessing the market in terms of competition, trade shows, insurance, financing, trend analysis, and strategy. Giving a picture of the progression of international operations is something that Export to Win! is particularly good at, relative to other resources.

Export to Win! pays great attention to detail, defining many important concepts throughout the simulation. A particularly useful aspect is that relevant terms are presented together, and comparisons made, so that you can decide in the context of XEBEC management decision making which choice is best for you.

Beyond a Textbook

A textbook presentation simply cannot contrast alternatives as well as the Export to Win! simulation can. Here, you have to make the tough decisions about putting the international marketing program in place. Experience is the best teacher, and experience is what Export to Win! offers.

While information might be available from a textbook and from Export to Win!, the simulation discusses the information when you need it. This means that you will not study Chapter 15, (e.g., logistics) and Chapter 21 (e.g., international accounting), as separate bodies of knowledge to be mastered for different midterm exams. Instead, the perspective of Export to Win! is that of the export manager, and definitions and information are presented at the point of the simulation where they are needed to make decisions. Thus, while your text and other assigned reading materials might have more detail on a particular topic than Export to Win!, the simulation tells you when, why, and how to use that information. It lets you "get your feet wet" in the overseas marketplace. The fact that the information is presented in a simulation, or game, format means that players who do their homework will be the ones that end up with the highest sales.

Students in international business courses find Export to Win! useful in areas other than their term project. They find it is a fun way to study material that might otherwise seem like just another 100 definitions. The clustering of important concepts and definitions makes Export to Win! a good tool for mastering the basics. Quizzes designed to test your retention are presented at the end of each of the five years of the simulation. Many suggested references and outside resources are listed in Export to Win! (just press F4). This feature could be very helpful to businesspeople seeking more in-depth information or personal contacts.

RUNNING EXPORT TO WIN!

Getting Started

The program takes about two minutes to load onto the hard drive for people who are inexperienced computer users. For those wishing to do so the program can be run directly from the master diskettes with either one of two floppy disk drives. Once it is loaded you enter the program by typing EXPORT and pressing the enter key. This brings you directly to the main menu. From there you make your choices from highlighted numbers or letters on the screen.

Entering the simulation, you are asked whether this is the first time you have run the simulation. If this option is selected, the "player" is taken, step by step, through a series of screens, called clusters in this simulation, designed to introduce the player to the simulated environment. There is even a sample decision available.

The Environment

You are the marketing manager for XEBEC, a manufacturer of industrial process control equipment with $13.5 million in sales. Your company is one of five major producers of this equipment worldwide. XEBEC has been active only in the domestic market, but your CEO is encouraging you to explore export markets. The four competitors are designed to provide the user with a broad range of competitive threats. One is a domestic producer, similar to XEBEC, selling only in the home market. This company provides a benchmark to judge your success against. The second company manufactures domestically, but markets its products worldwide. This is the market position desired by XEBEC. Your company also faces competition in the home market from a foreign company that produces in a foreign country, but sells worldwide. The final competitor is also a foreign company, but does not market its products in the United States.

As marketing manager you are instructed to develop a plan to export XEBEC's products. To accomplish this task you are guided through the process of developing and implementing a global marketing strategy. Your goal is to turn the company into a savvy global competitor. Step by step, the player is guided through the necessary decisions in developing a strategy.

Year One: Prospecting

The simulation starts each year's decision at a "home screen" which identifies the events and decisions which will need to be managed during the year. This provides structure to the simulation and guides the player through an increasingly complex decision-making process.

There are three decision/information clusters in year one: scenario, getting started, and trade show. In the scenario, the player is introduced to the company and its products; and is given an option to learn about the competition. If the player declines the option of learning about the competition, the following appears on the screen:

You have definitely made a fatal error. A basic rule in business is to know your competition . . .

After making the mistake, the simulation gives the player an option to amend his/her decision. The player is then asked whether he or she would like more information about exporting, or whether he or she knows enough already. There is a major emphasis in this simulation on being open to information, and willing to learn new methods of doing business. If the player declines the option of learning more about exporting, he/she is asked

". . . are you familiar with the following?" which is a list of critical factors such as: how to analyze foreign markets; how to develop entry strategy; possible risks–political changes, labor issues, and currency exchange; various approaches such as direct vs. indirect, joint ventures, etc., and information sources.

Since the player can get additional information on each of these topics, someone unfamiliar with exporting does not feel threatened or discouraged playing the simulation. An amazing number of terms are defined and clarified in the simulation, without the user feeling overloaded, or getting bored.

The main decision for year one is how the firm should respond to the opportunity to participate in various types of domestic or international trade shows. The choices include (1) attend a trade show to learn, (2) exhibit at a trade show to sell, or (3) participate in a trade mission. For example, under option 2 several choices are introduced. You can attend by yourself or through the Department of Commerce. After selecting a method of attending, the player must select among several types and costs of trade shows. Even for someone currently exporting, this thorough coverage of topics might help identify new opportunities currently being overlooked, such as participating in various kinds of foreign trade shows.

Year Two: Preparing an Offer

During the second year XEBEC attracts its first foreign prospect. Now decisions must be made on five fundamental factors in exporting: pricing, export licensing, financing, shipping, and insurance (see Figure 2). A thorough introduction is provided to each of these topics by asking the player a series of questions with alternative answers. The pricing decision is described so clearly that the various options both make sense and fit together. A weakness in the simulation is that the player can miss the information contained in a number of the clusters by choosing not to view it. However, the accompanying workbook contains a short quiz following each year's decision which, if used, will identify areas that have been missed, such as ex. works, f.o.b., c.f., c.i.f., etc. The importance of when the buyer takes title to the product is clearly identified.

The player is told why the U.S. government licenses exports, and why an exporter should inquire whether his/her product is subject to licensing. The simulation introduces (1) a general license, and (2) a validated license. Both types of licenses are explained. The simulation even gives the player the telephone number of the office of Export Licensing in Washington, D.C.

The financing section is very informative. It shows the prospective exporter that there is a solution to every problem; and that there is no reason to fear foreign sales, given that proper financing methods are selected. Several possible sources are introduced, such as commercial banks, export banks, the Small Business Administration, and others. Given the size of XEBEC the layer is directed to a commercial bank no matter which choice the player attempts. Several financing methods are introduced, and explained: cash in advance, letter of credit, documentary collection (cash against documents), and open account. Figure 3 displays a checklist of terms explained in the simulation for analyzing letters of credit.

Shipping is clarified with a number of simple, clear graphics screens. Although a freight forwarder may be the best option for a small exporter, one should be aware of the options, as well as the advantages and disadvantages of each option.

The simulation will show the player that insurance is needed, and why he/she needs it—a brief animation shows a sinking ship. Several

FIGURE 2. Pro Forma Pricing with Export Costs for the System 200

	PLUS COSTS	G&A OVERHEAD	MARGINAL COSTING

Ex-Factory with 30% Profit Margin	$ 5139.44
Shipping Costs	+ $ 513.93
FOB Cost	+ $ 5653.37
Ocean/Air Freight	+ $ 237.20
C&F Cost	= $ 5890.57
Insurance	+ $ 39.53
Cost C.I.F.	= $ 5930.11

COSTS TO SHIP F.O.B.

Crafting for Export	$	79.07
Forwarder's Fees	$	39.53
Banking Charges	$	237.20
Inland Freight	$	118.60
Pier Delivery Loading	$	39.53
Total F.O.B. Costs	$	513.93

{Press RETURN to continue}

{Select a letter or RETURN to continue}

options are given, showing a prospective exporter the possible solutions.

The final step in all years, after decisions are made, is to process the decisions. When this is done the simulation will comment on some of the decisions. For example, if an open account was selected as method of payment, the simulation will advise you that an open account may not have been the best financial arrangement in this situation.

Year Three: The Importance of Internal Development

How are exports to be handled by XEBEC? The player is provided with a thorough introduction to the factors to be considered in deciding how to manage exports.

There is a strong emphasis on market research, and the player is given several options of how to conduct the research. A short anecdote on the importance of understanding your market explains how

FIGURE 3

THE EXPORTER'S CHECKLIST FOR ANALYZING LETTERS OF CREDIT

Check the following to verify that all terms and conditions in the L/C agree with your Pro Forma Invoice and that you will be able to comply with the order as requested by the importer:

_ ✔ _ Identity of Parties	_ ✔ _ Preshipment Inspection Certificate
_ ✔ _ Confirmed & Irrevocable	_ ✔ _ Shipping Terms
_ ✔ _ Description of Goods	_ ✔ _ Shipping Date
_ ✔ _ Prices	_ ✔ _ Transport Charges
_ ✔ _ Amount	_ ✔ _ Partial Shipments
_ ✔ _ Currency of Payment	_ ✔ _ Transshipment
_ ✔ _ Sight or Time Draft for Payment	_ ✔ _ Consular Documents
_ ✔ _ Payment Terms (30,60,90, 180 days)	_ ✔ _ Presentation of Documents
_ ✔ _ Insurance	_ ✔ _ Expiration Date

{Press RETURN to continue}

---

someone trying to export household appliances to Brazil discovered that imports of most household appliances are not allowed. The message here is that a lot of time and effort can be saved by doing even a minimal amount of marketing research. In case the player decides not to do any market research, the simulation once again displays the message, "you may have made a fatal mistake." Again, the player is given a chance to correct the fatal mistake. The channel of distribution is explained. Notice the straightforward presentation of direct exporting and indirect exporting in Figure 4.

There are several alternatives under each choice in the selection of an agent, distributor, or a combination of both. The player is given access to definitions and explanations of each term. If indirect exporting is selected, the simulation explains to the player why that is not a wise decision. The simulation covers the advantages and disadvantages of using an agent vs. a distributor, and compares the

FIGURE 4

COMPARE THE TWO METHODS

Direct exporting	Indirect exporting
Poses higher financial risk because you are dealing with a foreign company	Financial risk is lower and/or more manageable since you are dealing with a U.S. based company
Requires higher marketing costs – for manpower – for foreign travel – in terms of time	Marketing costs are transferred to a third party, the exporter, usually at a constant level
The marketing function is more complex since you are dealing with many importers	The marketing function involves only one or a few importers, giving you more control
You have more leverage because you know what is happening in each market	You have less leverage when you receive information secondhand from an exporter

{Press RETURN to continue}

two methods. The importance of contracting, i.e., not relying on verbal agreements, is also covered.

The last part of year three is an introduction to export management companies. Addresses and telephone numbers where you can obtain further information are given. The player is presented with a list of what to look for in an EMC; what the EMC is looking for in you; and what kind of financial agreement an exporter might have with an EMC.

Several of the topics covered in year three build on the knowledge gained from the previous two years. Rather than covering all aspects of distribution, for example during year two, much of the detail was left for the discussion of channel design. This attention to making the information fit the situation is a definite plus for this simulation.

Year Four: Cultural Awareness

The fourth year focuses on travel, foreign cultures, currency exchange, and the marketing plan. Although the player cannot select the country he would like to learn about, the simulation does explain, by example, the importance of understanding the culture you are trying to do business with. The simulation stresses the importance of making a travel itinerary, prior to going overseas. Simple things in the cultural environment are often overlooked by inexperienced business travelers. It would be unwise to travel to France expecting to do business in August, when the bulk of the population is on holiday. Cultural sensitivity is brought home to the user in a way that holds one's interest. The brief introduction to cultural differences among countries also highlights important differences between low-context-cultures and high-context-cultures.

The player can select among France, England, Germany, and Japan for examples of cultural analyses, and will probably choose to study all four. The information given on each of these countries is very useful. It includes: visas, language, currency, customs and manners, and a map of the country. A very brief introduction to the customs and manners of each country includes how to greet clients in their language, and what to avoid when first meeting your clients. Sample travel itineraries include useful tips on: taxis and trains, reservations, business materials needed, service tips, and more. The simulation stresses the importance of making a travel itinerary before going overseas.

Foreign Exchange

The currency exchange section of this year's decision is strong. It includes the common methods of dealing with the risk of transactions exposure. Factoring and hedging and countertrade are covered, along with the easy method of simply quoting in U.S. dollars. The advantages and disadvantages of each alternative are given, and each alternative is explained in reasonable detail. Since most American students are not familiar with simple exchange rate calculations, they may need extra assistance with this important section of the simulation.

Year four ends with the development of a marketing plan for

international sales. The importance of a marketing plan is emphasized. Factors such as identifying markets, pricing, physical distribution, and promotion are covered. The concept of target market identification is presented as an analytical process involving a hierarchy of criteria. Weights are assigned to selected macro and micro indicators of alternative markets in order to assess market potential (Figure 5). A simple example of a weighting and ranking system is given. The user is guided through a sample market assessment.

The pricing section looks at ways to improve on the pricing decisions made in year two. By this point in the simulation the user is assumed to be familiar with the "standard" pricing/shipping terms and ready to consider the effects of alternative methods of handling these adjustments to the base price of the product on company sales.

The section on physical distribution highlights the importance of developing an efficient distribution system. Both cost reduction, and customer service levels in terms of product availability (lost sales due to stockouts) are emphasized.

The promotion section is concise, informative, and highly entertaining. The message is that effective cross-cultural communications require effort and attention to detail. Even though the culture the prospective exporter is entering does not seem much different from "ours," the results of poor preparation can be disastrous. The simulation gives the player a list of hilarious business briefs:
"Body by Fisher" became "Corpse by Fisher" in Flemish. The Pepsi slogan, "Come alive with Pepsi!" was translated in Taiwanese to, "Pepsi brings your ancestors back from the dead!" Procter & Gamble displayed a billboard in Saudi Arabia showing clothes entering the washing machine with Tide detergent and exiting clean at the end of the sequence. Arabic is read from right to left, so the billboard could be interpreted to mean that Tide would make your clothes come out of the wash dirty!

Examples appear to be an effective method for communicating the importance of these issues. Product image is also covered with examples as a major teaching aid.

The final part of year four emphasizes the importance of continuously updating the international marketing plan through intelli-

FIGURE 5

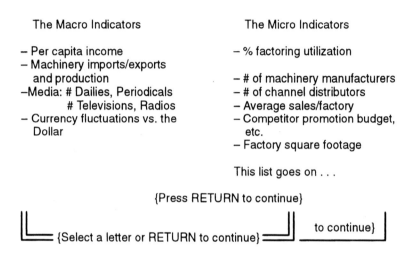

INTERNATIONAL MARKETING

SELECT MACRO & MICRO MARKET INDICATORS

The Macro Indicators

- Per capita income
- Machinery imports/exports
  and production
- Media: # Dailies, Periodicals
    # Televisions, Radios
- Currency fluctuations vs. the
  Dollar

The Micro Indicators

- % factoring utilization
- # of machinery manufacturers
- # of channel distributors
- Average sales/factory
- Competitor promotion budget,
  etc.
- Factory square footage

This list goes on . . .

{Press RETURN to continue}

{Select a letter or RETURN to continue}   to continue}

gence monitoring. Each aspect of intelligence monitoring is discussed and explained.

Year Five: Thinking Globally

The fifth year focuses on strategic thinking: product development, tracking trends, and global strategy. Under product development, issues such as product compatibility with European Community standards, environmental conditions, product life cycle, and customer satisfaction are discussed. Examples are used to emphasize the importance of adapting the product to market conditions, such as printing packages in a country's native language. Potential gains from the development of global products are also illustrated.

The importance of controlling the organization is a major focus in year five. Two methods of reducing corporate taxes and increasing cash flow are discussed: foreign sales corporation, and domestic international sales. Both options require more explanation than fit for this program, which is probably the reason why the mechanics are not explained. The importance of following trends in the marketplace is underscored. Again, marketing research is emphasized.

The final section of the simulation, Global Strategies, gives the player the option of taking credit for the success of the international operations, or reviewing procedures to encourage XEBEC's top management to think globally. The "business briefs" under global involvement give examples of several companies which realized early that they wanted to be involved in exporting. Several methods to cultivate global thinking within the company are presented, along with a list of sample global strategies to adopt. The list includes: global involvement; local distributor/foreign nationals; value-based services/products; boost market share over profits; alliances between competitors; and learn about exporting competitors. Under each strategy is a short discussion of the topic, and an additional business brief giving examples.

The Final Report

Once the final decision has been processed for year five, the player is either promoted to a Vice President–i.e., export revenues exceeded the $6 million goal–or recommended to go back to year one with the advice, ". . . appropriate efforts in the beginning will pay off in the long term."

Subsequent runs through the simulation will take the player much less time as many of the help screens can be skimmed, or skipped entirely. With some practice the simulation can be completed in less than one hour.

STUDENT COMMENTS ON EXPORT TO WIN!

Students enjoy playing Export to Win! Not only is the access to information easy, it is actually fun. Typical student comments include:

- the program is clear and straightforward, simple to use, and user-friendly
- the guide booklet explains the program sufficiently and provides good background material

- can be an integral first step in setting up an international business plan
- realistic interaction
- goals and objectives of the simulation are well explained
- new decisions are introduced in each year of the simulation

LIMITATIONS OF THE SIMULATION

Export to Win! is of course not perfect. Students complain that the simulation is fairly time consuming, especially since they probably will not really understand the strategic aspects of the game until the second time around. This problem is aggravated when students run the simulation directly off floppy disks, which increases the decision processing time greatly. The increasing prevalence of hard disk drives partially corrects this problem.

Because of the many screen overlays, it is better to use a color monitor to avoid confusion. The program does not have any way to let you print, other than mashing the Print Screen key. If the instructor wants to see the output from the simulation, this may cause a problem.

Decisions can be revised within each year until you are ready to proceed, but backtracking between years is not possible once a decision has been processed. The fact that there are only a few strategic options available (especially regarding your choice of markets), means that alternative scenarios are exhausted after only a few runs through the game. Usually, the simulation will not let you make what it calls "definitely fatal errors" in judgement. Students would like more flexibility to make stupid errors, but only if they have more flexibility to review their decisions.

CONCLUSIONS

Export to Win! is an entertaining way to gain a surprising amount of basic knowledge about exporting. The simulation is simple, yet full of useful information–both for laymen and professionals. The program introduces many of the factors involved in the process of exporting a product and/or service. Because it is so user-friendly the simulation provides a highly useful tool for an international business course, both at the undergraduate level and for beginning graduate students. The user gains a broad understanding of the terminology of exporting, and a feeling for how all these factors fit together. Export to Win! would probably fit best early in the semester, as an introduction to exporting and a foundation for further studies.

Even though Export to Win! is a good program, it is far from being perfect. The preselection of countries limits the possibilities of a global marketing strategy, i.e., different strategies for different countries. The preselection of countries also limits the professional use of the program. If more countries were included, the program could be used as an excellent information source, as well as a training tool. This could prove to be a major asset to any company beginning to export.

The almost foolproof design of the program also takes away from the learning value. It is practically impossible to make a major mistake–at least without knowing it. The program always tells you when you have made a major erroneous decision.

The Future

All in all, Export to Win! is an excellent introduction to exporting for beginners. An upgraded version, where the player would be responsible for much of the decision making, could be of even greater use to both classroom and professional settings. According to the publisher this is currently in the planning stage. Imagine Export to Win! II and III as more professional simulations, where the number of variables in the simulation could be adjusted according to the skill level of the player. In an advanced mode the player could be responsible for the bulk of the decisions. Players would also be allowed to make mistakes. This scenario begins to sound like a highly sophisticated computer game for business professionals. The player could also be responsible for selecting the countries in which to market Xebec's products.

The list of possible additions to Export to Win! is endless. That does, however, not diminish the usefulness of Export to Win!. It is meant to be an introduction, and as such it is excellent. Export to Win!

is user-friendly, informative, and entertaining. It is well worth the two to four hours required for an initial run through the simulation.

COMPUTER HARDWARE REQUIREMENTS

This program requires an IBM PC or compatible computer with 640 K RAM. The simulation works much faster when installed on a hard drive, but this is not necessary. On slower machines, such as those running on the 8086 chip, the hard drive reduces waiting time to a maximum of 15 seconds for the processing of each of the five yearly decisions. Users of machines with 486 chips should not notice that the computer is tied up during processing decisions.

Export to Win! requires 895,000 bites of hard drive storage space. The program comes either on two 3 1/2" diskettes, or two 5 1/4" diskettes.

Installation

This program is very easy to install on the hard drive. Simply insert the diskette marked #1 in your disk drive and type install. The rest is menu driven and requires surprisingly few decisions. The program will not let you make any major mistakes. It simply asks you which drive is the target and then proceeds to create its own subdirectory. From there on you simply type EXPORT to enter the simulation.

Ordering Information

The simulation was written by the Strategic Management Group, Inc. in association with the Port Authority of New York and New Jersey (1991). It has a retail price of between $20 and $25 per copy and can be acquired through:

South-Western Publishing Co.
Export to Win!
5101 Madison Road
Cincinnati, Ohio 45227

END OF CHAPTER QUESTIONS

1. What are the learning objectives of Export to Win!?
2. Name several financing methods available to exporters.
3. Give some examples of why cross-cultural understanding is imperative to an exporter.
4. Explain how this simulation will help the user understand exporting; when does the user know he/she is doing an acceptable job with the simulation?

Chapter 5

International Business Simulation II: The Global Market Place

J. A. F. Nicholls
Lucette B. Comer

INTRODUCTION

The Management of Strategy in the Global Market Place is an absorbing international business simulation developed by Dr. Ernest R. Cadotte at the University of Tennessee. The simulation is elaborate, with great attention to detail. Participants establish their own companies, analyze their markets, implement tactics, and develop strategy. They design and produce their own branded products, which compete against those of other companies in the international marketplace. In approaching this simulation, you, the student, may have a few concerns, such as:

- **Why do I need to use a simulation? Can't I just learn from books?**
  You will not get the same amount of involvement or have a hands-on experience with books. Nor will you develop a feel for the marketplace, have an opportunity to use your intuition, or gain a sense of accomplishment in trying out the job of an international manager.
- **Why can't I learn the material from other types of databases?**
  You can learn a great deal about international business from databases. The difference is that with a database you work on your own. With a simulation, you work with other people, just

101

as in the real world. You compete against some people and cooperate with others at the same time. These are extremely valuable experiences that are difficult to learn from databases (or books).

• **I'm a little nervous about computers. Can I handle a simulation?**

You will discover that if you follow some simple instructions and experiment with the program, it is quite easy to get up and running quickly. There is a learning curve, of course. However, as time goes on, you will begin to see interrelationships, master the computer software, and draw considerable satisfaction from what you are doing.

• **Are there materials to help me through this?**

Yes, there is a very complete manual that describes the simulation, and leads you through the necessary steps to complete your assignments.

• **Must I work with other people, or can I work by myself?**

In some simulations you can work by yourself, but this one is just too big for a single person to handle. You will need to cooperate with others. In the process you may well enrich your interpersonal skills. In business it is often necessary to work as a member of a team, so the development of team skills can be a helpful by-product of this simulation.

• **Do I need to know a lot about business before I start?**

The more knowledge you bring from the various business disciplines, the more benefit you will get from the experience. Depending on how your team is structured, you might have people from diverse backgrounds contributing different interests and strengths. If so, each will be able to "specialize" in his/her own area of expertise. If you start out with relatively little knowledge, you will have to work a little harder initially. However, you will wind up with a good idea of what knowledge and skills you need to function in international business later on. Moreover, you *will* develop a feel for what is involved in running a business internationally.

• **Will this help me in my future career?**

Absolutely. You will get a head start on other people in international business because you will have an opportunity to develop your management skills. You will act in varying capacities and learn how different functional areas of a corporation fit together. You will be able to apply material learned in other courses, and see how it comes together in running a multinational corporation. In the process, you will:

• Analyze and solve complex problems
• Think in strategic ways
• Integrate material across disciplines
• Execute decisions
• Respond to competitive moves and countermoves

Exhibit 1 shows you the scope of all of this. In manufacturing and distributing your products globally, you will be drawn into a complex web of decision making. Your team will make a set of decisions involving its corporate operations: production, distribution, marketing, and finance. You will seek to optimize your company's performance within this decision web. You will experience a definite sense of personal involvement and accomplishment as you outmaneuver your competitors and develop a successful business.

OVERVIEW OF THE SIMULATION

In the following sections, we are going to explain the major parts of the simulation and the opportunities it offers you for furthering your learning experiences. We will walk you through the process, so that you will be able to grasp the scope of the experience that awaits you.

The context of the simulation. The simulation divides the world into five geographic areas and is played out in the context of the global economy. Economic conditions mirror those prevailing in the real world. The program allows you to manufacture products in one global area and distribute them to others. Obviously, customers in different parts of the world differ in many ways. The program gives you the opportunity to consider cultural differences among people as you make your decisions. Naturally, currency differs from country to country, so exchange rates become an important consideration, as well as other aspects of international finance (for example, bonds or loans).

EXHIBIT 1. The Web of Student Decisions in the Global Business Environment Through Time

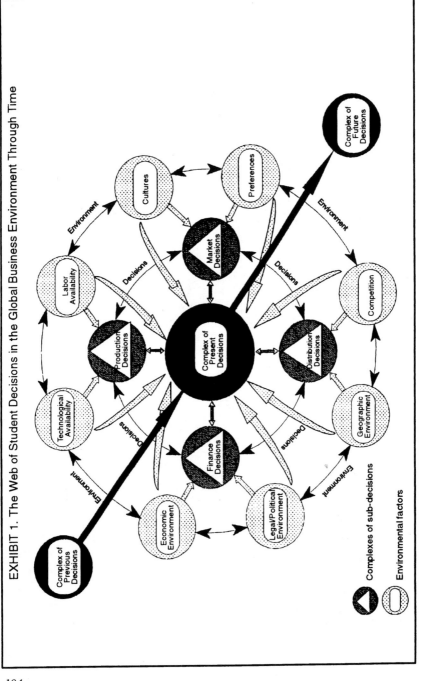

Organizing for the simulation. Your instructor will organize the class into a number of groups representing different companies. All of the companies compete against each other within the same industry, designing, manufacturing, and marketing brands of microcomputers.

Learning about the market. Since good marketing begins with an understanding of consumers' wants and needs, the program allows you to conduct consumer research to find out about these needs. You design and conduct a major consumer survey at the onset of the simulation. If you construct the survey well, you will obtain sufficient information to understand your market. You will then use this information to make decisions regarding target segments and product design.

Starting your operations. From an analysis of your research, you will uncover segments of consumers. You then design your products to match the requirements of those segments you decide to target. You plan to finance start-up operations. You locate your manufacturing plants geographically so as to reach your chosen target market most efficiently. You ship products from your manufacturing plants to outlets in the different regions of the world. You design advertisements to inform consumers of your product and convince them that it will, indeed, meet their needs. You also make decisions at the store level, considering such details as point of purchase displays, shelf location, brand assortment, and number of sales personnel.

Phases of your operations. The game simulates up to three years of business operations. You will face different problems each year. You will move from the start-up phase of your company, through a growth phase, to a stage where you are running a relatively stable business in a maturing market.

Evaluation of your operations. The program provides you with financial statements at the close of each quarter's operations. It also makes it possible for you to monitor your market to get a handle on how well consumers are reacting to your products. You can, then, revise and expand your strategies in the light of this information.

Interfacing with other teams. There may be negotiation between teams which will involve role play that transcends the computer aspects of the simulation. The program permits you to make contractual arrangements with other teams. For example, companies can license technology from other firms. Companies can even merge.

DETAIL OF THE SIMULATION

The software is described in the sections that follow.

The Context of the Simulation

Geographic areas. Exhibit 2 illustrates the geographic scope of the simulation, both the areas in which the products will be designed and produced and those to which they will be distributed and sold. There are five geographic areas, with four cities per area, providing 20 potential global locations for operations. Each of these can serve as either manufacturing or distribution points, or both. For example, participants might manufacture their microcomputers in Western Europe and market them in cities there (e.g., London, Rome, or Oslo), or they could transport them to cities in other regions (e.g., Mexico City, Hong Kong, or New York).

Cultural factors. Cultural differences are explicitly modeled into the program. The program considers cultural factors that may affect demand for microcomputers, so that some differences in preference segments can be detected among the regions. For example, in China several preference segments for microcomputers are similar to those found in other countries, including "people who need work stations" and "people who want a basic machine," but another segment found in many western countries, "people who require portability," is virtually unknown in China. By careful market analyses, participants can detect the presence or absence of these and other segments in the five regions.

Economic factors. Economic conditions vary among regions, as they do in the real world. Participants operate their companies without precise knowledge of market demand. The program, however, provides some aids for estimating how much they will be able to sell, such as product life cycle. Participants can develop forecasts based on their company's results as the simulation progresses. They can also predict overall demand or supply at the local store level. Economic uncertainty adds greater realism to the simulation.

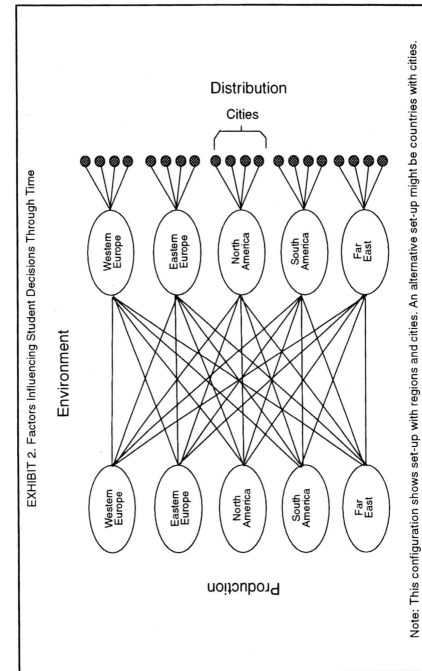

EXHIBIT 2. Factors Influencing Student Decisions Through Time

Distribution

Cities

Environment

Western Europe · Eastern Europe · North America · South America · Far East

Production

Western Europe · Eastern Europe · North America · South America · Far East

Note: This configuration shows set-up with regions and cities. An alternative set-up might be countries with cities.

Organizational Factors

In order to operate efficiently and effectively, participants must organize their companies. This occurs "outside of" the simulation. For maximum efficiency and effectiveness, responsibility for each aspect of operations should be assumed by a particular team member. This ensures a clear chain of command and coverage of all functional areas. In addition to a CEO, each company should have someone in charge of key areas, such as production, finance, and marketing.

Learning About the Market

In order to find out about the potential market for their product, companies must conduct consumer research. The software provides a menu from which participants can design surveys. A wide range of options are available, including such things as benefits sought by consumers, usage patterns, demographic characteristics, and buying styles (as shown in Exhibit 3). As in the real world, research information is not 100% accurate. There is always an error factor present, so participants can request their market research at a number of levels of accuracy. The more accurate the information, the higher its price. Thus, in designing their research, participants need to keep financial factors in mind, and decide whether the *value* of the information is worth its *cost*.

The program allows participants to request market research information broken down by a number of factors (e.g., city, geographic area). They receive research reports that enable them to identify relevant market segments. They might, for example, discover a segment of value conscious consumers, who want inexpensive machines that are easy to install and operate, and that are reliable.

Starting Your Operations

Design of products. The program offers a number of product features that teams can use to design their brands to match the benefits sought by their chosen target markets. The menu provides a

EXHIBIT 3. Examples of Consumer Research Available to Participants

Research Area	Examples of Research Categories Available
Customer needs/benefits sought	Speed of output Screen resolution Ease of operation Ease of installation Service response time Overall quality of service Local technical service Computers are the lowest price Reliability of the product Portability Can use on the road Established brand name [& 27 others]
Usage patterns	Industry category Size of firm Application Functional area
Decision-maker characteristics	Sex Age Education Employment Occupation Marital status Ethnicity Income Household size Residence type
Buying style	Economy-minded Experimenter Brand loyal Cautious Ecologist Style-conscious [& 7 others]

number of options including: memory capacity, type of disk drives, and monitors. Complicating the planning process, some of the features are not immediately available. They need further research and development (R&D), requiring lead time for production. It is also possible to develop any particular feature faster than usual by accelerating the R&D process. Speeding up R&D, however, is costly. So participants must consider another tradeoff, that between *production time* and *cost*.

Preferences for quality vary globally. For example, in eastern Europe, customers may be perfectly satisfied with a machine that has a 70% quality rating, but this would probably be totally unacceptable to those in the United Kingdom. Segments that are otherwise identical in different countries may differ significantly because of this quality issue. Participants are able to control production so as to produce their brands at different quality levels. Incorporating higher quality in production, however, increases costs.

Funding sources. Investment in R&D, market research, and factory construction requires funding, so participants must consider sources of start-up capital. Teams receive an equity allocation each quarter of the first year. Beyond that, they must depend upon the income they can generate, although they are able to get bank loans if they apply for them in advance. In the event that they miscalculate their financial position, they are able to get emergency loans, but must pay exorbitant interest rates. If they are fortunate enough to have excess funds on hand, they can invest them in short-term assets. All this is complicated by the fact that exchange rates fluctuate during the simulation. Companies can, however, protect themselves against loss by buying forward (purchasing foreign currency today, for use tomorrow).

Production and distribution. The software allows participants to establish their manufacturing plants in various parts of the world. In doing this, teams must consider market accessibility, as well as local industrial capabilities. When choosing retail locations, they must consider needs and preferences of consumers from many different cultural backgrounds. They must also consider logistical problems of moving products between production sites and distribution centers.

Marketing communication. The program allows participants to design individual advertisements for their different brands. They can design ads specifically targeted to different countries and to particular segments within countries. This is accomplished by use of a special menu from which they can select advertising copy. Twenty possible benefits are available for use in the ad copy, including such things as portability, price, and reliability (Exhibit 4). Participants place the advertisements in appropriate local, national, and international media throughout the world.

Scope of decision making. When designing their products, participants must consider the benefits sought by purchasers and match them with appropriate product features (Exhibit 4). They must make arrangements to manufacture their products (e.g., locate plants, arrange for financing). After the products are manufactured, they must let customers know about the availability of their products through advertising. They must determine which of the potential ad copy statements would stimulate the best response. Needless to say, participants must take into account *both* the benefits that these customers are seeking and the features of the product that they have designed and manufactured. All this takes considerable thought and planning.

In the stores. In addition to their larger-scale decision making, teams also deal with operations at the local store level. Participants are able to control a lot of detail, including number and location of point-of-purchase displays, shelf location, and brand assortment. They also decide upon the optimal number of salespersons at each outlet and whether to provide specialized training for them.

Assistance in making decisions. The program allows participants to perform "what if" analyses before finalizing their decisions. In the process, they can create pro forma income statements, balance sheets, and cash flow budgets which help them see where they are going and analyze the financial implications of their decisions.

Phases of the Simulation

Teams run their businesses for a maximum of 12 quarters. Each year of the simulation represents a different stage of the product life cycle (Exhibit 5). The first year might be considered an "emergence" or "getting started" phase. During this year, participants research the market, design their products, locate and construct their

EXHIBIT 4. Options for Consumer Benefits Sought, Product Features, and Advertising Copy

Consumer Benefits Sought	Product Features	Advertising Copy
Speed of output	Base components	Portability
Throughput speed	Memory: 640KB memory, 1MB memory	Low price
Amount of operator training required	Drives: 2 standard drives; 2 half-height	Been around for a long time
Resolution of screen	drives; 20MB hard drive; 40MB hard drive;	Technical leader
Color of screen	110MB hard drive	Do wide variety of tasks
Large size of screen	Expansion Slots: 2, 4, and 8	Tackle big problems
Ease of operation	Monitors: monochrome; color graphics;	Can be tailored to special problems
Aesthetics of product	high resolution color; super-twist LCD	High speed/execution time
Number and position of characters on	CPUs: 8/16 bit 8088, 16 bit 80286,	Easy to use
keyboard	32 bit 80288	Small footprint/size
Ease of Installation	Math co-processor	National sales/service network
Compatibility with other microcomputers	Keyboards: standard; enhanced	Local sales/training
Competence of service representatives	Graphics card	Wide variety of brands carried
Service response time	Factory power supply	Quick delivery–no stock outs
Service availability at point of need	Rugged carrying case	5% factory rebate
Overall quality of service	Mouse control cursor	Application: word processing
Local technical service	Built in modem	Application: finance/accounting
National support organization		Application: database management
Delivery lead time	Available only *after* R&D:	Application: portable computer
Ability to keep delivery promises		Can tie into other computers
Low price	4MB dynamic ram	Mention of specific brand name

EXHIBIT 4 (continued)

Consumer Benefits Sought	Product Features	Advertising Copy
Performance more important than price	Supertwist color LCD	
Offers a broad line of hardware	32 bit CPU 80386	
Vender visibility amount top management	Surface circuitry	
Financial stability of the manufacturer	Icon based DOS	
Been around for a long time		
Reliability of product		
Savings and operator cost		
Portability		
Ability to communicate with host computer		
Can tie into other microcomputers		
Can use on the road		
Vender as technical leader		
Established brand name		
Can handle large-scale technical problems		
Multipurpose workstation		
Small footprint/size		
Business graphics capabilities		
Computer-aided design capability		
Can be tailored to special applications		

EXHIBIT 5. Phases of the Simulation

Primary Concern	Emergence First Year (Quarters 1 to 4)	Development Second Year (Quarters 5 to 8)	Maturity Third Year (Quarters 9 to 12)
	Getting started	Becoming profitable	Extending global reach
Marketing	Design market survey Analyze market opportunities Select markets Design one or two brands Design ad copy Test market Enter initial markets Plan shelf allocations and POP displays	Evaluate initial strategies Expand product line Add new brands Select new markets Target new segments or regions Improve ad copy Develop media strategies Improve shelf allocations & POP displays Be aware of competitors' activities	Cognizant of complexities Evaluate brand mix Add new brands Refine ad copy Refine media strategy Refine shelf allocations Refine POP displays Monitor competitors' activities Intercompany negotiation
Production	Select initial plant location(s) Construct first facilities Consider R&D alternatives	Reevaluate plant locations and capacity Invest in R&D Construct new facilities Enlarge older factories	Invest in R&D Expand factories Consider buying plants Consider selling plants
Finance	Establish overall budget Develop pricing strategy Develop media budget Develop R&D budget Obtain initial financing	Monitor budget Obtain supplementary funding Apply for major expansion loan	Monitor budget Consider further equity/debt financing Allocate resources
Competition	Observe competition Monitor competitors' actions Check competitors' brands' consumer acceptance	Monitor competitors' activities Counter competitors' moves Preempt competitors' tactics	Monitor competitors' activities Counter competitors' moves Negotiate as necessary

production facilities, and test market their new brands. They are primarily concerned about getting their companies off the ground and operating profitably. The second year is a "development" phase. Participants normalize operations and become accustomed to making decisions. They begin their global "roll out" into broader markets. As operations become profitable, they may decide to expand their product line, adding brands targeted to the requirements of different segments or different parts of the world. They become aware of the activities of their competition and they begin to find out how successful they have been in their initial strategies. By the third year, a "maturity" phase, things are moving much faster. Participants are now aware of the complexities and possibilities of the simulation.

Operational Feedback

Financial reports. Each quarter, participating teams receive financial reports summarizing the results of their operations. The program automatically posts expenses and investments to the appropriate ledgers and adjusts income statements and balance sheets. This helps participants understand the financial impact of alternative marketing scenarios. An example of a balance sheet printout is shown in Exhibit 6.

Market monitoring. A menu is provided to offer a choice of market monitoring information. Participants can conduct "fast-tests" which give them a summary of customer perceptions of currently available brands, prices, and advertising copy. They are able to obtain ratings of, for example, how closely their brand matches the needs of the market segments and reactions of customers to brand price. This part of the program also provides quantitative data concerning in-store activities, market share, and advertising by competitors, as well as evaluations of the effectiveness of their own advertising.

Interfacing with Other Teams

The simulation is considerably enhanced if role playing is included. Intercompany negotiations add a realistic qualitative dimen-

---

EXHIBIT 6. Example of Balance Sheet Printout

QTR 3

Cash	$ 259,376
Fixed A.	$1,000,000
Mny Mkt	$ 150,000
A. R.	$0
Inv. FG	$0
Inv. WIP	<u>$1,542,284</u>
	$2,951,660
A. P.	$1,071,600
Loan C.	$ 420,000
Loan E.	$0
Stock	$3,000,000
R. E.	<u>($1,539,940)</u>
	$2,951,660

Legend

Fixed A.	=	Fixed Assets	A.P.	=	Accounts Payable
Mny Mkt	=	Money Market Funds	Loan C.	=	Conventional Loans
A.R.	=	Accounts Receivable	Loan E.	=	Emergency Loans
Inv. FG	=	Inventory (Finished Goods)	Stock	=	Common Stock
Inv. WIP	=	Inventory (Work in Process)	R. E.	=	Retained Earnings

---

sion. Power strategies emerge since companies can acquire each other. Participants learn the value of cooperation, as well as how to deal with conflict. Stronger groups may absorb the weak, so participants learn the consequences of both efficient and inefficient management. Licensing arrangements are also possible. Companies can license a component from a competitor–at a price. They may choose to formalize agreements through actual written contracts.

Competitors monitor each others' activities and lodge complaints when they believe advertising is deceptive or misleading. When a complaint arises, role play takes the form of investigative hearings. Guilty offenders face onerous penalties (e.g., fines, bans on advertising).

INSTRUCTIONS FOR USING THE SOFTWARE

Using IBM-compatible machines, participants "boot up" from their own self-contained diskette provided by their instructor. The main menu is composed of a series of decision categories, including brands, advertising, contracts, market research, production, and finance (Exhibit 7). Each of these accesses a series of sub-menus (see Exhibit 8 for an example). The menu system is quite complex, although the paths are easy to follow. After finalizing their decisions, participants record them on their diskette and return it to the instructor.

After the instructor has run the simulation, the diskettes are returned to the participants. These diskettes now contain the results of the quarter just completed. The content of some of the menus is changed by the results. For example, the "financial" report contains historical

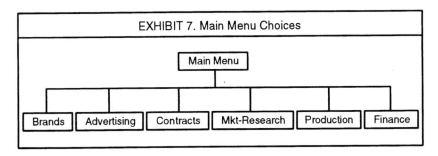

EXHIBIT 7. Main Menu Choices

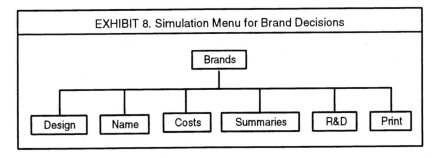

EXHIBIT 8. Simulation Menu for Brand Decisions

data updated by the running of the simulation. Participants print out what they want. Typically, this includes financial information, market share, etc. They then begin the analysis for the subsequent quarter.

ADVANTAGES AND DISADVANTAGES

Advantages

Participating in *The Global Market Place* can make a significant contribution to anyone's education in international business. The many advantages to using it are summarized, as follows:

- **A richly detailed simulation**
  The program is remarkable in its great attention to detail. It will be a challenge to participants throughout the term, regardless of their level of achievement. They will never become "bored" with the experience.
- **A comprehensive simulation**
  The complexity of the simulation imparts a real world flavor. It is neither quickly nor easily mastered. Participants develop a healthy respect for the game, and in the process, develop a sense of the complexity of the world of international business.
- **A tactical simulation that can become strategic**
  It is an operationally-oriented exercise that provides "practice" in the design, implementation, and control of international business strategies through the application of tactics. Participants make "middle management" type decisions and get involved with tactical issues.
- **Very involving**
  The simulation requires participants to become "totally immersed" in the business enterprise. This makes it particularly suitable for helping individuals master international business concepts. Participants are likely to become intensely preoccupied with it.
- **Provides insights**
  Participants develop insights into such things as how the components of international business fit together, how the results of research are utilized, how products must be developed and

distributed to meet the expressed needs of global consumers, and how the international marketplace changes over time. They also have the opportunity to see how unexpected events counteract the effectiveness of their decisions.

• **Provides feedback**
Participants can observe the impact of one proposed set of decisions, as compared with others. They can perform sensitivity analyses to help them optimize their decisions in advance of the simulation run. Thus, they receive two levels of feedback: one from performing "what if" analyses before the simulation, and the second through the results of the simulation, itself.

• **Provides personal development**
Participants also develop their personal skills while solving simulation problems. Making managerial decisions in a realistic setting provides them with a framework for developing decision styles that they will carry over into their real world careers.

• **Many purposes**
The simulation can be conducted in many settings. It was originally designed to accompany a course in international business at a university. It can also, however, be used as a training tool in a corporate setting to introduce neophyte managers to international operations.

Disadvantages

Despite these many advantages, there are also some disadvantages. Participating in *The Global Market Place* is not an "easy option." It is demanding, requiring time commitments by instructors and participants alike.

• **Prerequisite knowledge**
For optimal utilization, the simulation presupposes a certain amount of knowledge about business operations (finance, accounting, marketing). Beginners to these business disciplines will be at a disadvantage. They may need a good deal of supplemental or remedial work from their instructors.

• **Group activity**
The simulation requires participants to work in groups. This

necessitates interaction within and between teams. One person cannot run a company alone and a minimum of three companies are required to run the simulation.

- **Serious time commitments**
Participating in this simulation can be very time consuming. Individuals may find they do not have enough time to do a good job and also meet their other responsibilities. However, even though the time commitment is substantial, the end results are most rewarding, and well worth the effort expended.

SUGGESTIONS FOR TERM PROJECTS

The simulation can be used as the basis for term projects. Typically, these involve annual reports of company operations. In addition, participants can supplement the computer-based experience with library reports on related topics.

1. At end of the first year of play, prepare a First Annual Report, summarizing your goals, accomplishments, and shortfalls. Reports should include financial, managerial, and marketing data.
2. Before embarking on the second year of play, prepare a Two-Year Business Plan, detailing your proposed activities for years two and three. Reports should include a request for equity funding to support proposed activities.
3. At end of the second and third years of play, submit Annual Reports, summarizing goals, accomplishments, and shortfalls. Reports should include financial, managerial, and marketing data.
4. Conduct in-depth analyses of one of the different geographic regions in the simulation, including cultural aspects. Consult secondary sources in the library and interpret the feedback from the simulation in the context of this information.
5. Prepare a supplemental report justifying advertising decisions in the cultural framework of the different markets.
6. Perform an analysis of the advantages and disadvantages of licensing agreements versus independent operations.
7. Discuss the issue of policing worldwide deceptive advertising.

END OF CHAPTER QUESTIONS

1. What are the advantages of using a simulation model as opposed to other types of software?
2. How does a course using a simulation contrast with one based on lectures alone?
3. Is there any value to a simulation since it differs from the real world?
4. What are the major stages through which this simulation passes? How do they emulate the product life cycle?
5. What are the major areas of decision making in this simulation? How do these compare with the real world operations of a company?
6. What are the major cost trade-offs in this simulation?
7. What mechanisms does this simulation provide for evaluation of managerial efforts?
8. How can participants find out what benefits consumers are interested in; how can they use the information in ensuring the profitable operations of their companies?
9. How does role play enrich the computer aspects of this simulation?
10. Is there an ethical issue in having a lower quality for certain consumers or should one aim for higher quality for all consumers?

Chapter 6

Utilizing Databases in International Business I: National Trade Data Bank, World Trade Exporter, World Trader, and Core II

Edward W. Schmitt
Gary P. Kearns

INTRODUCTION

It has been acknowledged in the business, government, and academic fields that U.S. companies generally have underperformed in the exporting arena relative to their European and Asian counterparts. According to the U.S. Department of Commerce, only about 15% of all U.S. manufacturers export. Further, the percentage of the U.S. gross domestic product that comes from exports is less than 10%, about half the rate of most European countries. Kefalas and Carr (1988) state that a major cause of this subpar performance in international trade is a lack of knowledge on the part of many U.S. businesses about the exporting process. Weber (1991), supported by many references, argues that college and university curricula are inadequate in addressing international business issues.

Surprisingly, this subpar performance exists despite the U.S. government's extensive efforts to promote exporting. Part of the problem has been the inability to effectively package and distribute to potential users the tremendous volume of information on the exporting process maintained by public and private sources. Aided by the increased availability and acceptance of personal computers, however, several software developers and the federal government have recently introduced programs which are highly effective in organizing and retrieving the massive amounts of information available on the exporting process. This chapter analyzes four such software programs with an eye to their utility as teaching tools.

While there are other methods to teach about the exporting process (e.g., cases, videotapes, projects, lectures), software programs such as those analyzed herein are highly effective in organizing and retrieving fragmented information to meet the specific needs of individual users. Further, these programs can be utilized in conjunction with other teaching methods. Readers interested in a more detailed discussion of issues related to the use of computers and software in business education should refer to International Council for Computers in Education (1986) and Karakaya and Karakaya (1989).

The analysis of each software program addresses the following key points in this chapter:

- Program focus, objective, and targeted user market
- Stage(s) of exporting process addressed
- Program features
- Strengths and weaknesses
- Application to case studies

To facilitate comparisons among programs, the exporting process was divided into five basic stages:

1. *Internal Assessment* by the prospective exporter, including competitive strengths and weaknesses on both an organizational and product basis (Kennen International, Cavusgil, and The Dialog Systems 1991);
2. *International Marketing Research*, including the potential markets, competition, pricing, product planning, export and import trends, distribution, and demographics;
3. *Market Entry Strategies* such as distribution, acquisition, or joint venture strategies;
4. *Export Strategy Implementation*, including export documentation, licensing, insurance, financing, promotion, and trade leads;

5. *Ongoing Assessment of Success or Failure*, including performance measures and frequency of self-assessment process.

CASE STUDY APPLICATIONS

This chapter develops several hypothetical case studies to high-
light similarities and differences among programs and to serve as a
guide to potential users by category (e.g., educators, advisors, businesses). These cases are described in further detail below.

Case One

The first case study involves a U.S. manufacturer of spectrometers
(electronic components that measure energy emitted by certain
sources). The fictional company, Electronic Components Inc. (ECI),
does not presently export. ECI has $15 million in annual revenues
and 50 employees. It wishes to learn more about the exporting process, to determine its readiness to export, to learn more about potential markets, and to understand the risks involved. This company has
approached its local university which, as part of a graduate marketing class project, has assigned a team of students to assist the company. None of the students has any experience with exporting, and
must also educate themselves before assisting the company.

Case Two

The second case study involves a manufacturer of biotechnology
equipment which presently exports to several European countries.
This fictional company, Biotech Inc. (BI), wishes to search for
additional markets in the Far East, Latin America, and elsewhere,
but is uncertain about how to proceed. The company has contacted
its local Department of Commerce office about resources to assist
in the process, and has been informed that several software programs exist which can help it to assess these markets.

ANALYSIS OF PROGRAMS

The programs analyzed in this section are summarized in Table 1.

TABLE 1

Program Name	Developer/ Marketer	Program Description	System Requirements
National Trade Data Bank	Office of Business Analysis U.S. Department of Commerce HCHB Room 4885 Washington, DC 20230 Contact: Mr. Ken Rogers	CD-ROM based system which provides extensive economic and international trade data. Encompasses over 100,000 documents from 15 federal agencies; includes "how-to" guide for new exporters. Covers all stages of exporting process. Cost: $360/year or $35 for a single disk.	IBM PCs and compatibles. 640K available RAM. ISO 9660 CD-ROM reader (cost $500-800). MS-Software to access CD-ROM reader.
World Trade Exporter	National Technical Information Service and International Systems Development Corp. 2101 E. Jefferson St., Suite 210 Rockville, MD 20852	Reference tool focusing on federal and state agency information that provides assistance to exporters. Link to over 850 external databases. Covers all stages of exporting process, with emphasis on research. Cost: $250 for basic system; $545 includes package of quarterly updates, WorldNet password, $100 on-line credit.	IBM PCs and compatibles. Operating system PC-DOS or MS-DOS version 3.0 or higher. 640K available RAM; hard disk with approx. 4.52 MB free space.
World Trader	Gate Waze Inc. 66 Summer Street, P.O. Box 743 Manchester, MA 01944	Reference and planning tool covering all stages of the export process. Provides country profiles, trade data for the top 50 U.S. trading partners, key international trading contacts, an export reference guide, and hyper-menu linkages. Cost: $479 includes one year of quarterly updates and access to a toll-free hotline.	IBM PCs and compatibles. 640K available RAM. Hard disk storage space of 7 MB. EGA or VGA monitor.
CORE II	S. Tamer Cavusgil Michigan State University International Business Centers 6 Kellogg Center E. Lansing, MI 48824	Accesses a company's readiness to export (corresponds to stage one of the exporting process). Self-assessment tool. Cost: $295	IBM PCs and compatibles. 580K available RAM. Hard disk with 2 MB disk space. 132 column printer.

THE NATIONAL TRADE DATA BANK (NTDB)

The NTDB is a CD-ROM-based service provided by the Department of Commerce which contains over 100,000 documents of current international trade and economic data from 15 federal government agencies. The program addresses all stages of the exporting process, with exceptional coverage of references and resources available to assist in the process. The stated objective of the NTDB is to provide reasonable public access, including electronic access, to federal government data of the greatest interest to U.S. firms that are engaged in export-related activities (Cremeans and Williams 1991; Plant 1991). The NTDB's development was mandated by the enactment of legislation in 1988 that directed the Commerce Department to centralize the government's extensive trade and export promotion information resources housed in 15 separate agencies. The program is currently available at nearly 700 local libraries across the U.S. and is available free to any Federal Depository Library. The entire program is updated on a single disc each month and may be purchased as a monthly subscription or on a one-time basis. Its target market includes students and faculty of colleges and universities, businesses, and government agencies.

Program Features

The program is essentially a search and retrieval system for the extensive information maintained in the NTDB. It offers the user a choice of two search and retrieval features: "BROWSE," which is intended for users with basic computer skills and no specific knowledge of federal data; and "ROMWARE," a more complicated menu program that may be replaced in the near future. Both features search the NTDB database based on country, product, or topic criteria. This paper focuses on the BROWSE feature, a series of pyramid menu structures offering five different choices to access the database: *Source, Topic, Program, Subject,* and *Item.* Selecting *Source* produces a detailed list of agencies contributing to the NTDB and serves as a gateway to a more detailed sub-menu of program names produced by each agency. *Topic* enables access by general topic or category, while *Subject* allows a search for more specific items (e.g., product or country).

The NTDB includes a comprehensive, 100-page guide to exporting as well as most resources published or maintained by the federal government on exporting. Included are such features as The U.S. Industrial Outlook; the World Factbook published by the Central Intelligence Agency detailing political, economic, and cultural issues by country; market research reports on given countries and industries; and the Foreign Traders Index, which identifies over 50,000 foreign firms active or interested in importing U.S. products. The Foreign Traders Index also includes a description of each prospective importer by country and by product(s) desired, how long it has been in business, and the number of employees. The program is updated monthly.

Strengths

A key strength is the sheer volume of relevant, accessible trade and economic information housed in the program. As noted in the introduction of this paper, one of the critical gaps in export education to date has been organizing and distributing the volume of information maintained and assembled by the federal government. The NTDB addresses this problem in a surprisingly effective manner. The NTDB is especially appropriate for colleges and universities, many of which already have CD-ROM readers, for use in a broad number of curricula applications in economics, marketing, and finance. In addition, as noted in the case study section below, both the electronic components and biotechnology equipment companies can fulfill their particular exporting information needs solely from this program.

Weaknesses

The NTDB program features only U.S. government information, and does not incorporate access to external databases or resources like World Trade Exporter or World Trader. A Department of Commerce spokesman notes that this exclusion is due to a desire to keep the costs of the NTDB reasonable, something it could not do by paying royalties to third-party sources of information. The NTDB's search and retrieval software is also a bit more cumbersome than others. To be used effectively, the user must spend relatively more time reading the technical manual and working with the program, although the volume of information contained is also significantly greater and potentially more beneficial than in other programs. To use the database, one needs access to a CD-ROM reader, thereby excluding in the near-term many small and medium-sized businesses that have only basic personal computer setups. While these weaknesses may limit the program's effectiveness for business users, they do not diminish the appeal of this program for educational purposes. In addition, since the government applies no copyright protection to the information contained in the NTDB, it is expected (and encouraged by the Commerce Department) that a number of private software developers will begin to incorporate sections of the program relevant to small and medium-sized businesses into their current product offerings. The prices of CD-ROM readers are also expected to continue falling to more reasonable levels which, combined with more information becoming available on CD-ROM media, should encourage more businesses to purchase them.

Application to Case Studies

ECI would find enough information to sufficiently educate itself on the export process, although it would be advised to work through a regional U.S. Department of Commerce trade specialist to access this program. A first step of interest would be the 12 most common mistakes made by exporters, which is featured in the basic guide to exporting. For more specific information, the company could access the Foreign Traders Index to obtain a listing of spectrometer importers throughout the world. From a recent NTDB disc, this company would be given a listing of eight importers specifically interested in spectrometers located in the Netherlands, Canada, Japan, the United Kingdom, Saudi Arabia, France, Chile, and Belgium. No other program reviewed herein offers this level of detailed information. Market research could also be accessed by country. The program offers the ability to create mailing labels to companies on the Foreign Traders Index via WordPerfect version 5.1, a valuable feature.

The biotechnology company would similarly find a productive resource in the NTDB. In addition to detailed market research reports that could be accessed by product and country, it could access the

Foreign Traders Index for a listing of biotechnology equipment importers. From the NTDB disc, this company would be given a listing of 12 companies located in Denmark, Belgium, the Netherlands, Canada, Italy, India, the United Kingdom, and Japan. Again, no other program reviewed offered this detailed and productive level of information. Armed with the NTDB as a resource, the biotechnology equipment company could very quickly and efficiently conduct most steps of the market research process at a fraction of the cost in time and money of a third-party consultant.

WORLD TRADE EXPORTER

World Trade Exporter is a comprehensive tool which provides references, resources, and contacts dealing with all stages of the exporting process. The program's stated objective is "to assist small- and medium-sized U.S. businesses to become more competitive in the global business arena by providing the information critical to success in exporting." It is also recommended as an educational tool for universities and government agencies.

Program Features

World Trade Exporter has a superb menu-driven system which facilitates use and access of four main sections: Trade Topics, Trade Directory, Trade Bibliography, and NotePad. The *Trade Topics* section features 160 topics including a 44-page guide to the exporting process, a description of federal and state export assistance programs, a listing of products/services exported to major countries, and a calendar of trade fairs and shows. The *Trade Directory* is a name/address/telephone listing of 2,115 export-related agencies, organizations and contacts (public and private) in the U.S. and overseas that provide export information and assistance. The *Trade Bibliography* contains a listing of over 1,000 government and commercial on-line databases and 813 printed books and reports on international trade matters. The *NotePad* feature is a handy note-taking, recording, and editing tool for personal notes and messages while working with the program.

The program also includes features to help the user to quickly locate, display, and print out precise information through its powerful Search, Table of Contents, Glossary, Help, and Keyboard Index features. These features can be accessed at any time from the main menu sections. Of particular interest, the *Trade Glossary* contains 372 exporting terms, functioning as a pop-up menu which can be accessed at any time as needed. The *Search* function is by far one of the most beneficial features of the program, enabling the user to quickly find the information being sought. World Trade Exporter also features a gateway to external communications through its modem function, which allows automatic log-on to the Worldnet ($545 package only) and Department of Commerce databases. The 151-page User's Guide is an excellent reference which includes a detailed 44-page tutorial on using the system.

Strengths

The program is comprehensive in nature while relatively easy to use. Its menu, search, glossary, and communications features are powerful yet easy to use, enabling the user to quickly and efficiently find the information or resources sought. The program does not seek to contain all primary information available to current or prospective exporters, but rather acts as a comprehensive research and reference vehicle. The volume of information stored in the program is also impressive. The pop-up features were well thought out, especially the Glossary section which can be accessed when needed. The system is also updated quarterly, a service included in the $545 purchase price.

Weaknesses

No glaring weaknesses were found with this program. One mild bias is to point the prospective or current exporter mainly toward governmental resources, which the developer notes is a program objective. Given the high quality and low price of such resources this is not a weakness. However, the program could be strengthened by incorporating certain contacts and topics covered in more depth by the NTDB, especially the Foreign Traders Index. By combining

World Trade Exporter's search capability with the raw data contained in the NTDB, an even more outstanding program for educational, business and government users could be created. We understand that the developer is presently working to incorporate access to the NTDB into the program.

World Trade Exporter does not profess to go into the depth that some other systems do to exhaustively describe the exporting process, although it does devote 44 pages to an effective overview and provides extensive resources and references for additional information. ISDC also publishes the World Trade Director program which is similar to World Trade Exporter except that it addresses more of the process of exporting and less of the references and resources contained in World Trade Exporter. Given this similarity, World Trade Director was not reviewed in this paper.

Application to Case Studies

This program is highly relevant and beneficial to both case study examples. In the case of ECI, a review of the basics contained in the "Learning Exporting" section offered a good overview of the process and suggested an appropriate first step: using an export qualifier program (CORE II). To obtain a contact for CORE II, we used the search function in the Directory, where we found a telephone number for the U.S. & Foreign Commercial Services in Washington, D.C. Calling this number, we were immediately referred to the Philadelphia district U.S. Commerce Department office, which administers the CORE II program in our region. The program also directed ECI to a number of resources from which it could learn more about international market research, market entry strategies, financing, trade leads, and general success tips.

In addition to this general information, a more specific search of the Trade Topics and Bibliography sections under the general category "Components" directed the user to a number of resources including several state International Trade Administration offices and to countries which import components (Algeria, Australia, Austria, Canada, France, Israel, Singapore, Taiwan, and Thailand). The Trade Calendar section of the Trade Topics menu directed the user to six international trade shows featuring electronic components, including one in Seoul, Korea and one in Utrecht, Netherlands. In addition to these leads, a search of the Bibliography section produced 13 publications regarding foreign markets for components, such as export opportunities in Europe. These are excellent leads and exemplify the utility of this program, which also provides easy-to-use print capabilities to record these leads on paper. It should be noted that the World Trader program reviewed on the following page yields greater potential contacts in this specific case study than World Trade Exporter: a similar search of countries importing electronic components produced 21 countries and 13 trade shows versus nine and two, respectively, for World Trade Exporter. The reader should also keep in mind that the NTDB system is by far the most complete resource for investigating potential export markets, producing more potential and specific leads than either World Trader or World Trade Exporter.

For the biotechnology equipment company, World Trade Exporter is also a valuable source of data. Singapore and the United Kingdom are biotechnology equipment export markets mentioned in the Trade Topics section, while in the Bibliography section 18 publications regarding foreign markets were identified. In addition, this company was referred to the U.S. & Foreign Commercial Services' Comparison Shopping Service, which provides the detailed information needed to assess export markets in over 50 countries.

WORLD TRADER

World Trader is a comprehensive reference tool which assists its users in understanding the exporting process, identifying export markets, explaining important trade issues, and obtaining trade contacts in foreign countries. The program appeals to small, medium and large businesses; lawyers, consultants, accountants, and government agents who advise these businesses; and educators and students in business programs.

Program Features

World Trader is composed of four primary program segments: *World Atlas, Market Analyst, Info-Deck,* and *Export Reference*

Guide, which are integrated by *Quick-Link*, a powerful data-linking tool. *World Atlas* contains general information profiles on over 125 countries, including country overviews, import statistics, transportation and communication access, and regional maps. *Market Analyst* offers the ability to analyze trade data by country on such search criteria as prospects by product category, total imports, and total U.S. imports. This is useful for determining on a macro sense where the export markets are for various U.S. products. A charting feature facilitates organizing and presenting data for selected countries, while data can also be downloaded to ASCII, Lotus 1-2-3 or dBase files. *Info-Deck* is organized as an electronic file directory of over 3,500 U.S. and foreign trade contacts which can be printed from the Global Report Generator feature. The *Export Reference Guide*, a 677-page reference source on all stages of the exporting process, is included in the software. The guide is based on the publication *Exportise* by the Small Business Foundation of America, and is a 272-page written copy which is included in the User's Guide to World Trader. To provide an overview of the *Export Reference Guide*, the program offers a unique *Blueprint* feature which is a high level schematic of the exporting process linked to sections of the guide. It provides an excellent overview; the user can also access any stage of the exporting process shown in the schematic simply by moving the cursor and pressing return. *Quick-Link* enables the user to link data among the four program segments.

The program also features helpful pop-up utilities which include calculators for distance between any two cities in the world, weights and measures and foreign currency conversions, and time zone for any city; an easily accessible glossary of trade terms; and a search mode to access a detailed database of over 2,500 international trade show listings.

Strengths

World Trader is a well-designed reference tool packed with valuable features. Like World Trade Exporter, it is easier to learn and use to access trade information than the NTDB system, although this may be due in part to the fact that it houses about one-tenth the information of the NTDB. *World Atlas* is an excellent feature which can quickly educate the user on general matters about foreign countries, although it contains considerably less detail in this area than the NTDB. *Info-Deck* has excellent trade contacts arranged in a branching hierarchy for easy access, including for example a detailed listing of freight forwarders.

Weaknesses

Although the program does not contain any glaring weaknesses, several areas for improvement are suggested. First, the user searching for export markets can quickly generate a listing of all countries that import a general product category. It is not possible to view on screen a summary of the search findings for more than five countries at a time, however. Instead, the results must be output to a data file or to a printer. Data for a single country can be displayed, or up to five countries' import data can be compared on screen using the *Chart* feature. Second, the program offers good general information on countries importing a general product category (e.g., Electronics and Electronic Components), but offers neither the specificity of product (e.g., spectrometer) nor the vast importer contacts contained in the NTDB system. World Trade Exporter also shares this weakness. Both World Trader and World Trade Exporter would benefit from providing greater access to the NTDB system within their programs.

Application to Case Studies

The electronic components company and its student assistants would benefit significantly from World Trader. The trade references and exporting guide are outstanding and thorough. Regarding market research, World Trader offers a listing of 21 countries that import electronics and electronic components. This list is an excellent resource from which to conduct additional research. Interestingly, the list of 21 countries found by the program is much broader than the nine countries generated by the World Trade Exporter program, and the number of trade shows found is 13 compared with six for World Trade Exporter. World Trade Exporter's bibliography feature provides more external references to assist both case study companies, however. In summary, both the company and the students would find this program to be of great assistance.

The biotechnology company also found the program of assistance in its effort to expand international markets, and similar to World Trade Exporter found two countries (United Kingdom and Singapore) that represent potential new markets. The references in this program generally pointed our company in the correct direction, although the NTDB system offered more specific and detailed information, including importer contacts, as noted earlier.

CORE II (COMPANY READINESS TO EXPORT)

CORE II addresses internal assessment and positioning, the first stage of the exporting process. It is designed to be used as a management tool for assessing a company's readiness to export. The program's stated objective is to assist both potential exporters and advisors to exporters in developing a systematic, proactive approach to export market development. CORE II targets the following user groups: (1) individual companies interested in evaluating their own readiness to export; (2) export assistance agencies interested in helping their clients evaluate and prepare for exporting; and (3) colleges, universities, and seminar/workshop sponsors seeking an educational tool to explore the exporting process.

Program Features

The program starts by offering the user the choice of "novice" or "expert" mode, the difference being that novice mode offers additional instructions throughout the exercise. For an export assistance agency or consulting firm that regularly uses the program, this is a beneficial, time-saving feature. The user then starts from a Main Menu, the centerpiece of the program, which offers two principal choices: commencing the CORE II exercise (the evaluation of export readiness) or a step-by-step export guide. If the user is unfamiliar with even the basic concepts of exporting, the step-by-step tutorial guide serves as a good overview in outline form of all stages of the exporting process. It is by no means a comprehensive resource, however.

The CORE II exercise emphasizes up front that five factors are highly correlated with exporting success: (1) the organizational characteristics of the firm; (2) the motivation for going international; (3) top management commitment; (4) the company's product strengths; and (5) the suitability of its products for foreign customers. The user then provides responses to a detailed five section survey which corresponds to the five success factors. The program reminds the user to give candid responses in order to provide an objective assessment of the company's export potential. Once a section of the survey has been completed, a message appears on the screen summarizing what has just been covered and how it relates to exporting success. In addition, CORE II offers the ability to review and modify user responses at any time. After answering the first section dealing with background questions, the program points out three factors that are generally associated with exporting success: (1) risk taking attitudes of managers; (2) the firm's expansion in the domestic market; and (3) access to experienced personnel and resources. It also reminds the user that one must have a deliberate strategy to achieve specific goals in exporting. The user is then prompted to enter the principal product category of the firm, and is offered six choices: "Components, Commercial Products (e.g., office equipment, computers, furniture), Industrial Goods, Agricultural Goods, Final Consumer Products, and Services." Our hypothetical producers of spectrometers and biotechnology equipment might be confused about which category they fall under, and no assistance is offered by the generic help feature.

Once the five-part survey has been completed, the user proceeds to the *CORE II Evaluation*, which weights the responses given and generates both a graphical matrix and a more detailed written breakdown of the company's export readiness rating (high, moderate, or low) in two categories: Organizational and Product. These categories measure success factors such as previous international experience, strength of motivation for exporting, management commitment, product uniqueness, and product adaptability. The more detailed written breakdown offers readiness ratings and composite scores for the five success factors. Once the evaluation section has been started, the user is not allowed to return to the main menu until it has been completed.

Strengths

Depending on the accuracy of the answers to the survey, the program can provide a good assessment of how ready a company is to export before it haphazardly enters into the process. It identifies potential company weaknesses, which top management can address prior to entering international markets. It points out certain of the company's strengths which can be exploited in export markets. CORE II allows the user to choose different responses to the survey (e.g., higher or lower level of management commitment) and observe the changes in the degree of export readiness. It also provides a basic tutorial on all steps of the exporting process. For export agencies and consulting firms, the program offers the ability to provide a written input form to interested companies, a valuable feature that can save time as well as appeal to those with no desire or ability to use a computer. The help feature offers educational explanations of many topics, and is only infrequently too general to offer specific assistance. A written user manual is provided which has a helpful introduction and guide to using the program.

Weaknesses

The CORE II program is an effective tool for assessing the factors correlated with exporting success, and for identifying strengths and weaknesses of the prospective exporter. It is unlikely to be as valuable a learning tool for students of international business, however, unless a detailed case study can be prepared which provides input for the survey points. The detailed nature of the questions on the company, management's motivation and commitment, and product strengths do not lend themselves to reactive impulse answers, and little educational benefit is derived. The program offers only limited references to external information. In addition, the step-by-step tutorial is more of an outline and not of sufficient depth to provide a comprehensive education in the exporting process for students.

The written manual also notes that the program asks for limited information from the user company and that it provides only a tentative positioning of the company's organizational and product strengths and weaknesses. Accordingly, it advises that the program should be used with an experienced export advisor so that positive or negative results are not misinterpreted as conclusive. The risk, however, is that a prospective exporter without an experienced advisor might be dissuaded from further evaluation if a low readiness rating was received.

Application to Case Studies

CORE II is highly recommended for ECI and would be educational for the team of students involved in assisting the company. By design, the program is intended to address only the first stage of the exporting process, and ECI and the students must look to another program for assistance in other stages of the exporting process. Similarly, the step-by-step export guide discusses the overall process only in very general terms, and does not provide a detailed listing of external references and resources. In the second case, BI already exports and presumably meets the readiness tests. Therefore, CORE II would not have much apparent value to this firm. The program's developer, Dr. Cavusgil, commented however that it might be beneficial to have the managers of this company complete the CORE II assessment to compare their perceptions of success factors with the CORE II results and see if these coincide. In addition, Dr. Cavusgil noted that CORE II can be used as an assessment tool to delineate how individual managers perceive their company's strengths and weaknesses, with the results of each individual compared and contrasted with others.

SUMMARY AND RECOMMENDATIONS

Table 2 provides a summary which rates the relative proficiency of each program along two lines: (1) general features and benefits and (2) effectiveness in assisting the hypothetical case study companies. All the programs reviewed were generally found to be well designed and successful in meeting their program objectives. As noted in the introduction, this chapter is intended to meet the needs of educators and students in undergraduate and graduate business programs. It is also applicable to businesses looking to enter or expand into export markets and to government agencies and other

TABLE 2. Proficiency Ratings
(1 = Outstanding, 2 = Satisfactory, 3 = Below Average)*

	The NTDB	World Trade Exporter	World Trader	CORE II**
1. General Features/Benefits				
Stages of export process addressed:				
○ Internal assessment	2	2	2.5	1
○ Market research	1	1.5	1.5	
○ Entry strategies	2	2	2	
○ Strategy implementation	2	2	2	
○ Ongoing assessment	2	2	2	
User's guide/technical manual	3	2	1	2
Menu/help features	2	1	1	2
Data search feature	2	1	2	
Content: depth and breadth	1	2	2	1
Ease of navigating program	2	1	1	1
Teaching effectiveness	1	1	1	1
2. Case 1 Items				
Learn about exporting process	1	2	2	2
Determine export readiness	2	2	2.5	1
Learn about potential markets	1	2	2	
Understand risks involved	2	2	2	2
3. Case 2 Items				
Search for new export markets	1	2	2	

Notes:
*Proficiency ratings by the authors of this paper.
**This program does not attempt to address all stages of the exporting process and is evaluated only for criteria which apply.

advisors involved in export education and administration. Which programs are most appropriate for each of these groups?

Business school educators would be well served by investigating the NTDB system in greater detail. Many universities throughout the U.S. maintain CD-ROM readers in library reference areas, and the NTDB system could be used more broadly in economics, marketing, and international business curricula. World Trade Exporter should be investigated in part for its powerful search feature and extensive bibliography, as well as its ease of use. World Trader, similar to World Trade Exporter in certain respects, also merits evaluation.

Businesses would be advised to investigate (in the following order) World Trade Exporter, World Trader, and the NTDB. They should also keep in mind that CORE II is a recommended first step appropriate for every company considering exporting, and that the Passport system, although not reviewed herein due to its specialization, is a valuable aid in understanding foreign cultures and business practices (see Appendix A for a brief description).

Businesses should also seek to utilize the resources of the government provided through the Department of Commerce. As a general rule, a company seeking export information or assistance should first seek to take advantage of the vast resources, many of them free of charge, that are offered by the federal government. Many of these services are provided on a regional basis, supplemented by small business export development centers maintained in a number of universities around the U.S. These resources are well equipped to offer appropriate education and assistance, and frequently offer access to or use of many of the programs reviewed herein at a fraction of the charge of purchasing them outright.

Government agencies would be wise to invest the resources to promote more widespread usage of the NTDB and Export Qualifier (CORE II) programs by private sector software developers. In addition, government agencies should be aware of the private sector programs available so that they may be recommended where appropriate.

SUGGESTIONS FOR TERM PROJECTS

1. Select a country in either Africa or the Middle East and, using the World Factbook from NTDB, write an analysis of the

country's political, economic, and social stability. How would
you rank the country as a potential export market for either of
the case studies in the chapter (ECI or BI)?

2. Contact your local Commerce Department or International
Trade Administration (ITA) office and volunteer your assistance in working with a local company to evaluate its export
potential. Incorporate the five stages of the exporting process
in your work. Develop an organizational workbook to guide
you through the process.

3. Approach the publisher of one of the software programs reviewed in this chapter, and request the names of several corporations which use the software. Develop a survey to gather
information from these users, measuring the respondents' utilization of the software program, its effectiveness, and its
strengths and weaknesses. Based on the results of your survey,
offer suggestions for improvements.

4. Discuss the possibility of incorporating an expert system shell
into the NTDB program. Refer to Chapter 4 for references on
expert systems.

5. Using the Foreign Traders Index of the NTDB, select an importer of any manufactured product in either Canada or the
U.K. Contact this importer via fax or letter, inform them of
your involvement in an international marketing course, and
inquire about the most common mistakes the importer has
observed in dealing with U.S. exporters. Juxtaposition the results of your inquiry against the 12 most common mistakes
made by exporters as discussed in the NTDB.

6. Contact your local Commerce Department or International
Trade Administration (ITA) office. Arrange to work through
CORE II with a prospective exporter. Assist the prospective
exporter in completing the self assessment of CORE II. Comment on the utility of CORE II in accomplishing this task.

END OF CHAPTER QUESTIONS

1. How is the United States performing in the export arena? List
both your criteria for measuring this performance and your
sources.

2. Explain one aspect of the exporting process using the NTDB's 100-page Guide to Exporting.
3. Explain the importance of internal assessment by a prospective exporter. How would you go about this process? What major product and organizational variables would you measure?
4. What steps would you take to conduct international marketing research if you were new to the exporting process? Include references to price, planning, promotion, and product as covered in the NTDB Guide to Exporting.
5. What criteria would you use to evaluate the user friendliness of the NTDB? If you have access to other international marketing or exporting programs, make comparisons.
6. You have been asked to advise Electronic Components, Inc. (one of two case studies referenced in the chapter) on a market entry strategy to sell its products in Germany. Explain the alternatives available (e.g., joint venture, distributor, acquisition) and the relative strengths and weaknesses of each strategy.
7. What features would you consider adding to the NTDB? Provide explanations for your suggestions.
8. What are the characteristics of a good database? Using these characteristics, critically evaluate the NTDB.
9. Comment on the 12 most common mistakes made by exporters, as discussed in the NTDB.
10. Discuss the five factors that CORE II maintains are highly correlated with exporting success. Relate these factors to small business.

REFERENCES

Cremeans, J. and Williams, A. (1991). The National Trade Data Bank: A New Window on International Trade. *CD-Rom Professional*, (July), 76-80.
International Council for Computers in Education (Ed.). (1986). *Software Selection, Evaluation and Organization (and) Software Reviews. Article Reprints.* Eugene, OR: International Council for Computers in Education.
Karakaya, F. and Karakaya, F. (1989). Selection of Statistical Software Package for Marketing Research Course. In *Proceedings of the 1989 AMA Microcomputers in the Marketing Curriculum Conference,* Dwyer, F. R. & Steinberg, M., (Eds.), Chicago, IL: American Marketing Association, 237-244.

Kefalas, A.G. and Carr, H.H. (1988). Designing an Assistant Export Expert Information System (EXIS) for an International Manager. In *Proceedings of the Twenty-First Annual Hawaii International Conference on System Sciences IEEE*, Sprague, R., (Ed.), Washington DC: IEEE Comput. Soc. Press, 94-101.

Kennen International, Cavusgil, S.T., and The Dialog Systems Division of A.T. Kearny, Inc. (1991). CORE II USER'S GUIDE, Version 3.2.

Plant, M. (1991). The National Trade Data Bank: A One Year Perspective. *Business America*, (September), 2-5.

Weber, J. (1991). Global Business Simulation (GBSIM): A Simulation Exercise to Aid in Globalizing the Marketing Curriculum. In *Proceedings of the 1989 AMA Microcomputers in the Marketing Curriculum Conference*, Dwyer, F.R. and Steinberg, M., (Eds.), Chicago, IL: American Marketing Association, 59-71.

Chapter 7

Utilizing Databases in International Business II: Compact Disclosure and Disclosure/Worldscope

John William Clarry

In today's global economy, the demand for high-quality, easily accessible information on public companies worldwide is greater than ever.

Steven Goldspiel, late President, Disclosure Inc.

INTRODUCTION

Information is one of the most critical resources in today's global economy, and information technology is essential to attain and sustain competitive advantage (Porter 1985; Wriston 1992). Yet the optimal use of such information technologies also requires information databases that are timely, reliable, flexible, and accessible. Until recently, there were relatively few databases available for international business users that met these criteria. In this information vacuum, many student and practitioner users tended to rely on more general theories or rules of thumb for international business questions, without the data capabilities to test or analyze competitive situations more completely.

The increasing demand for information has stimulated the rapid development of databases and software in a variety of business and academic fields. Many of these databases can extend the reach and capabilities of end-users, but international business databases have often tended to lag behind the needs of users and developments in other fields. In this chapter, we will briefly review several types of databases available for international business studies, then focus on the content and capabilities of two databases from Disclosure.

TYPES OF INTERNATIONAL BUSINESS DATABASES

There are now a variety of databases available in different formats for international business users. Many of these databases are accessible on-line through DIALOG or similar gateway services; but some of the more recent products follow the user trends in information technology towards computer disk-read only (CD-ROM) formats for easier searching by end-users (Nahl-Jakobovits and Tenopir 1992). But whatever the format, international business databases reflect the critical variables and information sources of their suppliers. The challenge for end-users is to learn how to adapt the information available on different international databases to their own functional or project based needs.

One set of databases is constructed from geographically based information about specific nations or regions of the world. For example, there are databases about business in Britain (Montgomery 1990), Canada (Reed 1992; Merry 1989), China (Jackson 1991), France (Eichler and Pagell 1991), Germany (Ojala 1992), Japan (Miller 1991b), and the former Soviet Union (Klotzbucher 1992). There are also broader regional databases about the changing areas of Eastern Europe (Ojala 1991a), Asia (Ojala 1990), and the Middle East (Ellis 1991). However, there are few databases available on less developed countries in general, due to limited infrastructures and business information demand (Karake 1990). Despite the scope of geographic coverage of these databases, most still have only a domestic bias (Choi 1988), with a comparative rather than strictly foreign or international perspective; different data fields and definitions also limit the comparability of information across distinct databases.

Another set of databases with a more international emphasis tends to focus on trade and export statistics, either from source or destination countries; for example, shipping data are available in PIERS from the U.S. Department of Commerce (Bjorner 1992). Other large databanks are available from on-line services such as DIALOG, and many databases are offered by government sponsored agencies (Chadwick 1990). Although these on-line services may provide trade leads or business contacts, they are still limited mostly to host market situations or specific trade opportunities. More general information on international stock price movements, in menu driven or interactive formats, is also available (Graham 1992). News or event databases are accessible from the Financial Times on Data Star, or other bibliographic sources for mergers and acquisition announcements (Bell and Halperin 1991). Specific segment databases on international business have also been created for the auto industry (Ojala 1991b), and for Japanese technology applications (Coghlan 1992), or for current financial data and corporate news announcements on Extel cards. Yet these specialized databases are not necessarily comparable, and accessing them through other gateway services on-line can become expensive.

A third type of database combines the specific business and financial variables of comparative domestic products with the international scope and perspective of trade statistics or foreign news stories. Several corporate financial directory databases are currently available on DIALOG files or other formats, such as CD-ROM; most of these databases are composed of public firms, and include over 100 numeric data fields from a variety of sources. Yet there are still significant differences in how soon the latest data are available on-line, and variations in how the databases can be searched or displayed (Miller 1991a). For our purposes, there are also distinct differences in how much of the universe and how many of the data fields represent international business dimensions searchable by end-users. In order to apply these search skills for international business projects, this chapter will discuss two CD-ROM databases generally available for research purposes in many institutions; they are also available on-line through the Nexus service or by DIALOG, or on magnetic tapes.

Compact Disclosure

The CD-ROM databases of Compact Disclosure have been available in many academic and research institutions since 1985. The Disclosure universe is based on information compiled primarily from Securities and Exchange Commission (SEC) filings. Monthly discs are provided by annual subscription with information on over 10,000 publicly listed companies. The information for most companies is current and updated on a regular basis. While there is some variation of companies listed in each monthly disc, the total number of records available provides a wealth of readily available and timely data for many user projects. Much of this information is compiled from each subject company's annual report and 10-K filings, which are available to the public; but end-users often prefer the ease and control of searching for their own data through customized menus. The CD-ROM format is also becoming more popular than on-line searches (Nahl-Jakobovits and Tenopir 1992).

One of the strengths of Compact Disclosure's database products is the sophisticated and user-friendly software included. End-users can easily search the complete database by a number of different criteria such as company names, types of business classified by Standard Industrial Classification (SIC) two or four digit codes, textual descriptions of businesses, or industry groups. More specific search criteria for international business include country of parent incorporation and national currency listings. For example, a search of Disclosure's non-U.S. company sample would find the most firms to be incorporated in Canada (Clarry 1990); but non-U.S. currency searches will identify foreign exchange transactions in many different denominations. Financially oriented users can also search for samples of companies with specified performance, asset, or stock market data ranges updated weekly. Accounting users can examine companies by auditor or the content of auditor reports. Managers can search for companies by their number of employees or dates of recent acquisitions, or by the names and compensation levels of a firm's upper echelons of top officers.

The Disclosure software also allows users to conduct multiple step or "emulation" mode searches, either narrowing or augmenting their searches by listing additional search criteria. For example, users may begin by searching for all companies listed in a given business code or industry group; then perform additional searches by setting financial ranges or by other keywords from the corporate textual fields. A search of the pharmaceutical industry (SIC 2834) could be refined by delimiting the range of sales sizes or R & D expenditures; further searches could specify specific products or strategic keywords. While there are some restrictions on search procedures, users can also follow their own customized steps through Disclosure's "emulation" mode for more flexible searches. There is also a great deal of flexibility in the display of selected data after the search is completed. Formats can be specially designed and easily edited to display only desired data, which can be presented in user display formats or downloaded into a comma-delimited format for import into another spreadsheet program (Berry 1991).

Limitations

Despite the ease and sophistication of Compact Disclosure's software, there are still some inherent limitations in the database for international business users. First, since the universe is drawn from SEC filings, most of the firms in the large database are U.S. owned. There are over 300 non-U.S. owned firms that have filed American Depository Receipts (ADRs) in the U.S.; but this is still only a small proportion of all companies in Disclosure's population, and only a fraction of the foreign companies selling in the U.S. without issuing equity, and this could create significant biases. Moreover, there are often more missing data for non-U.S. companies because of different legal disclosure requirements. Separate databases on Canada and Europe have been created and marketed by Disclosure, but the main product is still based on U.S. SEC filings. This reliance on SEC filings of company 10-Ks can also delay the availability of some of the data (Miller 1991a). Finally, there are few specifically international statistics included in Disclosure's financial data for either U.S. or non-U.S. companies. In order to compensate for this omission, Compact Disclosure has recently formed a joint venture with another information firm to market another more international database.

Disclosure/Worldscope

The national limitations of Compact Disclosure's database are now offset by a new product jointly developed by Disclosure and Wright's Investor Service (1990). Wright's had previously marketed bound Worldscope volumes with international business data, and still publishes these volumes; but many users will find the new computerized access more useful and flexible. After offering a less flexible and successful product on disc with Lotus, the Wright's firm entered a joint venture with Compact Disclosure to market Worldscope products on CD-ROM disc.

The Disclosure/Worldscope database has many of the same features and software advantages as the Compact Disclosure product discussed above; but in addition, Worldscope offers much more data on non-U.S. companies. The Global database monthly discs include extracted data on over 9,000 companies from 25 different industries and 40 countries. The countries covered include not only the more developed OECD countries, but also fast growing nations like Hong Kong, Malaysia, Mexico, Singapore, and South Korea. This broader universe of nations provides a more comprehensive selection of companies to study, and can help to overcome some ethnocentric biases and information blinders of U.S. users.

While the broader universe of non-U.S. companies offers a better basis for studying international business, the differences in accounting practices and legal disclosure requirements make direct data comparisons more difficult. The Global Disclosure/Worldscope database tries to follow a unified format to adjust data for consistency, but does not attempt to "adjust away" any country specific accounting variations (Disclosure/Worldscope 1991). However, there are still many national and firm-specific variations in reporting and financial accounting, which must be kept in mind to discourage too many crude comparisons of data by users (Cf. Eiteman and Stonehill 1989: Chapters 19-20; Choi et al. 1983).

Detailed financial footnotes of accounting adjustments are also included to provide additional auditing details not disclosed in numerical fields. Some currency adjustments for non-U.S. companies are also necessary as key financial data are usually presented in the local currency of the company for the past ten years; but certain summary financial data are presented in U.S. dollar terms for annual or five year periods. Performance ratios are not impacted by different currency denominations, but may still reflect different accounting rules. A valuable feature for time series analysis of non-U.S. firms is Worldscope's inclusion of monthly and annual foreign exchange rates from Dow Jones to convert local currency data to U.S. dollars. However, the problems of comparing sales of companies with different exchange rate translations seem to be similar to Dun & Bradstreet's Market File products on DIALOG service (Pagell 1991).

The most valuable feature of Disclosure/Worldscope for students is the easy availability of numerous foreign and international business statistics for both U.S. and non-U.S. companies. These data include foreign assets, sales, income, return on assets, asset turnover and growth rates, sales and income growth rates, and ratios of foreign to total assets, sales, and income. In addition to annual international business data, there are also five year averages and growth rates reported for comparison. Although some companies do not always report these data for public information, there are still often sufficient numbers provided for a given year or total worldwide performance to determine national profiles of competitive advantage (Cf. Porter 1990; Clarry 1993). Other financial information is also reported on R & D or cashflow as a percentage of sales, sales per employee, and additional financial performance measures on both an annual and five year average basis.

Despite occasional or systematic data omissions by some companies, this kind of information is highly appreciated by international business users. It is also valuable evidence for growing numbers of non-U.S. MBA students or expatriate managers, who may be more interested in the performance and conduct of familiar national firms. Further enhancements are being offered to extend Worldscope's financial information by product segments, shareholder ownership, and additional stock price and trading data. Moreover, annotated corporate news headlines and citation references by firm or nation keywords have been added to the search menu for access to many topical international financial publications.

While the Disclosure/Worldscope product offers several features and a broader universe of global companies not accessible to Compact Disclosure users, as summarized in Figure 1, there are still some disadvantages for international business analysts. First, there are many different data fields available to users, but not all of them can provide a basis for sorting or reporting records. For particular relevance, these formatting options are not available for foreign business statistics or many financial liquidity ratios. Second, the keyword textual field searching capability is not as useful as it is with Compact Disclosure because there is not as much textual material included from annual reports, except occasional financial or accounting footnotes, or the annotated news headlines. Third, there are few ownership or subsidiary listings included for comparison of corporate governance or organizational structure arrangements. Finally, this database is new and relatively expensive for many institutions to afford at a time of fiscal austerity and corporate retrenchment (Cf. DeLoughry 1992). Unfortunately, despite a heightened

FIGURE 1. International Dimensions of Two Sample Databases

DIMENSION	COMPACT DISCLOSURE	GLOBAL DISCLOSURE/ WORLDSCOPE
Sample Size	10,000 +	9,000 +
Update Frequency	Monthly	Monthly
Universe Coverage	Public SEC Listing	Wright's Investor Service
Nationalities	Mostly U.S. Firms and American Deposits (ADRS)	Firms In 40 Nations and 24 Industries
Time Periods	Quarterly, Annual, 5 Yrs.	Annual, 5 Year Averages
Variables	Currency (Non-U.S.)	Foreign Sales (Percentage)
	Subsidiary List	Foreign Assets (Percentage)
	Text Dictionary (Nation)	Foreign Income (Percentage)
	Corporate Exhibits	Foreign Income Growth
	Financial Footnotes	Foreign Income Margin
		Foreign Return on Assets
		Foreign Asset Growth/Turnover
		Foreign Sales Growth

interest in international business, many educational organizations may be unable or unlikely to subscribe to both of these databases. Hence, end-users will have to learn how to either maximize the utility of what information is available, or appeal to Disclosure to broaden the availability of foreign business statistics, or to lower prices below their already discounted academic rates.

FUNCTIONAL APPLICATIONS
OF COMPUTERIZED DATABASES

The increased access to information on international business databases should help stimulate active interest in the theories and practices of firms involved in international business. However, the interest and applications of these databases will still be shaped by the existing functional orientations that users and corporate departments continue to follow, even as business schools and firms become more internationalized. In order to justify some of the resources and support required for international business databases, specific functional searches and projects should be designed which will more fully utilize the vast capabilities that international information systems allow. In the sections below, we suggest some projects that database users can pursue in different functional areas of international business.

Marketing

Much of the pedagogical material in international business involves cases and theories of what products to market where, or how to enter foreign markets. Even the standardization of global marketing programs requires accurate customer databases (Marketing News 1992: 21-22). But in order to examine the particular marketing mix and decisions of specific international firms, these two databases provide the current information and search capabilities that end-users will better appreciate. If firms practicing global marketing can be identified and distinguished from those that follow "multi-domestic" strategies (Cf. Prahalad and Doz 1987), other performance or corporate variables can be readily compared for paired sets or larger samples.

For example, both Compact Disclosure and Worldscope allow searches by primary business code or industry, which should help reveal the major competitors in a specific four-digit SIC coded market. Further elaborated searches could be added to narrow the criteria to certain size, R & D, or performance ranges which may be used to define distinct "strategic groups" in a given product market. Comparisons between U.S. and non-U.S. companies could also be made by separate searches of both databases, or an emulated two-step search for firms from specific parent country locations. Comparing primary and secondary business listings would show which firms have most of their sales in a specific product market. Segment data from both databases would also show the relative sales and profits earned by diversified firms in each distinct business; but these segments are often defined too aggregately or idiosyncratically to correspond with the SIC codes of product markets.

For distinctly international marketing issues, the shares of foreign to total business may offer additional competitive clues of a particular firm's international strengths and weaknesses. If users are interested in how much of Procter & Gamble's or Unilever's sales are derived in foreign markets, a search of these databases would reveal some current sales information. The Worldscope database is better for ascertaining the level and growth of a firm's international sales and income, either on its own or compared to others in its core business or parent nation. Firms that rely more on sales and income from their own domestic profit "sanctuary" (Prahalad and Doz 1987) would also be detected by foreign income, margins, and return on assets as a percentage of total operating income or assets. Five year averages of these foreign business statistics would also demonstrate trends or patterns, which may be associated with the levels of foreign competition, top management strategies, or the strength of a firm's domestic currency in price competitive markets.

The geographic configuration of a firm's sales and functional value added activities (e.g., Porter 1986) could also be measured by the dispersion and percentage of foreign to total assets, whether for a single firm or nation, or even a whole industry (Clarry 1992). For example, in the automotive vehicle parts industry (SIC 3714), the larger and more vertically integrated firms, such as Ford or Fiat, also have more foreign based assets than smaller firms, or those in other location bound industries, like Paper Products (SIC 2621); but until recently, Japanese owned auto parts firms have lower levels of foreign assets than U.S. or European owned firms. Users could then test whether marketing intensive or location bound businesses can rely more on export strategies to serve foreign markets than assembly oriented industries, without the risk or expense of large foreign asset investments.

While the Worldscope database provides abundant statistics on a firm's or an industry's total foreign business activities, there is less information within the database on specific geographic markets or operations. Disclosure has begun to segment the market for Worldscope by offering regional databases; for example, the Worldscope/Europe product contains some further breakdowns of sales and income from different European nations, but there is still a lot of missing data. Unfortunately, the data gaps tend to follow national origins and disclosure laws, so there is more missing data from German owned firms.

Although the Compact Disclosure database contains less general information on overall international performance than Worldscope, there are three features that offer access to specific market data. First, a lengthy listing of domestic and foreign subsidiaries provides evidence of the extent of market penetration and the scope of ownership presences established around the world (Miller 1991a). Users could focus on a specific product line or subsidiary incorporated under a different name, rather than searching whole company lists. Second, there is additional information often contained in corporate exhibits and SEC filings that announce planned or intended market entries and acquisitions; complete 10-K filings can be accessed separately on another data service, Compact D/SEC. Third, the dictionary listing of keywords to search by can offer some textual evidence of actions or results in specific product or geographic markets. For example, a keyword search for names of specific countries like China or Japan, or regions like the European market, will indicate which firms have a current presence or strategic interest in these geographic areas. Additional information from the Managerial Discussion section of annual reports may also provide current sales or competitive details from specific regions and product divisions of a firm.

Management

The management aspects of international business are often of special career interest to students and executives, but there has been only limited information available on more than an anecdotal or anonymous basis. The personnel or cross-cultural management practices of particular companies are not accessible to the general public, but some pertinent information can be ascertained by combining searches of our two databases. For example, both databases list the number of employees of firms in their universe, and Disclosure/Worldscope reports total employee growth rates on an annual and five year basis. Unfortunately, there is no breakdown of foreign and domestic numbers of employees in either database; but there are indicators of firm productivity and growth rates by employee to sales or asset ratios. Some information can be compiled by searching Compact Disclosure's list of a firm's subsidiaries, then matching the unit with data on employees, SIC codes, or performance levels from other corporate ownership directories (e.g., Wards).

There is somewhat greater information available on the top management officers in both databases; but Compact Disclosure also provides data on the age, title, and apparent compensation of officers for an "upper echelons" type of study (Cf. Hambrick and Mason 1984). Compact Disclosure also lists shares held by insiders and any recent trades, while Disclosure/Worldscope lists the number of common shareholders and closely held shares. This information could allow users to test assertions of the impact of financial ownership variables on sales strategy or stability of performance, or to compare domestic with more international firms. Broader relationships of corporate governance can also be examined with data on boards of directors, both insiders and outsiders, listed by Compact Disclosure. Managers and board members can also be selected by name, which permits algebraic identification of governance networks of interlocking directorates within specific industries or firms, or even within specific nations.

The annual report text information contained in Compact Disclosure may be used to analyze patterns of strategic change or corporate responsibility by firms, either with or without international business activities (Bowman 1984). Methodologies of content analysis can be employed through keyword searches to detect linguistic or attributional changes in corporate strategies (Huff 1990). Strategic changes may be shown by the incidence of keywords for international business, such as worldwide or global competition (Clarry 1990). These keyword indicators of any strategic change can also be revealed by the Corporate Exhibits or SEC filings sections, which cite significant announcements of acquisitions, divestments, new joint ventures, or licensing agreements. Comparisons of such announcements with degrees of international business, levels of R & D spending, or managerial changes will offer students a real current test of theories of internalization, governance, or upper echelon managerial behavior. Similar comparisons can also be made to identify patterns of corporate social responsibility or risk taking as revealed by content analysis of annual reports (Bowman 1984).

Finance

Both of the databases reviewed have substantial information on financial variables for research projects; but like many financial databases, there is somewhat of a domestic bias in either the reporting or the scope of company data extracted (Choi 1988). The Disclosure/Worldscope database has more explicitly international information due to its broader universe and many foreign business statistics. However, Compact Disclosure has some additional customizing options that will make it possible for users to select and partition samples of firms on different geographic or strategic criteria for further financial analysis.

One of the major financial features of Disclosure/Worldscope is its array of foreign business statistics and records for non-U.S. companies. This data has been difficult to obtain on-line before, and will now allow students to track and compare the international performance of different firms, industries, or parent nation composites. It is also possible to use this times series data for five year correlations with other firm or industry variables, such as R & D expenditures, capital investment or employee growth rates, acquisitions, etc. For example, competitive variations and longitudinal trends in R & D expenditures were shown across a cross-national sample of multinational firms (Clarry 1993). International income returns and growth rates may also be used to test financial effects of stability or risk reduction by diversified sales portfolios, either by geographic diversification or business segments (Eiteman and Stonehill 1989).

Another pertinent financial aspect of international business is the source of funds for multinational firms and their subsidiaries. Both databases have information on multiple sources of funds and cashflows from operations, as well as different uses of retained earnings such as dividends or capital expenditures, that can be compared by industry or other variables. Compact Disclosure also provides data on any loans or investments in a firm's subsidiaries, which may indicate the process of cross-subsidization of cashflows employed in global strategies (Cf. Prahalad and Doz 1987). The stock and debt listings for each company can also be used to compare the levels of leverage in different firms, and as a percentage of total capital or assets. Aggregating this data by nation or industry allows cross-sectional and longitudinal tests of the existence of distinct country norms for debt to equity ratios (Eiteman and Stonehill 1989).

A third critical aspect of international finance is the exposure of firms to possible foreign exchange losses, or perhaps gains. The increasing foreign exchange volatility of the 1980s has impacted the operations, cashflows, and occasionally the strategies of many multinational firms (Eiteman and Stonehill 1989). Sophisticated firms now try to hedge and manage their exposures more, but must still report any gains or losses for accounting and tax purposes. The Disclosure/Worldscope database has these variables available to report or sort by, and users can compare different industries or nationalities of firms for financial risk management (Wriston 1992). Monthly foreign exchange values can also be computed to ascertain the volatility of a given currency, and identify any adjustments taken by a specific firm; however, there are still caveats in comparing foreign exchange translations across firms and national databases (Pagell 1991). More detailed accounting information is often included on foreign exchange income in Compact Disclosure, but these data apply mostly to U.S. owned firms. However, further augmented searches by functional currency denomination can determine patterns by nationality within this database, too.

Accounting and Taxation

The accounting and taxation functions of multinational firms have always been important in international business, but have assumed a rather reduced role as functional courses have expanded coverage and accounting topics became far more specialized. For example, one of the leading texts in international business (Daniels and Radebaugh 1989) has reduced the number of pages and chapters devoted to accounting and taxation issues in its recent editions. Some other finance texts (e.g., Eiteman and Stonehill 1989) have included partial coverage of these issues; but effective databases offer more opportunities for projects that will stimulate user interest and demonstrate the material impacts that accounting and taxation procedures can have on international firms.

One of the problems of analyzing international business performance is the different accounting methods that may be used to report or consolidate worldwide income flows. While some progress has been made in harmonizing the accounting practices around the world (Daniels and Radebaugh 1989), users can easily detect variations in the reporting Worldscope database. Despite some efforts to create a common format, there are numerous reporting variations and omissions due to different legal disclosure requirements and accounting practices. These national accounting differences can also be employed to show the aggregated discrepancies of balance sheets and income statements across distinct origins of parent firms (Choi et al. 1983). For example, different ways of measuring debt and liquidity ratios can often be found by comparing financial profiles of firms in the same industry. Worldscope offers a separate field of company specific accounting for comparing terms in different industries. However, national variations in financial reporting rules still may confound cross-national comparisons of ratios in the same business.

A closely related accounting issue with widespread international business implications is the question of appropriate income taxes for multinational firms with dispersed sales and operations. The dispersed activities and high levels of intrafirm transactions provide opportunities for shifting income and profits to other tax jurisdictions, either by adjusting transfer prices or transfers of intangible property rights (Eiteman and Stonehill 1989; Daniels and Radebaugh 1989). Although international tax issues are not typically the most interesting functional questions, they do become more intriguing when databases can be used to discover and compare the incidence of reported tax liabilities or adjustments. Variations in pretax margins and effective tax rates can be found in Worldscope by searching across industry, nationality, or other criteria. Searches by each firm's auditor or opinion of the auditor's report can also reveal tax problems.

While these tax variations do not necessarily indicate suspicious transfer pricing behavior, they can be used to establish benchmarks or comparables for other firms with tax audits or challenges. In the U.S., the Internal Revenue Service's own IRC 482 regulations (IRS Manual 1985) use several criteria to establish comparability for determining appropriate arm's length transaction prices; and the databases under review both provide substantial information on pricing, margins, and selling or distribution expenses to identify suitable transfer pricing comparables. The detailed information in Compact Disclosure is more relevant for establishing comparable companies in U.S. inbound transfer pricing cases; once a set of firms has been isolated, it is often easier to download necessary data on spreadsheets, or from Compustat (Berry 1991). In addition, users can also employ the keyword search capabilities of Compact Disclosure to locate firms with tax audit problems or reallocations; and they could then create their own sample for investigation by identifying firms with subsidiaries in Puerto Rico, Ireland, the Cayman Islands, or other alleged tax havens.

Finally, perusing the Corporate Exhibits and SEC 10-K filings on Compact Disclosure may allow users to find lists of firms with licensing agreements or transfers of technology between related and unrelated parties. Extracting data from these filings has formed the foundation for the IRS's recent "White Paper" on 482 regulations for intangible property tax transfers (Touche Ross 1988); and all users can follow these database tracks to learn more about the many complex tax and accounting rules governing international business, without being overwhelmed by written law cases. Moreover, law firms now often use corporate databases and legal services software to edit and retrieve clauses from a variety of contracts (Business Week 1992), which should also facilitate the frequent comparisons or revisions of international business contracts. All of the various functional uses of our international databases are summarized in Figure 2.

CONCLUSIONS

In order to meet the growing interest in international business and complement the functional orientations of most practitioners, there should be greater access to and utilization of computerized databases about the operations of multinational firms. This chapter has compared the features and capabilities of two relevant databases available on CD/ROM or Nexus in many institutions: Compact Disclosure and Disclosure/Worldscope. Both databases have their strengths and weaknesses in coverage or search capabilities; but when combined, they offer a valuable contribution to international business students and academic or practitioner researchers. Specific functional applications were suggested for possible database use, and greater utilization will help to justify and incorporate this essential but expensive investment into international business analysis. Thus, the benefits of these and other databases for international business will be more interested students and better trained managers, who will be aware of and prepared for the possible opportunities and threats in a more integrated and information rich global economy.

END OF CHAPTER QUESTIONS

1. Industries vary in their forms and extent of international business transactions, but how could you identify the most internationally active firms in a particular industry?
2. How can firms implementing global marketing strategies be identified?
3. What variables can be compared to measure patterns of international management and organizational structure?
4. How can firms with large foreign exchange exposures or losses be identified?
5. Which companies and industries have the highest potential opportunities for international tax avoidance by adjusting their transfer pricing?

FIGURE 2. Functional International Business Project Applications

BUSINESS PROJECT APPLICATION	DATABASE VARIABLES
MARKETING	
Competitor Analysis	SIC Groups, Product Segments
International Sales Profiles	Foreign Sales, Income % Foreign Subsidiary Listing
Geographic Configuration	Foreign Assets, Margin, ROA
Trends, Strategies	5 Year Foreign Averages Keywords and Exhibits
MANAGEMENT	
Employment Profiles	Number of Employees
Productivity	Employee/Sales Ratios
Top Management Control	Officers and Compensation Boards of Directors
Governance	Insider, Stock Ownership
Strategic Change	Keyword Text 5-Year Foreign Averages
FINANCE	
Risk and Corporate Performance	Foreign Business Statistics
Sources of Funds	Debt, Equity Ratios Cashflows, Foreign ROA
Use of Funds	Dividends, R & D, Capital Expend.
Stock Listings	Stock Ownership Profile
Foreign Exchange Exposure	Footnotes on Gains/Losses
ACCOUNTING AND TAXATION	
Different Accounting Standards	Disclosure Variations Accounting Practice Footnotes
Income Tax Rates	Payable, Deferred Taxes Pretax, Net Margins
Transfer Pricing Practices	Industry Comparables Benchmarked Costs
Intangible Asset Values	Corporate Licensing Exhibits Keywords in Text

REFERENCES

Bell, S. J. and M. Halperin. (1991). "M & A moves abroad: Databases for researching cross-border deals," *Database* (October), Vol. 14, No. 5, pp. 20-24.

Berry, Dixon. (1991). "Post-processing data from Compact Disclosure using spreadsheets," *Database* (April), Vol. 14, No. 2, pp. 58-61.

Bjorner, Susan N. (1992). "Import-export reports: Choose your output from on-line, disk, or CD-ROM," *Online* (November), Vol. 16, No. 6, pp. 94-98.

Bowman, Edward H. (1984). "Content analysis of annual reports for corporate strategy and risk," in *Readings in Strategic Management,* Arnoldo Hax (Ed.), . Cambridge, MA: Ballinger.

Business Week. (1992). "How many lawyers can you fit on a floppy disk?" (December 21), p. 63.

Chadwick, Terry Brainerd. (1990). "International trade information: Other business databases online," *Database* (August), Vol. 13, No. 4, pp. 26-29.

Choi, Frederick D.S. (1988). "International data sources for empirical research in financial management," *Financial Management* (Summer), Vol. 17, No. 2, pp. 80-84.

Choi, Frederick D.S., Hisaaki Hiro, Sang kee Min, San Oh Nom, Junichi Ujiie, and Arthur I. Stonehill. (1983). "Analyzing foreign financial statements: The use and misuse of international ratio analysis," *Journal of International Business* (Spring/Summer), Vol. 12, No. 2, pp. 114-131.

Clarry, John W. (1993). "Innovation and national advantages in global competition," *Journal of International Consumer Marketing,* forthcoming special issue.

_____ . (1992). "Industry and national determinants of international organizational configurations," Unpublished manuscript.

_____ . (1990). *The Sectoral Distribution of Global Competition.* Paper presented at the Academy of Management annual meetings, San Francisco.

Coghlan, Jill. (1992). "The business of technology in Japan: A review of the Japan technology database," *Database* (April), Vol. 15, No. 2, pp. 42-46.

Daniels, John D. and Lee H. Radebaugh. (1989). *International Business: Environments and Operations.* (5th edition). Reading, MA: Addison-Wesley.

DeLoughry, Thomas J. (1992). "Recession spurs changes in college market for computer technology," *The Chronicle of Higher Education* (December 9), p. 22A.

Disclosure/Worldscope. (1991). *Disclosure/Worldscope Global: Database Supplement to User's Manual.* Bethesda, MD: Disclosure Inc.

Eichler, L. and Ruth Pagell. (1991). "Delphes: A French boutique database," *Online* (July), Vol. 15, No. 4, pp. 36-38.

Eiteman, David K. and Arthur I. Stonehill. (1989). *Multinational Business Finance.* (5th edition). Reading, MA: Addison-Wesley.

Ellis, L.M. (1991). "Middle East information online: The Arab Information Bank on DIALOG," *Online* (March), Vol. 15, No. 2, pp. 41-43.

Graham, Catherine. (1992). "International stock prices: Getting them in the U.S." *Database* (August), Vol. 15, No. 4, pp. 64-70.
Hambrick, Donald and Phyllis Mason. (1984). "Upper echelons: The organization as a reflection of its top managers," *Academy of Management Review.* 9: 193-206.
Huff, Anne Sigismund (1990). Mapping strategic thought. In *Mapping Strategic Thought,* A.S. Huff (Ed.), New York: John Wiley.
Internal Revenue Service. (1985). *Internal Revenue Service Field Audit Guidelines, Exhibit 500-1.* Washington, DC: Tax Management, Inc., Bureau of National Affairs.
Jackson, S.F. (1991). "China information at your fingertips: An ever growing amount of data is available on-line," *China Business Review* (November-December), Vol. 5, No. 1, pp. 10-13.
Karake, Zeinab A. (1990). International market analysis through electronic databases. In *Global Business Management in the 1990s,* Fariborz Ghadar, Phillip D. Grub, Robert T. Moran, and Marshall Geer (Eds.), Washington, DC: Beacham Publishing, Inc.
Klotzbucher, Werner. (1992). "Online communication with the ex-USSR," *Online* (September), Vol. 16, No. 5, pp. 106-109.
Marketing News. (1992). "Kotler: Future marketers will focus on customer databases to compete globally," (June 8), Vol. 22, No. 12, pp. 21-22.
Merry, S. (1989). "The Canadian connection: Business online," *Database* (October), Vol. 12, No. 5, p. 15.
Miller, Carmen. (1991a). "U.S. company financial databases on DIALOG," *Database* (June), Vol. 12, No. 5, pp. 24-29.
_____ . (1991b). "Teikoku databank: Japanese companies," *Database* (December), Vol. 14, No. 6, pp. 51-54.
Montgomery, Susan. (1990). "British databases: A comparison of Reuter textline and Profile information," *Database* (April), Vol. 13, No. 2, pp. 28-32.
Nahl-Jakobovits, Diane and Carol Tenopir. (1992). "Databases online and on CD-ROM: How do they differ, let us count the ways," *Database* (April), Vol. 15, No. 2, pp. 42-47.
Ojala, Marydee. (1992). "German company information online," *Online* (November), Vol. 16, No. 6, pp. 83-87.
_____ . (1991a). "Communing with Eastern European business information," *Online* (January), Vol. 15, No. 1, pp. 39-40.
_____ . (1991b). "Driving data: The automotive industry online," *Database* (October), Vol. 14, No. 5, pp. 76-79.
_____ . (1990). "Information sources for the Pacific century," *Database* (April), Vol. 13, No. 2, pp. 81-85.
Pagell, Ruth A. (1991). "It's Greek to me! Exchange rate translations and company comparisons," *Database* (February), Vol. 14, No. 1, pp. 21-28.
Porter, Michael E. (1990). *The Competitive Advantage of Nations.* New York: Free Press.

_____. (1986). Competition in Global Industries: A Conceptual Framework. In *Competition in Global Industries,* M.E. Porter (Ed.), Boston: HBS Press.

_____. (1985). *Competitive Advantage.* New York: Free Press.

Prahalad, C.K. and Yves L. Doz. (1987). *The Multinational Mission.* New York: Free Press.

Reed, William. (1992). "Dun & Bradstreet's online services: A central source for business searchers," *Database* (June), Vol. 15, No. 3, pp. 84-88.

Wright's Investor Service. (1990). *Worldscope Industrial Company Profiles.* Bridgeport, CT: WIS.

Wriston, Walter B. (1992). *The Twilight of Sovereignty: How the Information Revolution is Transforming Our World.* New York: Simon & Schuster.

Chapter 8

Utilizing Databases in International Business III: One Source CD/Corporate International Public Companies

Kate Jones-Randall

INTRODUCTION

The One Source family of products on compact disc encompasses a wide variety of business information. Although it is most commonly found in corporate settings, many U.S. colleges and universities also have it available for use by students, faculty, staff, and the general public. Users find the unique combination of annual report, current and historical financial data, and news and announcements paired with sophisticated searching and formatting capabilities particularly useful when incorporated into a single product. Additionally, One Source allows for the transfer of text and numeric data into 1-2-3 spreadsheet format as well as a number of other popular software programs. This makes retyping columns of numbers unnecessary and greatly reduces the possibility of errors.

THE CD/CORPORATE FAMILY OF PRODUCTS

While only the CD/Corporate: International Public Companies[1] will be discussed in any depth here, it is essential to note that it is one of five products available under the CD/Corporate label, and one of two which are international in scope. CD/Corporate includes U.S. Public Companies, U.S. Private +, U.S. M&A, U.K. Public Companies, U.K. Private +, and European M&A. One of the three available compact disc products from CD/Investment, International Equities, also has an international focus; the other CD/Investment products include U.S. Equities and U.S. Research. CD/Banking, the other financial group of One Source products, consists of Commercial Banks, Bank Holding Companies, Savings and Loans, Savings Banks, and Branches.

CD/Corporate: European M&A (Mergers and Acquisitions) contains in-depth information on over 10,000 United Kingdom and European mergers and acquisitions, including target and acquiror company information, deal terms, advisors and target company financials, and takeover techniques and defense tactics. Data is compiled from the IDD United Kingdom Mergers & Acquisitions and IDD European Mergers & Acquisitions on-line databases, provided by IDD Information Services, Inc., a member of the United Newspaper Group.

CD/CORPORATE: INTERNATIONAL PUBLIC COMPANIES

In all the One Source products, the menus and screens are consistent and well-designed, offering an identical interface in style if not content from product to product. International Public Companies is no exception. The left side of the screen lists the available menu choices, while the right side of the screen describes in detail whichever menu choice is highlighted. Once the data is loaded into the "workspace," the split screen disappears, and One Source presents the information either in paragraph or tabular style.

While it is not possible to disable or bypass the menus and utilize a command-driven interface, the function keys make the passage from one set of menus to the next relatively simple. The F2 key allows for quick return to the main menu, while the Escape key lets one back up one screen at a time, from any menu choice. This is particularly advantageous when using the Screening menu function, where search parameters can be changed or edited without beginning the entire search over again. In this way, the baseline search, such as country, or line of business, etc., does not have to change or be chosen again while various fields of financial data, for example, can be rearranged or manipulated to suit the searcher. The ease of use coupled with the depth of information available makes it possible to perform complex company and industry analyses quickly and effectively. International Public Companies is updated monthly. Student usage typically includes all types of business majors, from accounting and taxation to management and marketing, depending upon course requirements.

INTERNATIONAL PUBLIC COMPANIES

Data Source

CD/Corporate International Public Companies on compact disc utilizes data from Extel Financial Card Services, of Extel Financial Limited, an authoritative on-line source of international company financial information.

Applications

CD/Corporate International Public Companies' broad applications include the following: investment analysis, whereby one can identify and evaluate investment opportunities based on one's own financial criteria; merger and acquisition analysis, particularly in regard to acquisition history; corporate finance and historical financial analysis, using the income statements to determine the financial health of international companies; industry research and sector analysis, incorporating the SIC code search capability to evaluate industry performance and then perform competitive analysis by ranking individual companies within an industry on selected financial criteria; and valuation studies, whereby company capital structure can be analyzed to determine financing needs and appropriate valuation for new debt or equity issues.

Contents

Approximately 9,000 companies are included, with data from company annual reports and accounts (income statements), historical financials, corporate background, consolidated profit and loss accounts (income statements), and interim reports and news items available. The historical financials date back five years, with ratios available in local currency. United Kingdom conventions for financial data format and wording are followed for all of the standardized information fields. All standardized financials are also available for sorting and report formatting in British Pounds Sterling, U.S. dollars, and the local currency for each company.

General information, such as name, address, telephone number, is presented, as are listings of subsidiaries, profit and loss statements, balance sheets, industry-specific financial items, other financial items such as contributions, etc., annual growth rates, financial ratios, and share-related items for a more in-depth profile of each company.

Features

All of the above items are available for use within the Screening menu, which involves the creation of combinations of different fields within a single search, by choosing "and" or "or" between fields. "And" restricts the results of each search to only those companies which contain all of the items requested; for example, only those companies which are located in New Zealand and have more than 100 employees. "Or" broadens the search results, for example, to include those companies which are located in either New Zealand or Australia and have more than 100 employees. This form of combining fields is called Boolean searching, arising from Boolean algebra. The searching is done by the user; the algebra by the computer. The Screening menu readily allows variation within certain fields as well as across them.

Sample Searches

Users searching for international company information in CD/ Corporate: International Public Companies will find that company name searches retrieve the largest quantity of data on individual companies. The full report on any given company can include the items listed in Figure 1a. Sample screens illustrating the depth of company information involved in the different company reports are shown in Figures 1b, 1c, and 1d.

SEARCHING INTERNATIONAL
PUBLIC COMPANIES BY SIC CODE

Searches by SIC (Standard Industrial Classification) Code or description will retrieve all companies which are identified by a particular code number or alphabetic description, such as 3740 for Clocks, Watches & Other Timing Devices, as their *primary* line of business (see Figure 2b). The total number of companies in the database which are identified by that SIC code number is listed, and an explanation of the scope of the SIC code number is given. Figures 2a, 2b, and 2c show some examples.

SEARCHING INTERNATIONAL PUBLIC COMPANIES
BY NEWS AND ANNOUNCEMENTS

Searching the News and Announcements field updates the Extel data on each company in the database (similar to Securities Exchange Commission [SEC] filings). The entire list of companies in the database are included in these topics: Capital Restructuring, Management Statements, and Financials. The total number of announcements is given, as well as broken down chronologically to the past month, the last three or last six months. See Figures 3a, 3b, and 3c. If one would prefer to view news and announcements for specific companies, it is easier and faster to search the News & Announcements listed under the specific company name entries.

FIGURE 1a

Main Menu	
Company	After selecting one or more companies,
SIC Code	you may choose from the following
SIC Description	report options
News & Announcements	● Participants List (sorted in GBP or USD)
Screening	● Company Summary
Database Glossary	● Profile
Quit	● Reported Financials
	● Comparative Financials
	● Subsidiaries & Related Companies
	● Capital Structure
	● Share Performance
	● Management Discussion
	● Recent Announcements
	● Full Report (GBP, USD, or Local)
	● Postscript Full Report (GBP, USD, or Local)
	● Custom Profile
	● Custom Report
	● Announcement Search
	● Mailing List

Select item: Item 1 of 7
Press F9 or ENTER to select
F1-Help   Int'l Public Cos – 1 December 1992

Figure 1a illustrates the various types of report options available from the Company search menu. The options are self-explanatory, with the Full Report inclusive of all the listed options. The Custom Profile or Custom Report options allow the user to choose from various field elements, while the other report options offer pre-formatted contents.

FIGURE 1b

Company List	Company

Ableserve PLC
ABM Investments Ltd
ABN Amro Holding NV
ABP Holdings LTD
Abrafract Holdings Ltd
Abtrust Atlas Fund
Abtrust Holdings Ltd
Abtrust New Dawn Invest
Abtrust New European In
Abtrust New Thai Inves
Abtrust Preferred Incom
Abtrust Scotland Invest
ABU Dhabi Investment Co
ABU Dhabi National Hote
Acal PLC
Acatos & Hutcheson PLC
Acciaierie E Ferriere L

Acco-Rexel Group Holdin
Accor

ABP Holdings Ltd
Stokes House
College Square East
Belfast BT1 6HD

Tel: 0232 243377

FYE: 12/31/88 Num of Employees: 1,146
Turnover (Local '000): 192,771
(GBP '000): 192,771
(USD '000): 348,686
Pre-Tax Profit (Local '000): 1,766
(GBP '000): 1,766
(USD '000): 3,194
Last annual: 9/27/90
Last updated: 9/27/90

Select company: Item 97 of 9,404
Press F9 or ENTER to select
F1-Help   Esc – Main Menu   Int'l Public Cos – 1 December 1992

Figure 1b illustrates the initial screen which appears when one searches the Company list menu. The company information here includes the address and telephone number or the company, the fiscal year end, number of employees, sales (turnover), pre-tax profit, and dates of the most recent annual report. The companies are listed alphabetically, and users may select up to 250 companies from this menu.

FIGURE 1c

Company Reports	
Company	

	This report contains the list of companies

Participants List (GBP)   This report contains the list of companies
Participants List (USD)   selected, ranked by normalized turnover in
Company Summary   thousands of GBP currency, including for
Company Profile   each company:
Reported Financials
Comparative Financials   • Currency and Scaling Factor
Subsidiaries & Related   • Normalized Turnover in Thousands
Capital Structure   (in GBP)
Share Performance   • Most Recent FYE
Management Discussion   • Turnover in GBP
Recent Announcements   • Pre-Tax Profit in GBP
Full Report (GBP)   • Turnover in Local Currency
Full Report (USD)   • Pre-Tax Profit in Local Currency
Full Report (Local Currency)   • Turnover in USD
PS – Company Reports
Custom Profile
Custom Report
Announcement Search
Mailing List

Select report: Item 1 of 19
Press F9 or ENTER to select
F1-Help   Esc – Company List   Int'l Public Cos – 1 December 1992

Figure 1c illustrates the Participants List screen which appears when one chooses that option from the Company Reports menu. The report information here includes the list of companies selected, arranged in tabular format by the elements listed above on the right side of the screen, and ranked by normalized turnover (sales) in thousands of GBP currency.

FIGURE 1d

Company Reports	Company

Participants List (GBP) This report contains a profile of each company,
Participants List (USD) including:
Company Summary
<u>Company Profile</u>
Reported Financials
Comparative Financials   – Basic Identification
Subsidiaries & Related   – Activities
Capital Structure   – Additional Co. Identification
Share Performance   – U.K. SIC Codes
Management Discussion   – Key Financials in 3 Currencies
Recent Announcements   • Local
Full Report (GBP)   • GBP
Full Report (USD)   • USD
Full Report (Local Currency)
PS – Company Reports
Custom Profile
Custom Report
Announcement Search
Mailing List

Select report: Item 4 of 19
Press F9 or ENTER to select
F1-Help   Esc – Company List   Int'l Public Cos – 1 December 1992

Figure 1d illustrates the Company Profile screen which appears when one chooses that option from the Company Reports menu. The report information here includes a profile of each company selected, consisting of name, address, telephone number, etc. (basic information); company line of business (activities); additional company identification such as SEDOL or Valoren numbers, primary and secondary U.K. SIC (Standard Industrial Classification) codes identifying the company's product or service, and key financial data in three currencies.

FIGURE 2a

Main Menu

Company   After choosing a SIC code, you may choose
SIC Code   from the following report options.
SIC Description
News & Announcements   • Participants List (sorted in GBP)
Screening   • Participants List (sorted in USD)
Database Glossary   • Company Summary
Quit   • Announcement Search
                        • Custom Report
                        • Mailing List
                        • Portfolio

Select item: Item 2 of 7
Press F9 or ENTER to select
F1-Help   Int'l Public Cos – 1 December 1992

Figure 2a illustrates the report options available once the user chooses
a SIC code. As previously stated, the left-screen menu choice is explained
in the right-screen box: this repeats throughout the database. Each subsequent menu choice following *Company* has fewer, but relevant, report
options. Notice that only seven of the 16 report options offered at the
Company menu are available here. In addition, no subsequent fields may
be incorporated into these searches as is possible in the Screening menu.

FIGURE 2b

SIC Code List	SIC Code

3521 – Motor Vehicle Bodies
3522 – Trailers & Semi-Trail
3523 – Caravans
3530 – Motor Vehicle Parts
3610 – Shipbuilding & Repair
3620 – Railway & Tramway Vehi
3633 – Motor Cycles & Parts
3634 – Pedal Cycles & Parts
3640 – Aerospace Equip Mfg &
3650 – Other Vehicles
3710 – Measuring, Checking &
3720 – Medical & Surg Equip
3731 – Spectacles & Unmounte
3732 – Optical Precision Ins
3733 – Photographic & Cinema
3740 – Clocks, Watches, & Oth
4115 – Margarine & Compound
4116 – Processing Organic Oi
4121 – Slaughterhouses

3740 – Clocks, Watches & Other
Timing Devices

Number of Companies: 24

This SIC includes establishments
engaged in manufacture of clocks
and watches of all types (including
instrument panel clocks for aircraft
and motor vehicles), timing devices
and time switches (including parking
meters and time clocks). Also
includes manufacture of movements
and cases.

Select SIC code: Item 136 of 335
Press ENTER to make first selection
F1-Help   Esc – Main Menu   Int'l Public Cos – 1 December 1992

Figure 2b illustrates the SIC Code List. In this case, U.K. SIC Code 3740 is selected, including 24 companies which are engaged in the manufacture of clocks and watches of all types, etc. Note that 335 total U.K. SIC codes are available to be searched from this menu choice.

FIGURE 2c

SIC Reports   SIC Code

Participants List (GBP)   This report is a custom row by column report
Participants List (USD)   with company names by report items selected.
Company Summary   All financial figures are in 3 currencies. Local,
Announcement Search   GBP, and USD. Thecategories of items which
Custom Report   can be selected include:
Mailing List
Portfolio

　　　　　　　　　　　　　　• General Information
　　　　　　　　　　　　　　• Profit & Loss Items
　　　　　　　　　　　　　　• Balance Sheet
　　　　　　　　　　　　　　• Industry-Specific Financial Items
　　　　　　　　　　　　　　• Other Financial Items
　　　　　　　　　　　　　　• Annual Growth Rates
　　　　　　　　　　　　　　• Financial Ratios
　　　　　　　　　　　　　　• Share-Related Items

Select report: Item 5 of 7
Press F9 or ENTER to select
F1-Help   Esc–SIC Code List   Int'l Public Cos – 1 December 1992

Figure 2c illustrates the SIC Reports options. The user may choose one of seven options. In this case, *Custom Report* is highlighted, and the right screen explains that this report is tabular in style, and allows the user to choose from among the listed items above. Some or all of the items may be incorporated into the report which is then assembled in the "workspace," and may be printed or transferred after it appears on the screen.

FIGURE 3a

Main Menu

Company
SIC Code
SIC Description
News & Announcements
Screening
Database Glossary
Quit

Allows you to retrieve information updated
since the most recent Extel Annual Cards for
companies in the database. You may choose
from the following update categories:

● Capital Restructuring
● Management Statements
● Financials

Select item: Item 4 of 7
Press F9 or ENTER to select
F1-Help   Int'l Public Cos – 1 December 1992

Figure 3a illustrates the update categories available to the user from the News & Announcements menu. The information included here reflects only the most recent updates from the Extel Annual Cards.

FIGURE 3b

Topic List	News & Announcements
CAPITAL RESTRUCTURING	CAPITAL RESTRUCTURING
Bid Situation	
Fund Raising	in the database. You may choose from
Liquidation Statement	the following update categories:
Loan Capital	
Share Capital	● Capital Restructuring
Trading Facility	● Management Statements
MANAGEMENT STATEMENTS	● Financials
Activities	
Annual General Meeting	
Approach	
Awards (News)	
Company Particulars	
Contract	
Discussions	
Group Organisation	
Litigations	
Name Change	
Negotiations	

Select topic:	Item 1 of 31
Press ENTER to make the first selection	
F1-Help Esc – Main Menu	Int'l Public Cos – 1 December 1992

Figure 3b illustrates the topic list choices available to the user from the News & Announcements menu. *Capital Restructuring* is highlighted here, and the user will note that the broad update categories are further broken down into specific elements of capital restructuring, management statements, and financial data, such as *fund raising*. Multiple elements may be selected from this menu.

FIGURE 3c

Topic List	News & Announcements

CAPITAL RESTRUCTURING   Topic: Activities
Bid Situation
Fund Raising   Total Number of Announcements: 2450
Liquidation Statement
Loan Capital
Share Capital   Number of Announcements in last
Trading Facility   month: 120
MANAGEMENT STATEMENTS   Number of announcements in last 3
Activities   months: 393
Annual General Meeting   Number of Announcements in last 6
Approach   months: 828
Awards (News)
Company Particulars
Contract
Discussions
Group Organisation
Litigations
Name Change
Negotiations

Select topic: Item 9 of 31
Press ENTER to make the first selection
F1-Help   Esc – Main Menu   Int'l Public Cos – 1 December 1992

Figure 3c illustrates the specific topic from *Management Statements* from the News & Announcements menu. *Activities* is highlighted here, and the user will note that the total number of announcements in the entire database is given, and then broken down chronologically for ease of use. Multiple elements may be selected from this menu.

SEARCHING INTERNATIONAL
PUBLIC COMPANIES BY SCREENING

A Screening search involves combining multiple fields to retrieve very specific results. For example, searching for companies in Germany that manufacture motor vehicles and parts, with a turnover of at least $10,000,000 retrieves only seven companies. Screening searches may combine any number of available fields; each field choice *reduces* the total number of companies retrievable by using the Boolean "and" operator; the "or" operator *increases* the possible number of companies to be retrieved. Particularly useful are the financial data fields, which may be searched in a comparative manner. All search results may be formatted into reports of the searcher's choosing, either into ranked columns or by text paragraphs, including participants' listings, company summaries, customized reports, mailing lists, or by specific items chosen into a "portfolio." See Figures 4a, 4b, and 4c.

INTERNATIONAL PUBLIC COMPANIES:
DATABASE GLOSSARY

The Database Glossary is an especially useful feature, providing definitions and explanations of the terms used in the database, such as TOPIC codes; Valoren, Registration, SEDOL and Extel Reference numbers; as well as explain SIC codes and descriptions. "Print Lists" allows one to retrieve a report containing a complete list of the items offered in the glossary, and save, print, or transfer the report to other software programs. This is particularly helpful for users unfamiliar with international coding schemes. See Figures 5a and 5b.

INTERNATIONAL PUBLIC COMPANIES

CD/Corporate: International Public Companies is limited, if at all, only by the number of publicly-held international companies; certainly this is not a failing on the part of Lotus Development

FIGURE 4a

Main Menu

Company   Allows you to search for companies that meet
SIC Code   your choice of criteria. You may select as
SIC Description   many items as you want from the following
News & Announcements   categories:
Screening
Database Glossary   ● General Information
Quit   ● Profit & Loss Items
                            ● Balance Sheet
                            ● Industry-Specific Financials
                            ● Other Financial Items
                            ● Annual Growth Rates
                            ● Financial Ratios
                            ● Share-Related Items

Select item: Item 5 of 7
Press F9 or ENTER to select
F1-Help   Int'l Public Cos – 1 December 1992

Figure 4a illustrates the Screening main menu. The user will note that the broad categories will further expand, as did the topic list choices in News & Announcements, into specific elements of profit & loss, balance sheets, annual growth rates, financial ratios, etc. The *Screening* "workspace," however, differs from the other left- and right-screen boxes because of the multiple variable choice.

Screening Menu						Screening

GENERAL INFORMATION

So far you have selected 4 items:

Activity
Activity Vocabulary
Primary SIC Desc
Secondary SIC Desc
Country
Address
Address Vocabulary
Number of Employees

Motor Cycles & Parts – 3533
Motor Vehicle Bodies – 3521
Motor Vehicle Parts – 3530
Motor Vehicles & Their Engines – 3510

Select item: Line 2 of 5

SET	VARIABLE	AT LEAST	AT MOST	N/A	NOT	PASSED
A	Country	Germany		no	no	310
A	Primary SIC Desc 4 Selections			no	no	18
A	Turnover (USD'000)	10,000,000		no	no	7
					Total:	7

Screen: A

or

Type text or press SPACE to edit current criterion or press F9 to continue
F1-Help   Esc – Main Menu   Int'l Public Cos – 1 December 1992

Figure 4b illustrates the Screening menu above. The Screening "workspace," however, differs from the standard left- and right- screen boxes because of the multiple variable choice. In this case, *Primary SIC Desc* is highlighted, with four selections listed from the alphabetic SIC menu. Previously, *Country* (Germany) and a *turnover* (sales) figure of at least $10,000,000 were also selected. The initial choice of the 310 German companies in the entire database is reduced to 18 when the SIC description is applied, and further reduced, to seven, when a specific sales figure is stipulated. This is the feature of the Lotus One Source family of products which is the most valuable and attractive to users.

FIGURE 4c

Report Items	Custom Report

GENERAL INFORMATION
Activity
Primary SIC Desc
Secondary SIC Desc
Country
Local Currency ✳
Address
Number of Employees
Year Established
Regist & Comp History
Additional Company ID
Subsidiaries
Directors
Shareholders
Management Discussion
Extel Reference Number
Registration Number
Registration Date
Calendar Year

In addition to this category, there are seven other major categories:

● General Information
● Profit & Loss Items
● Balance Sheet
● Industry-Specific Financials
● Other Financial Items
● Annual Growth Rates
● Financial Ratios
● Share-Related Items

Press "+" key to move to the next category
Press "–" key to move to the previous category

Select item: Item 1 of 199
Press ENTER to make the first selection
F1-Help   Esc – Screening Reports   Int'l Public Cos – 1 December 1992

Figure 4c illustrates the *Custom Report* option from the Screening menu. Other reports available include the *Participants' List* (see Figure 4d), the *Company Summary*, etc., just as the *Company Report* options are listed. In this case, the eight *Custom Report* broad categories expand significantly to encompass many possible report elements, all chosen at the users' discretion.

FIGURE 4d. Participants List (Sorted in USD)

SCREENING SUMMARY

Type of Criteria	Criteria	Companies Passing Screen
SET A:		
Country	Companies in: Germany	310
Primary SIC Desc	Companies in: Motor Cycles & Parts – 3633, Motor Vehicle Bodies – 3521, Motor Vehicle Parts – 3530, Motor Vehicles & Their Engines – 3510	18
Turnover (USD'000) (USD'000)	At least 10,000,000	7
	Total Companies passing screen:	7

Sorted by: Turnover (USD'000)

Rank	Company Name	Country
1	Daimler-Benz Ag	Germany
2	Volkswagen Ag	Germany
3	Robert Bosch GmBh	Germany
4	Bayerische Motoren Werke Ag	Germany
5	Adam Opel Ag	Germany
6	Ford-Werke Ag	Germany
7	MAN Ag	Germany

Fiscal Year End	Turnover (USD'000)	Pre-tax Profit (USD'000)	Turnover (Local'000)	Pre-tax Profit (Local'000)	Turnover (GBP'000)
12/31/91	62,569,000	1,963,000	95,010,000	2,981,000	33,513,000
12/31/91	50,257,000	1,176,000	76,315,000	1,785,000	26,919,000
12/31/91	22,127,651	1,119,079	33,600,400	1,699,300	11,851,990
12/31/91	19,651,000	1,030,000	29,839,000	1,564,000	10,525,000
12/31/91	17,879,000	1,123,000	27,149,000	1,706,000	9,576,000
12/31/91	14,725,118	−135,069	22,359,800	−205,100	7,887,053
6/30/91	10,489,000	413,000	19,031,000	749,000	6,479,000

Pre-tax Profit (GBP'000)

1,051,000
630,000
599,400
552,000
602,000
−72,346
255,000

Figure 4d illustrates a Screening Summary by Participants' List of the companies retrieved in the Screening search performed in Figure 4b. A condensed print option on the printer attached to the CD/Corporate workstation will avoid any tabular printing problems.

FIGURE 5a

Main Menu

Company	Allows you to look up or print information
SIC Code	about items used in the database. You may
SIC Description	choose from the following options:

Company
SIC Code
SIC Description
News & Announcements
Screening
<u>Database Glossary</u>
Quit

Allows you to look up or print information about items used in the database. You may choose from the following options:

- Screening/Report Items
- TOPIC Codes
- Valoren Numbers
- Registration Numbers
- SEDOL Numbers
- Extel Reference Numbers
- Print Lists

Select item: Item 6 of 7
Press F9 or ENTER to select
F1-Help   Int'l Public Cos – 1 December 1992

Figure 5a illustrates the Database Glossary main menu screen. Users may look up or print a concise explanation of the items attached to the broad categories listed.

Corp. There are approximately 9,000 companies listed in the database as of December 1992; CD/Corporate: U.S. Public Companies lists just over 12,000 publicly-held U.S. companies by comparison. Also, while some countries may appear in the country list available through the screening menu, in some cases no companies are listed for that country. For example, Mexico lists no publicly held companies at this time. International privately held companies are similar to their U.S. counterparts in that information on either is more difficult

FIGURE 5b

Database Glossary	Database Glossary

Screening/Report Items
TOPIC Codes
Valoren Numbers
Registration Numbers
SEDOL Number
Extel Reference Numbers
SIC Codes
SIC Descriptions
Print Lists

Provides a menu of TOPIC codes, displaying each code's associated company:

TOPIC is the company's TOPIC code
identifier. This is the company code used
by subscribers to the London Stock
Exchange's TOPIC information service. It
stands for Teletext Output of Price
Information Computer.

Select item: Item 2 of 9
Press F9 or ENTER to select
F1-Help   Int'l Public Cos – 1 December 1992

Figure 5b illustrates the Database Glossary screen, featuring TOPIC codes, one of seven glossary choices. The Glossary and the explanations are generally straightforward, and can be extremely beneficial to users.

to obtain, as it is not readily available through governmental channels. CD/Corporate: U.S. Private + and U.K. Private + are welcome resources in this regard.

The real strength of International Public Companies lies in the depth of financial information available, in the ease of use of the compact disc system, and in the presentation format that is readily understood and arranged to the searcher's needs. In particular, the ability to work either from British Pounds Sterling, U.S. Dollars, and/or local currencies makes International Public Companies very valuable. As a student resource, it is nearly a "one-stop shopper's" paradise.

INTERNATIONAL PUBLIC COMPANIES: TECHNICAL REQUIREMENTS

One Source requires the following hardware: one compact disc drive per product, 1 MB of RAM; a hard drive; and a 386-level or higher, at least 25 Mh IBM-compatible computer, for the best results. Any One Source product may be networked as well, providing for simultaneous multiple users. If a modem is present in the computer system, users may go on-line directly to update the information contained on the compact disc.

END OF CHAPTER QUESTIONS

1. What report lists the companies which have been selected and ranks them by normalized turnover?
2. What is a company's TOPIC code, and where in the One Source CD Corporate: International Public Companies is it explained?
3. Where is the most recent information concerning capital restructuring, management statements, and/or financial updates to be found?
4. Companies may be selected by name, by SIC code, or by SIC description. What method is used to combine variables and search for companies that meet your choice of criteria?
5. What are the different broad categories under which you can search to create custom profiles or custom reports?

NOTE

1. Literature from Lotus Development Corp. in addition to use of the *CD/ Corporate: International Public Companies* compact disc database in actual practice contributed to the writing of this chapter. Screen facsimiles from *International Public Companies* are printed with permission of Lotus Development Corp.

Chapter 9

Electronic On-Line Data Retrieval in International Business

Fred Miller
Linda Gillespie Miller

INTRODUCTION

As the research topic for your international business course the question is posed, "Should Pepsico attempt to build on the success of its clear cola product in the United States by introducing the brand in Japan?" To answer this question, you must gather reliable, timely information on the firm, its financial position, competitive strengths and strategies. You must also gather the most recent available data on the beverage market in Japan, including major competitors, their brands, market positions, marketing strategies, and competitive practices. Immediately you foresee visions of countless hours of searching in your library's print indices, sorting through current editions in the periodical stacks, and ordering numerous articles from Interlibrary Loan to be delivered the day before your paper is due. Surely there must be a better way!

Fortunately, in fact, there is; electronic data retrieval in the form of CD-ROM databases or on-line electronic data retrieval. Several chapters in this volume describe some CD-ROM databases and how to use them. This chapter discusses on-line electronic data retrieval and how you can use it to help you gather information for this and other assignments.

WHAT IS ON-LINE ELECTRONIC DATA RETRIEVAL?

On-line electronic data retrieval involves accessing, searching, and extracting data from databases which are stored electronically in central locations. The key component in this system is the information service, which either compiles databases of its own, or collects databases from other information vendors. In the latter case, the vendors are responsible for maintaining and updating the databases they provide. Users who subscribe to the information service use dedicated terminals, or more commonly, personal computers, to access the databases they require. This system is illustrated in Figure 1.

In an era in which most information is produced in electronic form before it is converted to print, the range of electronic information providers has expanded greatly. Several newspapers and academic journals, for example, offer their publications electronically as well as physically. Market research services, financial information providers and securities firms all use electronic information services to expand the reach of their services. In addition, several information vendors offer databases exclusively in electronic form, creating research possibilities for which there are no print equivalents.

WHY ON-LINE ELECTRONIC DATA RETRIEVAL?

On-line electronic data retrieval offers several advantages over manual research methods and CD-ROM products alike. Compared to manual research, both CD-ROM and on-line techniques offer advantages of efficiency, comprehensiveness, and timeliness. The efficiency benefit is a function of the ability to search several years accumulation of data at one time, with a single search strategy. These research methods are more comprehensive in that electronic databases are usually broader in coverage than corresponding print versions. Indeed, some electronic databases have no print equivalents at all. These measures produce more timely results, as they are updated more frequently, and the updated information disseminated more rapidly, than similar print databases.

On-line electronic data retrieval also has some advantages relative to CD-ROM methods. First, the number of databases available is quite large. The service used in the example below, DIALOG, offers access to over 250 databases. Even if all were available on CD-ROM, which is not the case, a collection of this size would be prohibitively expensive for most organizations. Second, access to

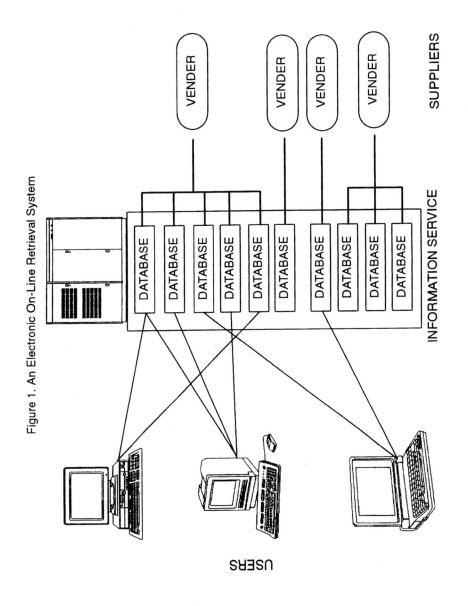

Figure 1. An Electronic On-Line Retrieval System

on-line databases does not depend on physical access to a CD, allowing more people in an organization to use the services simultaneously. Third, some services, including DIALOG, allow users to search several databases simultaneously with a single search strategy. This is not possible in a CD-ROM format. Finally, the updating of on-line databases is done systematically, with no additional cost or effort required of the user. For example, to update CD-ROM databases, users must replace old CD's with new ones on a continuous basis. The timeliness of data available from the database is dependent upon the interval of that replacement process. On the other hand, providers of on-line databases typically update them on a regular basis ranging from daily to annually. As soon as these updates are made, the new data is available to all system users immediately. While the actual advantage here depends upon the updating procedures of the database provider, new information is generally available more rapidly and at less cost through an on-line system rather than a CD-ROM system.

On the other hand, there are some disadvantages to on-line data retrieval. First, costs are directly dependent upon utilization. Thus extensive or inefficient searching in a database can produce excessive costs quite rapidly. This also creates learning costs for the novice researcher or the researcher who is exploring a new database. In a CD-ROM system, the cost of acquiring the database is fixed, so researchers can learn the system thoroughly without incurring additional costs as a result. On-line retrieval systems entail security problems. With CD-ROM systems, the CD itself must be protected. In on-line systems, anyone with access to the account number and password can use the system at will, incurring sizable unauthorized costs. Finally, access to large numbers of databases does not mean that the researcher can easily search all of them effectively. The data structures and coding systems of these databases vary considerably. This requires the collection of documentation and instruction manuals for the databases used most extensively.

In sum, on-line electronic data retrieval is best used as a complement to CD-ROM systems. It can be used to search databases not held by the organization in CD-ROM format, or to update searches performed in CD-ROM systems. It can also serve as a means of evaluating a database considered for CD-ROM acquisition, or as the sole method of searching seldom used databases. It is clearly the quickest way to gather the most up-to-date information on a selected topic, industry, or firm.

SYSTEM REQUIREMENTS

On-line electronic data retrieval requires relatively little investment in personal computer hardware and software. Virtually any PC equipped with an internal or external modem will meet the hardware requirements. While a 2400 baud rate is the current standard for most on-line services, higher speed modems which also offer send and receive fax capability are also available at little additional expense. Many on-line services offer their own software packages for telecommunications. However, any general communications package which offers data capture capability (the ability to store data in memory for subsequent transfer to a printer or disk file) is acceptable. As data files may be stored to disk and printed at a central facility, no printer is required in this basic system.

In addition to this basic system, users must also establish subscriptions with on-line information services and acquire the documentation for those services. This is necessary for access to the remote system as well as cost assessment and assignment within the organization. In addition, for effective searching, users should acquire documentation for the specific databases they plan to use. This documentation is available directly from the firm which maintains and updates those databases rather than the central information service. That is, documentation for the extensive Predicasts series of databases on the DIALOG service is purchased from Predicasts, not DIALOG.

DIALOG'S "CLASSROOM INSTRUCTION PROGRAM"

The remainder of this chapter will focus on applications using databases within the collection provided by DIALOG Information Systems Inc., of Palo Alto, California. While this firm has several competitors in the information services market, its databases selection is sufficiently broad and its educational rates sufficiently affordable to render it a most cost effective service for international business applications. Through the firm's "Classroom Instructional Program," students may use most of the firm's hundreds of electronic databases at a flat rate of $15 per hour. Moreover, the menu systems used in the search process allow novice users to attain worthwhile results very quickly. This is especially true of the "DIALOG Business Connection," a menu system for searching in several business related databases simultaneously. In addition, more experienced searchers can focus on very precise information in specific databases using the command structure of the DIALOG system. Both menu-driven and command search techniques are illustrated below.

DIALOG DATABASES IN INTERNATIONAL BUSINESS RESEARCH PROJECTS

This section describes ways in which databases from the DIALOG information system may be used in international business courses and assignments. While not comprehensive, Figure 2 lists the DIALOG databases which are most relevant for research in international business courses. Many of the databases in Figure 2 are included in the DIALOG Business Connection system, rendering them easily available to inexperienced searchers.

There are four general types of international business research projects in which electronic data retrieval can be useful. They are: (1) market assessment; (2) financial analysis of companies; (3) identifying potential opportunities, support services, customers, partners and/or competitors; and (4) competitive analysis. In the market assessment research, students evaluate foreign countries as markets in general or for specific products. Any of the databases offering business, economic, social, political, or general news are useful for this purpose. However, *PTS PROMT* and *INFOMAT World Business* are particularly valuable here. These are very extensive databases which index and summarize articles from business, trade, and professional journals from around the world. Many of these journals are very difficult to find and are not indexed anywhere else. Moreover, article summaries are written in English,

FIGURE 2: Selected DIALOG Databases with International Business Information

Database (DIALOG Number)	Geographic Focus	Type of Information
ABI Inform (15)	International	Academic literature in business
AGRIS International (203)	International	Agricultural literature
Arab Information Bank (465)	Arab world	Economic, political, social trends
Asia Pacific (30)	Asia/Pacific rim	Business and economic news
Business International (627)	International	Economic, political, social, & business trends
Canadian Business and Current Affairs (262)	Canada	Business and general news
CANCORP Canadian Corporations (491)	Canada	Corporate directory
Corporate Affiliations (513)	International	Corporate parent/subsidiary relationships
D&B Canadian Dun's Market Identifiers (520)	Canada	Corporate directory, some financial information
D&B European Dun's Market Identifiers (521)	Europe	Corporate directory
D&B International Dun's Market Identifiers (518)	International	Corporate directory
Delphes European Business (481)	Europe	Business and economic news (French language)
DIALOG Company Name Finder (416)	International	Identifies databases with information on a selected company
European Directory of Agrochemicals (316)	Europe	Directory of agrochemical products
Extel International Financial Cards (500)	International	Financial information on companies
Extel International News Cards (501)	International	Company news
Facts on File (265)	International	Short news items
Financial Times (622)	International	Business and financial news
Harvard Business Review (122)	International	Full text of HBR articles
Hoppenstedt Directory of German Companies (529)	Germany	Corporate directory
ICC International Business Research (563)	International	Financial analysts' reports

FIGURE 2: (continued)

Database (DIALOG Number)   Geographic Focus   Type of Information

IDD M&A Transactions (550)	International	Merger and acquisition activity
Industry Data Surveys (189)	International	Information directory
INFOMAT International Business (583)	International	Industry and product news
INVESTEXT (545)	International	Company and industry financial analyses
Japan Economic Newswire (612)	Japan	Business, economic and general news
Japan Technology (582)	Japan	Research, technology and business news
Journal of Commerce (637)	International	Trade and transportation information
Knight-Ridder Financial News (609)	International	Financial and business news
KOMPASS Europe (590)	Europe	Corporate directory
KOMPASS UK (591)	United Kingdom	Corporate directory
Management Contents (75)	International	Academic business literature
Moody's Corporate New–International (43)	International	Business and financial news
PAIS International (43)	International	Public policy related topics
PAPERS	International	Full text of several U.S. newspapers
Piers Exports (571,572)	United States	U.S. export shipping records
Piers Exports (573,574)	United States	U.S. import shipping records
PTS International Forecasts (83)	International	Economic and industry forecasts
PTS Marketing & Advertising Reference Service (570)	International	Marketing and advertising information
PTS New Product Announcements (621)	International	New product information
PTS Newsletter Database (636)	International	Economic, social & political trends
PTS PROMT (16)	International	Industry and company information from trade and business journals
Teikoku Databank: Japanese Companies (502)	Japan	Corporate directory, financial information
Trade Names Database (116)	International	Directory of 280,000 brand names & owners

though many of the original articles are in other languages. Specialized event and product codes allow searchers to seek general information or target articles on a specific product and/or business function.

Financial analysis assignments require the collection of financial data as well as financial news and analysts' opinions about a company. Many of the corporate directory databases contain limited financial information about the companies they describe. Extel International Financial Cards contains more extensive information. Several databases, including Financial Times, Knight-Ridder Financial News, and Moody's Corporate News–International contain financial news about companies. Two databases, INVESTEXT and ICC International Business Research contain financial analysts' evaluation of specific companies.

The corporate directory databases are the best sources of information about companies who are potential customers, partners, and/or competitors. Students may extract lists of companies by industry, including any selective criteria on size, number of employees, and/or geographic presence they deem advisable. Resources include worldwide directories such as D&B International Dun's Market Identifiers, and country-specific databases such as the Hoppenstedt Directory of German Companies or the Teikoku Databank: Japanese Companies.

Competitive analysis research projects require students to identify the major competitors and competitive practices within a global, regional, or country-specific industry. In addition, the strategies, plans, strengths, and weaknesses of major competitors must also be assessed. All of the databases described thus far may be used in this process. There are others which are also of value in competitive analysis. For example, Industry Data Surveys identifies the sources of information available for a particular industry, while PTS Marketing and Advertising Reference Service indexes articles on marketing and promotional activities of firms in various industries. By identifying all the DIALOG databases that contain information on a particular company, the DIALOG Company Name Finder can help locate comprehensive information on a selected competitor.

These examples describe the application of electronic data retrieval techniques to the basic types of research projects in international business education. These techniques may also be used in support of other class activities. Students may use database searches to update or expand the information used in case analysis assignments. These resources may also be used to gather practical examples of course concepts, identify articles for class discussion, or provide background information on firms being studied. Of course, the academic literature databases, ABI Inform and Management Contents, are invaluable for the traditional research paper assignment.

In short, the databases listed in Figure 2 may be used to support a wide range of learning activities in international business courses with wide access and very reasonable cost.

SAMPLE SEARCH USING
THE "DIALOG BUSINESS CONNECTION"

The following pages are printed versions of the screens encountered in the process of searching in the "DIALOG Business Connection" system. This system is completely menu-driven. At each stage, users are presented with a list of choices from which they indicate their preference by the appropriate response. In this sample session, the strings of asterisks indicate breaks between different screens within the system. Text in regular print represents the content of the screens. Bold text represents user selections from the menu options. Explanatory notes are in italic text.

This search addresses the problem posed in the opening paragraph in this chapter. It uses the "DIALOG Business Connection" system to extract financial and competitive information about Pepsico, as well as the reports of financial analysts on the firm. Note that the system extracts information from several different databases, though the searcher requires no knowledge of the content or information structure of any of them. This makes this system a most powerful tool for novice searchers.

Notice that the system guides the searcher through the process of focusing the search on the exact information required. Each additional screen allows the searcher to define the desired information more precisely. In addition, the system allows easy flow from one type of information to another. In this sample, the transition from the composite package of information on the firm to the reports of financial analysts is accomplished by two simple menus.

While this sample illustrates the search process, it does not contain the data retrieved by that process. In actual searches, several pages of data would be sent to the screen at the points indicated in the search. Searchers should save this data to diskette using the log or data capture feature in the telecommunications software being used. These files may then be edited with a word processor or printed with the DOS print command.

This is the opening menu of the DIALOG Business Connection. The sign-on procedure used to reach this menu depends upon your communications software and user profile on the DIALOG system.

****

DIALOG Business Connection
Main Menu

1 Worldwide Corporate Intelligence (Select Specific Company)

2 U.S. Financial Screening (Select Financial Variables)

3 Products and Markets (Select Industry or Product)

4 Worldwide Sales Prospecting (Select Companies by Geography, Size and SIC Code)

5 Travel Planning (OAG Electronic Edition)

6 Dialog Business News Flash (View The Latest Business News)

* Dialog Alert Service (Weekly Clipping Service)

Enter option number, or /H for help:

?1 *Indicates the portion of the DIALOG Business Connection you wish to use.*

****

Worldwide Corporate Intelligence
Company Selection

The following options can be used to select a company:

Company Name

Ticker Symbol

Enter a Company NAME, press ENTER to go to Company/
Ticker Symbol Finder or /H for help:

?PEP *The ticker symbol for Pepsico, typing the firm name would also work.*

****

Worldwide Corporate Intelligence

Continuation Options

There are 3 companies that match on PEP.

1 View Matching Company Names

2 Restrict by State of Company Location (US only)

3 Restrict by City of Company Location (US only)

4 Restrict to Headquarters (US only)

5 Consult Company Finder

6 Start with New Company

Enter option number, or /H for help:

?1 *To view the company names which match the search criteria.*

****

Worldwide Corporate Intelligence

List of Companies (3 companies, in alphabetic order)

Location data may include city, state or country.

Company/Location

----

1 P E P INC / FORT WAYNE / IN / SINGLE

2 PEPSICO INC / PURCHASE / NY / HEADQUARTERS

3 POSITIVE ENERGY PRODUCTS INC / RICHMOND / BRIT-
ISH COLUMBIA /

Enter option number(s), HALT, or /H for help:

?2 Indicates the firm on which you wish to receive information.

****

Worldwide Corporate Intelligence
Application Menu
Company: PEPSICO INC

1 Composite Financial Report

2 Composite Overview Report

3 Background and Location

4 Company News

5 Financial Reports

6 Analysts' Reports

7 Stocks, Ownership and M&A Activity

8 Products and Lines of Business

Enter option number, /H for help, or press ENTER to Go to Company Finder:

?1 Indicates the type of information you wish to receive.

****

Information includes data from the following sources:

Standard & Poor's Corporation

Disclosure Incorporated

Moody's Investors Service, Inc.

Media General Financial Services

The price for this Composite Report is $27.80

Do you want to receive this report? YES/NO

?Y

****

Several pages of information and financial reports follow.

****

Press ENTER to proceed

? Hit the 'Enter' Key

****

Worldwide Corporate Intelligence–Composite Report

Supplementary Data

Company: PEPSICO INC

Ticker: PEP

1 Composite Overview Report

2 News

3 Analysts' Reports

4 Financial: Management Discussion (when available)

5 Financial: SEC Filings and Dates

6 Stocks: M&A and Divestiture Activity

7 Stocks: Daily Price History

* Stocks: Institutional Owners

* Stocks: 5% Owners

10 Products: New Product Announcements

* Products: Detailed Lines of Business

12 Products: List of Manufactured Products

13 Background: Corporate Structure

* Background: Name and Address for All Locations

15 Price and Source

Enter option number, HALT, or /H for help:

?3 *This selection searches for published reports of financial analysts on the firm.*

****

Worldwide Corporate Intelligence

Analysts' Reports Available (350 company reports, most recent first)

350 reports on the company are available. The titles are listed below in reverse chronological order, along with the length and source of the report. The figure 921105 after the title of the first report is the date of issue, November 5, 1992.

Company: PEPSICO INC

Ticker: PEP

Report Title / Date / Investment Banking Firm / Number of Pages

----

1 PepsiCo, Inc.–Company Report / 921105

MARKET GUIDE INC. / 5 Pages

2 PepsiCo–Company Report / 921104

SHEARSON LEHMAN BROTHERS, INC. / 10 Pages

3 PepsiCo Inc.–Company Report / 921029

DEAN WITTER REYNOLDS / 2 Pages

4 PepsiCo–Company Report / 921027

BROWN BROTHERS HARRIMAN & CO. / 18 Pages

5 PepsiCo, Inc.–Company Report / 921020

PAINEWEBBER INC. / 8 Pages

Enter option number, HALT, /H for help, or press ENTER for next screen:

?2 *Indicates the number of the report to view.*

****

Worldwide Corporate Intelligence–Analysts' Reports

Display Options–Company Reports
Company: PEPSICO INC
Ticker: PEP

1 Table of Contents

2 Total Report (10 Pages)

3 Price and Source

Enter option number, HALT, or /H for Help:

?1 *To view the Table of Contents*

****

Table of Contents selection 1 of 1

03053004

PepsiCo–Company Report

SHEARSON LEHMAN BROTHERS, INC.

Coury, J., et al

NEW YORK (STATE OF)

DATE: November 4, 92

INVESTEXT(tm) REPORT NUMBER: 1273613, PAGE 0 OF 10, CONTENTS PAGE

This is a(n) COMPANY report.

SECTION/TABLE HEADINGS: Pages

------------------------------   -------

Stock Price, Earnings Data And Rating 1991-93   1

Summary And Recommendation   1-3

Enter option number, HALT, or /H for Help:

?2,3,4,7,8,9 *Indicate the page numbers you wish to see.*

****

The selected pages are sent to the screen.

****

SAMPLE SEARCH OF A DIALOG DATABASE AT THE COMMAND LEVEL

While the "DIALOG Business Connection" system is effective and easy to use, it can be difficult to gather very specific information using this system. For this purpose, it is often more efficient to search a single database using the DIALOG command system rather than a menu-driven system. The second part of our sample project, the collection of competitive information about the soft drink market in Japan, exemplifies this situation. The need here is for precise information about a relatively narrow market. The PTS PROMT database on the DIALOG system is a rich source of such information. This database indexes over 1,500 trade periodicals and journals from around the world, with article summaries in English no matter the language of the original article. This database, number 16 on the DIALOG system, is the target of the search strategy which follows.

Though more focused in its results, command level searching requires more knowledge and skill of the user than do the DIALOG menu-driven systems. It also requires more reference material on the database being searched. Specifically, the user requires; (1) the DIALOG "Bluesheet" on the database, (2) reference manuals on the database being searched, and (3) knowledge of the basic search commands. Excerpts from the bluesheet for the PTS PROMT database are contained in Figure 3. Bluesheets for DIALOG databases are available on-line in a database aptly entitled DIALOG BLUESHEETS or by mail from the firm. Reference manuals must be ordered from the information vendor. Figure 5 contains an excerpt of the PTS User's Manual, which covers all the Predicasts databases provided through DIALOG and other information services. Finally, the search commands described below are extracted from the Pocket Guide to DIALOG, a short reference manual provided by DIALOG Information Services.

The PTS PROMT bluesheet excerpts in Figure 3 describe the content, sources, and vendor of the database, as well as information about its indexing structure. The latter information is used in constructing search commands for the database. Each of the two letter codes described in the bluesheet refers to a particular field in the database. Search commands look for records with specified values in those fields and extracts those which meet the search condition. Thus, they are vital in extracting relevant records from over 3,000,000 contained in the database. Some of the fields can be searched without access to the reference manual. For example, CN=CHILE and PY=1991 search for

FIGURE 3. PTS PROMT BLUESHEET

PTS PROMT – File 16

FILE DESCRIPTION: Predicasts Overview of Markets and Technology (PROMT) is a multiple-industry database that provides broad, international coverage of companies, products, markets, and applied technologies for all industries. PTS PROMT is comprised of abstracts and full-text records from the world's important trade and business journals, local newspapers, regional business publications, national and international business newspapers, industry newsletters, research studies, investment analysts' reports, corporate news releases, and corporate annual reports. PTS PROMT abstracts and full-text records cover the international events and activities of public and private companies throughout the world.

SUBJECT COVERAGE: PTS PROMT is used for in-depth research on companies, products, and markets. Information found in PROMT includes: – Capital Expenditures – Financial Reporting – Industry and Business Issues – Management Procedures – Market Plans and Strategies – Market Size/Shares/Trends – Mergers and Acquisitions – New and Expanded Facilities – New Products and Technologies – Product Sales and Consumption – Research and Development – As a multiple-industry database, PTS PROMT offers comprehensive coverage of more than 60 manufacturing and services industries, including: – Advertising – Aerospace and Aircraft – Agriculture – Apparel – Automotive – Biotechnology – Chemicals – Communications – Computers – Construction – Defense Products and Systems – Electronics – Fabricated Metal Products – Financial Services – Food and Beverages – Furniture – Industrial Machinery –Instrumentation – Medical and Health Services – Mining – Petroleum and Energy Products – Pharmaceutical – Plastics – Printing and Publishing – Pulp and Paper – Rubber – Software – Textiles – Tobacco – Transportation – Wholesale and Retail Trade – Wood and others

SOURCES: PTS PROMT contains abstracts or the complete text of articles from a broad range of worldwide business publications. The scope of sources covered by PTS PROMT includes: trade and business journals, local newspapers and regional business journals, national and international business newspapers, industry newsletters, research studies, investment analysts' reports, corporate news releases, and corporate annual reports.

FIGURE 3 (continued)

DATES: 1972-present   **FILE SIZE:**   2,954,900 records, 2/92
UPDATE FREQUENCY: Daily
ORIGIN:

North America and Other Countries:	Europe:
Predicasts	Predicasts Europe
on-line Services Department	8-10 Denman Street
11001 Cedar Avenue	London W1V 7RF
Cleveland, OH 44106	United Kingdom
TELEPHONE: 800-321-6388	71-494-3817

SEARCH OPTIONS: BASIC INDEX	ADDITIONAL INDEXES
SEARCH DISPLAY FIELD	SEARCH DISPLAY FIELD
NAME/	NAME/
SUFFIX CODE	PREFIX CODE
INDEXING/EXAMPLES	INDEXING/EXAMPLES
/AB AB Abstract, Short Text ($<$ 450	
words)	CN= CN Country Name
S SALES(W)TARGET/AB	S CN=MEXICO
/DE DE Descriptor-2,3 Word &	PC= PC Product Code
Phrase	S PC=30754
S MARKET??/DE	PY= PY Publication Year
/TI TI Title	S PY=1989
S COMPETITION/TI	

OUTPUT OPTIONS:

Format 1 DIALOG Accession Number
Format 2 Title, Annotated Title,   Format 6 Title, Annotated
    Source, Language (if non-English),   Title, and Word Count
    Word Count, and Descriptors   Format 7 Title, Abstract or
Format 3 Bibliographic Citation,   Excerpt, and Source

    including Annotated Title and   Format 8 Title, Annotated Title,

    Word Count   Indexing, and Word
Format 4 Title, Source, and Abstract   Count
    or Excerpt   Format 9 Full Record
    Format 5 Full Record except Long Text

Source: *DIALOG BLUESHEETS* Database, DIALOG Information Services.

records related to Chile and records published in 1991 respectively. Other fields, such as the PC (Product Code) field require reference to the PTS User's Manual to use properly. Figure 4 contains a sample page from this manual which illustrates the product coding system. Patterned after the SIC code system, this system uses a cascaded structure in which codes with more numerals focus on increasingly narrow product categories. Thus PC=2085 would extract all records related to the broad product category "Liquor," while PC=2085316 would extract only those records related to the more narrow category "Scotch." All the records contained in the latter data set would also be

FIGURE 4. Selected PTS Product Codes

20	BEVERAGES	2086	Canned & Bottled Soft Drinks
2082	Beer and Malt Beverages	208601	Bottled Soft Drinks
20821	Canned Beer and Ale	2086011	Bottled nondiet colas
2082	Bottled Beer and Ale	2086015	Bottled nondiet root beer
20823	Beer and Ale in Bulk	208605	Canned Soft Drinks
2083	Malt and Malt By-Products	2086051	Canned nondiet colas
2084	Wine and Brandy	2086058	Canned nondiet colas
208401	Table Wines	208609	Fruit Drinks (Noncarbonated)
208402	Dessert Wines		
208403	Effervescent Wines	21	TOBACCO PRODUCTS
2085	Liquor	2111	Cigarettes
208531	Bottled Liquor	211101	Filter cigarettes
208531	Bottled Whiskey	211102	Nonfilter cigarettes
2085311	Straight Whiskey	21103	Low tar cigarettes
2085312	Blended Whiskey	2121	Cigars
2085314	Canadian Whiskey	2131	Chewing, Pipe, Snuff Tobacco
2085316	Scotch	2151	Synthetic tobacco

Source: *PTS User's Manual*, Predicasts, 1989, p. 5-14.

in the former, but the reverse is not true. Thus, these codes can be used to gather data on markets defined either broadly or narrowly.

These codes are incorporated into search strategies using the search commands of the DIALOG command structure as described in Pocket Guide to DIALOG. The search command relevant for our sample search are the SS, AND and T commands. The SS command means "search and assign to sets" and is used to create groups of records which meet specified criteria. The AND command is a logical operator which indicates that selected records should meet two or more specified criteria. Other logical operators, OR and NOT, extract records which meet either of two conditions (OR) or which meet one condition but not a second one (NOT). The OR and NOT commands are not used in the next sample search. The T command causes the DIALOG system to display selected records on the screen. It specifies the data set of the selected records, indicates the format in which the user wishes to see the information, and the number of records to be displayed. There are several other commands in the DIALOG command system, but these are the ones needed for the sample search below.

As in the previous search, regular text represents messages displayed by the system, bold text represents input by the user, and italics are explanatory comments on the search process. Only opening and closing screen markers are used here, as the command-driven search process is continuous and does not move from one full display screen to another. As before, the illustration begins after the user has logged on to the DIALOG system.

****

?b 16 = *BEGIN 16, indicating the specific DIALOG database you wish to search.*

File 16:PTS PROMT - 72-93/January 8

(Copr. 1992 Predicasts)

**FILE016: New FULL TEXT titles added: Derivatives Engineering & Technology, Manufacturing Technology, NDT Update, Wall Street Network News

Set Items Description

?SS PC=2086 AND CN=JAPAN = *SEARCH AND ASSIGN TO SETS all records with the product code (PC) '2086' (soft drinks) and the country name 'Japan'*

S1 14109 PC=2086   *There are 14,109 records covering soft drinks.*

S2 232387 CN=JAPAN (9JPN)   *There are 232,387 records on Japan.*

S3 515 PC=2086 AND   *There are 515 records which are CN=JAPAN   in both sets above.*

This data set is too large to be useful, and must be further narrowed. One way to do this is to select the most recent articles. This is accomplished by a command which limits the set to articles published in selected years.

?SS S3 AND PY=1992:1993 = *SEARCH AND ASSIGN TO SETS all records in Set 3 above, which were published in the years 1992 through 1993.*

515 S3   *The same 515 records found for Set 3 above*

S4 649123 PY=1992 :   *There are 649,123 records published in 1992 and 1993*
PY = 1993

S5 133 S5 AND   *There are 133 records on soft drinks in Japan published in 1992 and 1993.*
PY = 1992:1993

?T S5/4/1-133 = *DISPLAY ON THE SCREEN records 1-133 of Set 5 using report format number 4 (the contents of each report format are listed in the DIALOG* Blue Sheet *for that file). The 'Log' or 'Data Capture' feature of your communications software should be activated prior to issuing this command.*

At this point, records 1-133 will be displayed on the screen and stored by the PC as directed in the communications software. This file may be printed subsequently using the DOS "Print" command or edited with a word processing package which can import a DOS text file.

****

The result of these two sample searches is a substantial body of information related to both aspects of the research assignment. You should be aware of two potential pitfalls in your use of this data. The first is the potential problem of plagiarism. Any material you use from the searches should be documented properly in your project report. Use the records themselves or the bluesheets of the databases to identify the sources of the information you use. The second potential problem is copyright infringement. Generally copying or disseminating the results of data searches will constitute copyright infringement. Sometimes, simple long-term storage of search results on data diskette rather than a single printed copy can also be restricted. These precautions are especially important for searches performed under the Classroom Instruction Program. Be sure to familiarize yourself with these restrictions and observe them in your handling of search data.

SUMMARY

Due to advantages of timeliness, comprehensiveness, and simplicity, electronic data retrieval is increasingly replacing print-based research methods. Of these techniques, on-line data retrieval offers advantages of breadth of coverage, timeliness, and low cost of access, while suffering from disadvantages of system security and cost of learning search tools. The system requirements are modest in cost and may be added to existing PCs quite easily and cost effectively. The DIALOG "Classroom Instruction Program" offers access to most DIALOG databases at deeply discounted prices for instructional applications. Many of the databases available through this program are of great value for various types of international business research projects. For these applications, the most appropriate search tool for novice users is the "DIALOG Business Connection." This system covers many different databases and allows users to search them using a subject-oriented menu system which does not require extensive training in search methods. On the other hand, individual DIALOG databases may be searched using the system's command structure. This approach requires more knowledge on the part of users, but also offers the ability to focus search strategies on exactly the type of information sought. Both systems provide access to substantial amounts of data for use in international business courses very quickly and cost-effectively.

END OF CHAPTER QUESTIONS

1. Evaluate the advantages and disadvantages of electronic data retrieval relative to research in print resources.
2. Evaluate the advantages and disadvantages of on-line electronic data retrieval relative to CD-ROM based research methods.
3. Find a personal computer magazine. Using the ads in the publication, construct a cost estimate for a system (hardware and software) capable of on-line electronic data retrieval. Include a CD-ROM drive as an optional component in this system. Construct a second cost estimate for upgrading an existing PC with these capabilities.
4. Describe the roles of the information service and the database vendor in an electronic on-line data retrieval network. Whom would you contact with questions about the coverage and structure of a specific database? Whom would you contact for information on telecommunications settings and search procedures?
5. You wish to gather information on the financial strength of Mazda of North America. Which of the DIALOG databases would be the most likely sources of useful information? Which menu selections from the "Dialog Business Connection" system would you use? Explain your answers.
6. You wish to gather competitive intelligence on the market for VCRs in Germany. Which of the DIALOG databases would be the most likely sources of useful information? Which menu selections from the "Dialog Business Connection" system would you use? Explain your answers.
7. The following are search commands within the system used by the PTS PROMT database described in this chapter. Explain the meaning of each command.
   a. SS PC=20821   d. SS CN=FRANCE AND PC=2111
   b. SS CN=BRAZIL   e. SS CN=FRANCE OR CN=SPAIN
   c. SS PY=1989:1991   f. T S3/4/1-25

8. Using the search commands described in the chapter, construct a search strategy for the PTS PROMT database to extract records related to the wine and brandy market in Spain that were published in 1992.

BIBLIOGRAPHY ON ELECTRONIC DATA RETRIEVAL

Barcellos, Silvia de Oliveira, August 1990. A project for improving interaction between users and information centers: Public access to databases in Brazil. *Electronic Library*, 224-227.
Bardes, D'Ellen, July/August 1986. Attention novices: Friendly intro to shiny disks. *Library Software Review*, 241-245.
Chen, Ching Chih and David I. Raitt, 1990. How optical products have been used in the U.S. and western Europe. Paper presentation at the National on-line Meeting. EDRS Reports.
Cohen, Elaine and Margo Young, November/December 1986. Cost comparison of abstracts and indexes on paper, CD ROM, and On-line. *Optical Information Systems*, 485-490.
Daniels, Craig E., August 1984. On-line information retrieval: An underutilized educational tool. *Information Services and Use*, 229-243.
Desmarais, Norman, May 1986. Laser libraries: Publishers are providing information on optical disks. *BYTE*, 235-46.
_____ , December 1986. Buying and selling laserbases. *Electronic and Optical Publishing Review*, 184-188.
Pocket Guide to DIALOG. DIALOG Information Service.
Doney, Lloyd D. and Steven C. Ross, February 1987. A set of basic computing capabilities for undergraduate business students. *Journal of Education for Business*, 215-217.
Drucker, Peter, June 5, 1985. Playing in the information based 'orchestra.' *Wall Street Journal*.
Dyer, Robert F, Summer 1987. An integrated design for personal computers in the marketing curriculum. *Journal of the Academy of Marketing Science*, 15; 10-15.
Edyburn, Dave L., Summer 1988. Examining the successful retrieval of information by students using on-line databases. *School Library Media Quarterly*, 256-259.
Ekwurzel, Drucilla and Bernard Saffran, December 1985. Online information retrieval for economists: The Economic Literature Index. *Journal of Economic Literature*, 1728-1763.
Helgerson, Linda W., Summer 1986. CD ROM search and retrieval software: The requirements and the realities. *Library Hi Tech*, 69-77.
Johnson, Charles M. 1989. Online corporate intelligence in marketing research courses. *Proceedings*. American Marketing Association Microcomputers in the Marketing Curriculum Conference, 66-73.

Kurtz, David L. and Louis E. Boone, Summer 1987. The current status of micro-computer usage in the marketing programs of AACSB-accredited colleges and universities. *Journal of the Academy of Marketing Science*, 10-15.

Lambert, Steve and Suzanne Ropiequet eds. 1986. *CD ROM: The New Papyrus: The Current and Future State of the Art.* Redmond, WA: Microsoft Press.

Large, Andrew J., August 1990. The foreign language barrier and electronic information. *Online Review*, 251-266.

Laub, Leonard, May 1986. The evolution of mass storage. *BYTE*, 161-172.

Luhn, Robert, April 1987. PC World CD ROM forum: CD ROM goes to work. *PC World*, 220-231.

McGinty, Tony, March 1986. Text crunching: Publishers squeeze volumes onto laser read disks. *Electronic Learning*, 22-26.

Miller, Fred, Fall 1985. Integrating the personal computer into the marketing curriculum: A programmatic outline. *Journal of Marketing Education*, 7-11.

Miller, Fred, May 1989. Integrating electronic information retrieval techniques into the business classroom. *Journal of Education for Business*, 376-380.

Miller, Fred, 1989. Suggestions for using DIALOG's CIP in Seven Marketing Courses. *Proceedings*. American Marketing Association Microcomputers in the Marketing Curriculum Conference, 59-65.

Miller, Tim, March/April 1987. Competitive intelligence: Staying alive in the jungle. *Online Access Guide*, 44-52.

Nace, Ted, February 1986. Lighting a path to the future. *Macworld*, 100-106.

Nicholls, Paul and Shaheen Majid, August 1989. The potential for CD-ROM technology in less-developed countries. *Canadian Library Journal*, 257-263.

O'Connor, Mary Ann, July/August 1986. Education and CD ROM. *Optical Information Systems*, 329-331.

O'Leary, Mick, September 1986. DIALOG Business Connection: DIALOG for the end user. *Online*, 15-24.

Oley, Elizabeth, April 1989. Information retrieval in the classroom. *Journal of Reading*, 590-597.

Plant, Mark W., September 23, 1991. The National Trade Data Bank: A one-year perspective. *Business America*, 2-5.

Salton, Gerard, September 1987. Historical note: The past thirty years in information retrieval. *Journal of the American Society for Information Science*, 375-380.

Sehr, Barbara K., November 1, 1986. High noon for CD ROM. *Datamation*, 79-88.

Spickard, Jim, April 1987. Information please?: Getting facts on-line. *Profiles*, 20-27.

Thompson, N. J., May 1989. DIALOGLINK and TRADEMARKSCAN-FEDERAL: Pioneers in Online images. *on-line*, 15-26.

Whieldon, David, December 2, 1986. Look at optical storage. *Computer Decisions*, 58-60.

Wiley, Gale, Summer 1989. On-line references become available through CD ROMs. *Journalism Educator*, 67-68.

Zoellick, Bill, May 1986. CD-ROM software development. *BYTE*, 177-188.

Chapter 10

International Accounting in the Information Age

Beryl Barkman

INTRODUCTION

In production, transportation, communication, and raising capital in global markets, the barriers of national borders are rapidly falling. Cross-border transactions are not only possible but, for companies seeking to expand the markets for their products and services, global transactions have become increasingly desirable. It is obvious from readily available statistics on world trade and the world's capital markets that national barriers are collapsing and the world has become interrelated to a degree never before experienced. And we have only seen the beginning of these global activities.

Evaluating foreign investments for possible acquisition or disposition, for entering into joint ventures, for making market surveys, for comparing operations of a foreign holding with a domestic entity, or any other cross-border arrangement ultimately requires financial information for decision making regarding the particular venture under consideration. International investors, regulators, and rating agencies also use the international financial information. Fortunately, the developments in communication and computer technology makes such information readily available in a timely manner in international financial databases. However, since companies are not required to report financial information in accordance with international accounting standards, the information in the databases may need to be restated before it is used to make decisions.

In this chapter our main objective is to make the reader aware of problems that must be resolved before using the international financial information for decision making. These problems arise, not because the information in the databases lack validity or reliability but, because financial information originating in different countries may differ simply because it has been prepared to conform to accounting principles that differ in their approaches. Suppose, for example, you are a business executive in the United States and have decided to expand operations by acquiring a company overseas. You have narrowed your options to two companies; one company in Country A and one company in Country B. Your investigation shows that the companies are comparable as far as non-financial factors such as culture, politics, and economic stability of the two countries are concerned. In other words, the risk of the investments is the same. In this situation then, your choice between the two companies will be determined by deciding which of the two companies is going to make a higher return on your investment. To determine which is the better investment you are now comparing the financial reports of the two companies for the last five years and the reports they have projected for the next five years. However, for the investment decision to be reliable, the financial information prepared by the two companies must conform to the same accounting principles. If the financial information does not conform to the same accounting principles, the information you are comparing is not comparable. Not having comparable information could result in a poor decision regarding the two companies.

The diversity of accounting principles among the nations creates the problem of comparability of information. Since each country develops its own generally accepted accounting principles and auditing standards, the recording and reporting of financial information varies greatly from country to country. This diversity can easily lead to misinterpreting information that has been prepared in another country. In the scenario given above, you as the business executive in the United States, should first determine if the financial information for the companies under consideration has been prepared according to accounting principles and auditing standards of the United States. If not, the financial information should be restated for differences in accounting principles between Countries A and B and the generally accepted accounting principles (GAAP) established in the United States. Once this is done, performance measures of the respective companies will be on the same basis and it will then be possible to make valid comparisons of their operations and investment opportunities. Throughout this chapter we stress the importance of restating international financial information for cross-border comparisons before making any final evaluations.

In the first section we will consider how international accounting is affected by recent developments in computer and communication technology. The next section will provide an overview of some of the current problems in international accounting followed by a summary of what is being done to improve the practice of international accounting and how some users cope with these problems.

SOME EFFECTS OF RECENT DEVELOPMENTS IN COMPUTER AND COMMUNICATION TECHNOLOGY ON INTERNATIONAL ACCOUNTING

Before the rapid technological developments of the last two decades in communication the accountant, more often than not, was preparing financial reports for domestic readers. The preparer and the user of the financial information spoke a common language and had the same national culture. Over the years, standards and policies have been established to make these financial reports relevant and reliable and, therefore, useful for the decision maker. Since auditing standards and accounting principles quite generally keep pace with the economic development of a country, the more highly developed countries have the most highly developed accounting principles and auditing standards. Countries in which economic activities have been slow to develop have simple accounting principles and auditing standards in place. This difference is quite understandable. The United States, for example, which is considered to have one of the most highly defined set of accounting principles and auditing standards among the nations, has only recently defined a conceptual framework of accounting qualities. The Conceptual Framework Project was undertaken by the Financial Accounting Standards Board (FASB) in the 1970s and now consists of six Statements of Financial Accounting Concepts (SFAC) Statement No. 2 (see Exhibit) identifies the accounting qualities established in the United States.

In the diagram of SFAC No. 2, the decision maker is at the top to emphasize the fact that financial accounting is to serve the needs of users. The information must be relevant which means it should help the user develop evaluations about the outcomes of the past and the present and make predictions of future expectations. The financial information must also (1) be reliable, which means it measures what it purports to measure; (2) be capable of being verified; and (3) tell it like it is, i.e., it is not developed for any individual purposes. Unfortunately for decision makers, accounting concepts and standards have not been standardized for the international community. Actually, at the present time, there is a great diversity among the nations in their respective accounting concepts, principles, and standards.

Accounting principles in other highly developed countries have some of the same principles, standards, and concepts that have been established in the United States. However, financial reports, i.e., balance sheets, income statements, statements of cash flow, and supplemental information prepared by companies in these countries also differ in the way the financial information is prepared and reported. Underdeveloped and developing countries have even greater diversities.

Because there is no common global accounting language there is reason to fear that there will be problems understanding and interpreting the accounting reports outside the country in which the report was prepared (Foust 1990). Not only does accounting language differ from country to country but the stage of economic development, culture, business environment, regulatory-setting bodies, and social policies—macro or micro—also differ. These differences affect, to a greater or lesser degree, the way the accountant records and reports financial information from country to country. These conditions have a great deal to do with the question of financial reports from different countries being equally relevant. What is important in one country may not be important for information users in another country. Whenever financial reports have been prepared according to different standards, the reports must be restated to a common set of principles to make the information comparable, i.e., capable of being compared. This is usually called "harmonization," a term commonly used to describe the process of restating financial reports to make them comparable.

CURRENT PROBLEMS IN INTERNATIONAL
FINANCIAL INFORMATION

The problems for the preparer of international financial information arise primarily out of the differences in accounting principles, differences in auditing standards, and differences in disclosure requirements from country to country. For internal use the accountant must prepare the information to conform to the generally accepted accounting principles of the country where the company is domiciled. But he/she may also be required to restate the report to conform to standards of another country. This would be the case if the company wants to list its stock on a foreign exchange or raise capital from other foreign sources. Restating reports to conform to the standards of another country or to the requirements of a foreign regulator is not impossible but it is time-consuming and costly. Some companies find the cost of such restatements greater than the anticipated benefit and choose not to get involved in cross-border ventures requiring restatements.

The problems for the users are somewhat different. They must make every effort to harmonize differences between cross-border financial reports for any venture they are considering. First of all, they must determine if there are any significant differences in the way the companies present the financial information. If there are differences, the users must determine if they are the result of (1) accounting measurement differences, (2) business environmental differences or, (3) real differences. Determining the effect of the underlying differences between two cross-border financial reports is often a major problem.

Consider the problem an investor has in comparing the 1992 balance sheets of Company A, domiciled in The Netherlands, with the 1992 balance sheets of Company B domiciled in the United States. (The Netherlands allows upward revaluation of assets; the United States requires the historic cost approach for valuation of assets.) An analysis of fixed assets reveals the following information:

In 1990 both companies purchased land and buildings valued at $1,000,000 in U. S. currency. With the exchange rate at 1.79 guilders to one U.S. dollar, the Company in The Netherlands recorded the purchase at 1,790,000 guilders.

In the two years since the purchase, the assets in The Netherlands have increased in value by 20 percent and have been evaluated upward on the 1992 balance sheet at 2,148,000 guilders to reflect this increase.

The assets in the United States have also increased in value by 20 percent but revaluation upward is not permitted. In fact, the historic cost has been reduced by $50,000 for two years of depreciation on the buildings. Land and buildings are reported in the 1992 balance sheet at $950,000 net.

To compare the financial information of the two companies, a U.S. investor would probably restate the information from the company in The Netherlands to dollars. Assuming the exchange rate is still 1.79 (i.e., 1.79 Guilders = 1 U.S. Dollar), the assets of the Dutch company are restated at $1,200,000 (2,148,000 guilders/1.79 = $1,200,000.) Now, compared to the U.S. Company, the Dutch company would appear to own assets worth $250,000 more than the assets of the U.S. company. Yet the difference is created by different accounting methods, not by any real difference in the economic value of the companies. Restating cross-border financial reports to a common currency is only the first step in harmonizing the information. The next step is to analyze every item with a material difference to see what causes the difference.

Measurement differences illustrated by this simple example are really very complex. Financial information in each country is prepared according to the legal system, culture, general business environment, type of regulation, and level of the accounting profession of the country in which the information is prepared. While financial information may be adequate and well understood domestically, it may not be interpreted properly in another country. Some of the areas in which differences are troublesome are

1. multinational consolidations;
2. valuation of fixed assets;
3. deferred taxes and pensions;
4. foreign currency transactions and translation;
5. intangible assets, especially goodwill; and
6. inventory valuations and provisions.

It is outside the scope of this chapter to discuss the many differences and all the possible effects these differences might have for the reader of international financial information. However, an overview of some of the differences and their effects will be helpful in providing an introduction to the problem of harmonizing international financial information. In the discussion that follows we have selected the intangible, goodwill, valuation of fixed assets, and inventory valuations to illustrate the necessity to determine what accounting principles are used to prepare the financial information and, to demonstrate that when differences are present, adjustments must be made to make the information comparable.

Differences in Accounting Principles

Goodwill. Goodwill, in this context, is defined as the amount the purchase price exceeds the fair market value of the assets for the bidding company. The different accounting methods and tax treatments of goodwill across nations will have a two-fold effect: (1) upon reported earnings which includes earnings per share and (2) upon bidding against foreign interests for takeovers in which there is a common interest. The U.S. accounting rules for goodwill under Opinion No. 17, issued by Accounting Principles Board (APB) in 1970, requires that goodwill be capitalized and written off annually against earnings over 40 years unless a shorter period for economic life is justified. However, accounting standards for reporting goodwill in other nations may depart rather radically from the U.S. standards.

Prior to July 1990, International Accounting Standard (IAS), No. 22 issued by the International Accounting Standards Commission (IASC) recognized the alternatives of reporting purchased goodwill as an asset to be amortized over its useful economic life, or an immediate write-off of purchased goodwill against equity. In July 1990, IASC issued a Statement of Intent that to comply with IAS No. 22, purchased goodwill should be capitalized and amortized on a systematic basis over a period of five years unless a longer period of life is justified and explained in the financial statements. In any event, the longer period should not exceed 20 years. However, since the IASC has no authority to make nations adopt their statement, compliance with IASC Statements is voluntary. Individual countries may adopt fully, adopt in part, or completely disregard the IAS statements. The differences in accounting principles for goodwill in Japan, Germany, The Netherlands, the United Kingdom, and the United States focuses on the effects these differences have when comparing operations and values of companies in these countries.

In Japan, prior to the July 1990 statement of IASC, the acquisition was considered an investment and the total investment was recorded at cost. There was no allocation of the cost of the investment between assets acquired at fair market value and goodwill for excess of cost over the fair market value. Consequently, in subsequent years following a purchase acquisition, the Japanese company would not reduce annual earnings with a write-off of goodwill. On the other hand, the U.S. company would have an annual charge for goodwill. The net result is that the Japanese company would report higher earnings and lower total assets than the U.S. company. If the information is not restated to reflect the difference in accounting for goodwill, the analysis of the operations of the two companies is misleading. Since Japan has adopted IAS No. 22, financial reports issued after the effective date of IAS No. 22 should now be reporting purchased goodwill in the same manner as the United States. However, anyone making a trend analysis of the operations of a Japanese company should adjust for differences in purchased acquisitions before and after IAS No. 22 became effective.

In West Germany, prior to July 1990, the total acquisition cost was capitalized. No write-offs were made unless it became apparent that, on a long-term basis, the acquisition was not worth the additional cost. Generally, then, there were no write-offs against earnings (Ernst and Whinney 1988a). Again, the financial information user comparing financial reports prepared in Germany with financial reports prepared in another country under different rules for accounting for goodwill must adjust the reports to harmonize the information. And, as noted with Japan, accounting for goodwill before and after July 1990 in Germany itself could be on a different basis. Making a trend analysis of a German company would require adjusting financial reports prepared prior to the adoption of IAS 22 with reports prepared after the adoption of IAS 22. (Germany now allows goodwill to be recognized as an asset and amortized or written off against shareholder's equity.) Similarly, in the Netherlands, goodwill may be capitalized (recognized as an asset) and written off over a period of five years. However, it is generally written off immediately to stockholder equity reserves (Ernst and Whinney 1988b).

In the United Kingdom, goodwill in the purchase of any acquisition must be recognized as an asset and written off immediately to reserves against stockholder's equity. The effect is to eliminate the annual operating expense of amortizing goodwill and to reduce total assets by the amount of capitalized goodwill. The U.K. company will report higher earnings and lower net assets than will be reported by a comparable company that capitalizes goodwill and writes it off periodically as an operating expense against income. The foregoing comments on goodwill are summarized in Table 1 for information prepared before Statement of Intent to revise IAS No. 22 was issued.

A simple example can demonstrate how these differences in accounting measurements of goodwill changes financial reporting. Company A is domiciled in a country that does not require goodwill, (i.e., the excess of the market price over the fair market value of the assets), to be capitalized and written off periodically against earnings. Company A is earning $2,000,000 annually with assets having a fair market value of $14,000,000. If Company A is ac-

TABLE 1. Comparison of Selected Countries to the United States for Effects of Differences in Accounting for Goodwill on NA, EPS, ROI, and ROE (based on principles in effect prior to July 1990)

	NA	EPS	ROI	ROE
Japan	the same*	higher	higher	higher
West Germany	the same*	higher	higher	higher
Netherlands	lower	higher	higher	higher
United Kingdom	lower	higher	higher	higher

*Note: Would be the same when acquisition was recorded but would be higher as U.S. made annual write-off.

NA: Net Assets
EPS: Earnings per Share
ROI: Return on Investment
ROE: Return on Equity

quired for $20,000,000, the acquisition price is 10 times the annual earnings ($20,000,000/$2,000,000 = 10).

Company B is domiciled in a country that requires that a company report acquisitions at fair market value and record goodwill for the amount that an acquisition price exceeds the fair market value. Goodwill is then to be written off periodically against earnings over a time period of not more than 40 years and not less than five years. Company B is also earning $2,000,000 annually with assets having a fair market value of $14,000,000. If Company B is acquired for $20,000,000, the goodwill of $6,000,000 will be capitalized and written off periodically against earnings. If Company B amortizes goodwill over the maximum period of 40 years, it will report earnings after the acquisition of $1,850,000 ($6,000,000 goodwill/40 = $150,000 a year write-off for goodwill subtracted from $20,000,000). The price earnings ratio will be 10.8 times (the $20,000,000 purchase price divided by the yearly earnings of $1,850,000). Amortizing over 20 years instead of 40 would result in a price earnings ratio of 11.8 times and amortizing over five years would result in a price earnings ratio 25 times. Although the two companies are operating in an identical manner, they report different earnings because of the different accounting policies for recording and reporting acquisitions at prices above the fair market value of the assets purchased.

Since the price earnings ratio is one measure of the payback or length of time to recover the investment, a lower price earnings ratio indicates a quicker recovery of an investment than a higher price earnings ratio. In this example, although Company B is making the same return as Company A, the writeoff of goodwill for company B increases the price earnings ratio and makes it appear from this measurement that Company B is not as good an investment as Company A. In reality, the investment opportunities of the two companies are the same. It is only that conformity to different accounting standards for goodwill has the result of giving different information when, in reality, the event has been the same. The difference is one of form rather than substance. However, it should be noted that since these differences in reporting goodwill do not affect cash flow, some analysts question whether these accounting differences for goodwill actually affect decisions on acquisitions.

Valuation of fixed assets in United States versus other countries.
Fixed assets are assets acquired for use over long periods of time
often classified as land, buildings, machinery, and equipment. In
order to match the capital expenditure with revenues, companies
record the expenditure as an asset and periodically write off the
depreciable assets to depreciation expense over the estimated useful
economic life of the asset. There are two primary issues involving
fixed assets that all firms face. They are (1) in what periods fixed
assets should be expensed for accounting purposes (depreciation
methods) and, (2) at what value should fixed assets be carried on
the balance sheet. The way companies resolve these issues has a
direct affect on many of the analytical procedures used in measuring the value and performance of an enterprise. These differences
can affect financial decisions for management as well as for the
potential investor. Therefore, comparing cross-border international
financial reports requires investigating and adjusting the information for the effects of any differences in the depreciating methods
used for the respective reports. In addition to adjusting for the effect
of differences in depreciation, it is also necessary to adjust the fixed
assets on the balance sheet for differences in valuation. The effect
of differences in depreciation methods is discussed first.

Some methods of depreciation are straight-line, units of use, and
sum-of-the-years-digits (S-Y-D). Although the total depreciation
over the life of the asset is the same, there are timing differences for
the amount of depreciation expense in any given year depending
upon the method of depreciation. These timing differences affect
operating income and net value of the fixed assets over the economic
life of the asset. In general, S-Y-D and accelerated depreciation
methods write off more depreciation expense in the early years and
less in the latter years of use than the straight-line depreciation.
Straight-line depreciation recognizes the same amount of depreciation expense each year. This means companies with the same assets
and comparable levels of operation will report different earnings in
any given year simply because they use different depreciation methods. The result, if the reports are not adjusted for differences in the
depreciation methods used, is that performance measurements will
be different even though the operations are the same.

To adjust for the effects different depreciation methods have on financial information, the decision maker must first determine what method of depreciation the company used to make the financial reports. If a particular country requires one method of depreciation, as in Brazil where all companies must use straight-line depreciation, all companies will be on the same basis for depreciation expense. No adjustment will be necessary for comparison of the domestic companies. The only adjustment to be made will be with foreign companies that use some other method of depreciation. However, if a country recognizes alternative methods of depreciation (as in the United States), a determination of the depreciation method used by the enterprise in the country with acceptable alternative methods must be made. Then the differences in cross-border information in reporting depreciation expense can be reconciled. For example, when comparing a U.S. enterprise using S-Y-D or an accelerated method of depreciation with an enterprise in Brazil, the cumulative effect of the difference in depreciation methods on operating income must be made. Adjustments must also be made for the effect the different depreciation methods have on the book value of the fixed assets.

Book value is the net amount at which an asset or group of assets appears on books of account as distinguished from market value or some intrinsic value. The book value is derived by decreasing the original cost of the asset by the amount of accumulated depreciation. This is known as the historical cost method of asset valuation. Some countries that use historical cost are the United States, Canada, Germany, and Japan (Choi 1991, p. 4-9). Other countries allow companies to revalue assets upward and downward to current market value or replacement cost. Replacement cost is the current cost of replacing an existing asset with one of equivalent productive capacity. Brazil, France, Italy, The Netherlands, Switzerland, and the United Kingdom are some of the countries with accounting principles that allow some form of revaluation (Choi 1991, p. 4-10). Thus, the carrying value of the assets as reported in the financial statements differs depending on whether the historical cost or the replacement cost method is used to value the assets. The different accounting methods used to value the assets now indicates two different values for the comparable assets when, in reality, there is no real difference. In such cases, if the difference is significant in amount, adjustments should be made to make the values comparable before comparing the operation and value of the companies.

Differences in inventory valuation. The effect of differences in inventory valuation is very similar to the differences in fixed asset valuation. The differences affect most of the financial, profitability, and activity ratios widely used in the United States to measure the performance and value of an enterprise. Since for many companies inventory is one of the largest assets on the balance sheet, differences in the accounting method for inventory values can be very significant. If prices fluctuate throughout the reporting period, the value of the ending inventory will depend on the accounting method in use to allocate product cost to cost of goods sold on the income statement and to ending inventory on the balance sheet. The most common methods for allocating product costs are First In, First Out (FIFO), Average Cost, and Last In, First Out (LIFO). See Table 2 for the effect different inventory valuations have on reporting profits and inventory values.

The statement by the Institute of Certified Public Accountants (AICPA), "Financial statements prepared in conformity with accounting principles generally accepted in another country ordinarily are not useful to U.S. users." (AICPA 1986, p. 4) makes it very

TABLE 2. Allocation of Inventory Costs*

	Cost of Goods Sold (Income Statement)	Gross Profit	Ending Inventory (Balance Sheet)
Company A (FIFO)	$4,500	$5,500	$6,500
Company B (LIFO)	$6,500	$3,500	$4,500

*

Company A uses FIFO for allocating cost and valuing inventory.
Company B uses LIFO for allocating cost and valuing inventory.

Both companies acquire inventory at the same cost.

Purchase #1	50 units @ $40 ea.	$2,000.
Purchase #2	50 units @ $50 ea.	2,500.
Purchase #3	50 units @ $60 ea.	3,000.
Purchase #4	50 units @ $70 ea.	3,500.

Both companies sell 100 units for $10,000.

clear that statements prepared outside the United States need to be restated to be useful to U.S. users. Generally, for information to be relevant, reports prepared outside the user's country must be adjusted to the standards of the user's country before measuring and comparing operations and values of enterprises domiciled in a different country. Every item of financial information that has been prepared to conform to different accounting principles and is of a significant amount (by significant, we mean an amount such that, if it is changed, could change a user's decision) should be harmonized. Differences for amounts that are not significant can be disregarded as not being relevant. A second area for differences in international financial information is the business environment.

Differences in the Business Environment

By "differences in the business environment" we mean differences in the way companies may conduct business. Acceptable ways or methods of doing business vary across the nations. For example, in some nations, bribes or payoffs are a part of the way of doing business but the practice is illegal in another nation. What is considered a conflict of interest in some countries is perfectly acceptable in another. Such differences will impact on whether the financial information prepared in one country will be considered reliable by the standards of another country. For the purposes of this chapter the significance of business environment on financial information will be discussed as it affects auditing and disclosure of financial information.

Auditing standards. The auditor is often considered to be the credibility link to the financial report for the interested reader. Decision makers like to have an objective and independent view of the financial information. The auditor's statement that "the financial statements present fairly, in all material respects, the financial position, results of operations, and cash flows of the entity in conformity with generally accepted accounting principles" insures the reliability of the information. Within the reader's own country this is generally true but their is a danger in naively applying the same reliance on audited statements prepared outside the country.

Auditing standards develop over time as the business environment (made up of cultural, legal, political, and economic variables) changes. Since these changes come from both the public (government) and private sectors, it is easy to see that auditing standards are likely to differ from country to country. There are many reasons for the differences. Some countries rely on law for auditing standards while others rely on professional associations. The education and experience necessary to qualify as an auditor varies from country to country. So does the licensing procedure and the requirements for continuing education. Chapter 6 of Choi's *Handbook of International Accounting* summarizes differences in qualifications of auditors and the attest function for 18 selected countries. His summary shows very clearly that a decision maker should not assume that an auditor's opinion of the financial statements has the same significance from country to country. The AICPA has addressed this issue for U.S. auditors.

The guidelines of the AICPA (SAS No. 51) for U.S. auditors reporting on financial statements prepared for use in other countries recognizes that differences in auditing standards may cause misunderstandings (AICPA, p. 4).

> ... Therefore, if financial statements are needed for use both in another country and within the United States, the auditor may report on two sets of financial statements for the entity–one prepared in conformity with accounting principles generally accepted in another country for use outside the United States, and the other prepared in accordance with accounting principles generally accepted in the United States. ... If dual statements are not prepared, or for some other reason the financial statements prepared in conformity with accounting principles generally accepted in another country will have more than limited distribution in the United States, the auditor should report on them using the U.S. standard form of report, modified as appropriate for departures from accounting principles generally accepted in the United States. ... (p. 4, item 8).

* * *

The auditor should consider whether the standard report of another country or the financial statements may be misunderstood because they resemble those prepared in conformity with U.S. standards. When the auditor believes there is a risk of misunderstanding, he should identify the other country in the report AICPA, (p. 5, item 11.).

* * *

> The auditor should recognize that the standard report used in another country, even when it appears similar to that used in the United States, may convey a different meaning and entail a different responsibility on the part of the auditor due to custom or culture (pp. 5-6, item 12.).

However, in order to modify or restate a financial report for departures from accounting standards familiar to the decision maker, the accounting principles used in preparing the original report must be disclosed. Disclosure is the essential link in harmonizing international financial information for differences in accounting principles and auditing standards.

Standards for disclosure. The term "disclosure" may be applied to any fact, opinion, or detail required or helpful in the interpretation of a statement or report. Full disclosure includes all information useful for investment, credit, and similar decisions. As such, disclosure is reporting the effect of various contingencies on financial condition, the methods of valuing assets, and the companies' contracts and agreements as completely and intelligently as possible. This information may be in parenthetical explanations, notes, cross references to contra items, and supporting schedules.

The need for full disclosure to harmonize international financial information is self-evident. Since acceptable accounting standards often recognize alternative methods of reporting information, disclosure is needed to inform the user of the method used for a particular financial report. The footnotes, for example, tell how the inventory and fixed assets are valued. By comparing the notes of different reports, the user will know if they have been prepared according to different principles. However, if notes are not required and therefore not provided, the user will not know if the information is relevant or not. The link that provides the information-user with the knowledge to determine the relevancy and reliability of the information he/she is using is disclosure. Unfortunately, because of differences in business environment and culture, disclosure is not uniform throughout the nations. For an insightful summary of accounting diversities, the reader is referred the *Handbook of International Accounting* (Choi 1991, Chapter 7).

In this chapter we have been emphasizing that each nation has its own accounting principles and standards for reporting financial information. Before using financial reports prepared in different nations to evaluate companies, the information must be harmonized, i.e., made comparable. In the next section we summarize efforts to harmonize cross-border financial reports and report on how some information users cope with the current diversities in reporting financial information.

Harmonizing Accounting Principles; Coping with Diversities

International financial information will be harmonized if accountants everywhere prepare reports according to an international accounting standard. But developing a set of standards for diverse nations to adhere to is a gargantuan task and efforts to establish international standards are moving slowly. Compliance is voluntary but progress is being made.

Attempts to harmonize accounting principles. In 1972, the Tenth International Congress of Accountants formed the International Accounting Standards Committee (IASC) and established the International Coordination Committee for the Accounting Profession (IC-CAP). In 1973 representatives of professional accounting groups from nine countries met to establish the IASC. The IASC completed a conceptual statement in 1988 similar to FASB's conceptual statement (See Exhibit 1) and they are now working on a comparability project.

Both the United Nations and the International Organization of Securities Commission (IOSCO) are interested in international accounting standards and support the work of the IASC. By the mid 1990s, the IASC expects to have a framework in place to address new issues and a body of standards that will replace their older and, more general accounting standards. If these new accounting standards meet the approval of the IOSCO for presentations of multinational security offerings, they have indicated they will make every

EXHIBIT 1.

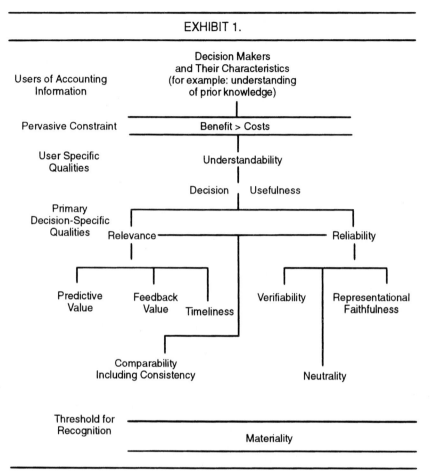

Source: SFAC 2, p. 15.

effort to have members report financial information according to the IASC accounting standards. This would, of course, be a major step in harmonizing international financial information.

Another organization, the International Federation of Accountants (IFAC) was formed in 1977 by 63 professional accountancy bodies from 49 countries. The overall objective is to develop a worldwide profession with harmonized standards. According to the

Handbook (Choi, 1991), current membership comprises 105 accounting bodies from 79 countries. Members work to encourage harmonization standards of financial accounting and reporting worldwide and attempt to implement standards and guidelines of both the IFAC and IASC.

Progress with harmonization. The subtitle to an interview entitled "Ralph Walters on Harmonization" succinctly states what is probably a good evaluation of the current attitude to harmonization of accounting principles: "Everybody wants to harmonize, but nobody wants to change" (Bisgay and Jayson 1989, p. 22). The interview with Ralph Walters, then chairman of a key IASC subcommittee, closes with these words, "I am convinced harmonization is the right thing to do, and, therefore, it will ultimately be accomplished. But my experience tells me that it will take a long time and will face many obstacles. It will not be a nice, neat transition" (Bisgay and Jayson 1989, p. 24).

The emerging countries and countries that have not already established their own accounting principles and auditing standards are adopting the standards of the IASC and the IFAC. The countries with well developed standards are the ones who are reluctant to change to global standards. Each believes it already has the best standards and wants global standards established to conform to its own standards. Obviously, these countries will have to make some concessions if the present diversities in accounting and auditing standards are to be replaced by uniform international standards.

Coping with the present diversities. The summary of how some groups are responding to the diversities in international financial reporting is adapted from "Behavioral Effects of International Accounting Diversity" (Choi and Levich 1991). Choi and Levich surveyed Institutional Investors, Corporate Issuers, Underwriters, Regulators, and Raters and four organizations that wished to remain unidentified.

Diversity is a problem. Of the 52 respondents taking part in the study, 24 responded that their capital market decisions were affected by accounting diversity. Of the institutional investors, nine of the 17 stated "that accounting differences make it more difficult for them to measure their decision variables and ultimately affect their investment decisions." Of the corporate issuers, nine of the 15 reported that GAAP differences did not affect their funding decisions but differences in disclosure requirements did make a difference. Issuers domiciled in Japan and West Germany were identified specifically as being affected by disclosure requirements. Accounting diversity is regarded as an issue for seven of the eight underwriters in the sample. The eight regulators in the sample did not report any particular problem with diversity in accounting information.

Coping with diversities. The manner in which some of the groups cope with the problems of diversity is interesting. Of the nine institutional investors who considered diversity to be a problem, seven restate the foreign accounts to a more familiar framework. Two adopt different investment strategies. One chose to limit foreign investments primarily to government bonds. The other follows a strategy of first selecting promising countries and then diversified investments within the selected countries. Of the seven who responded that diversity was not a problem, four had developed a system to familiarize themselves with "foreign accounting principles and adopted a local perspective," three rely on less sensitive information and one uses "sociological trends." Visiting the corporation is a frequently used coping mechanism. For the corporate issuers, some avoid raising funds or listing securities where accounting diversity would cause a problem, others restate fully or in part to meet requirements. Underwriters cope in different ways. One, who responded that diversity was not a problem, tries to avoid the problem by soliciting only top-tier firms, using credit ratings, and evaluating foreign capital via private placements. Of the other seven, five restate accounts to local GAAP, one restates accounts to both local and U.S. GAAP, and one examines rates of change in original accounting data. Five request additional information, one obtains guarantees from the parent company or a third party, and two avoid the U.S. market for a less demanding one.

SUMMARY

In this chapter we emphasize that financial reports prepared in one nation may be misunderstood in another nation. Even when the reports appear to be similar they may convey a different meaning because of differences in national customs, culture, and generally acceptable accounting and auditing standards.

As accounting principles and auditing standards become standardized, financial information will be harmonized. However, until global standards are the rule, rather than the exception, information-users must realize that reports prepared by the accountants in one country may differ in meaning from reports prepared by accountants in another country. To make cross-border comparisons, financial reports prepared in a foreign nation should be restated to conform to the accounting standards familiar to the information user.

It is paramount that the one using financial information from an international financial database first determine if the financial data conforms to a common set of accounting standards. If a common set of accounting standards has been used, the cross-border financial information is comparable. However, even though the financial reports conform to a common set of accounting standards, for the reports to be useful the standards must be familiar to the one using the reports. If the accounting standards used to harmonize the data are not standards familiar to the user, the reports should be modified to conform to accounting standards familiar to the one using the reports.

If the financial data in the international financial database has not been restated to conform to a common set of accounting standards, the information must first be restated to accounting standards familiar to the information user. Although the process of harmonizing cross-border information is time consuming and costly, it is imperative that cross-border financial information be comparable before the information is used to make any global decision. Decisions involving global transactions will be greatly improved by simply using information that means the same thing from nation to nation.

END OF CHAPTER QUESTIONS

1. Why is comparing cross-border financial information more difficult than comparing financial information of two domestic companies?
2. Discuss what is meant by "harmonization" of financial information. Give an example.

3. Compare the historic cost method of recording assets to replacement method of recording assets. What effect do these two methods have when comparing cross-border financial information?
4. You are performing a trend analysis of operating statement items of a foreign company. Is it necessary to restate the information to U.S. dollars before making the trend analysis? Why or why not?
5. What is meant by "disclosure" of financial information?
6. Why is full disclosure necessary for cross-border comparisons of financial information?
7. Define "goodwill."
8. Why is it necessary to disclose the accounting principles relating to goodwill when comparing cross-border financial information?

REFERENCES

AICPA, "Statement of Auditing Standards," No. 51, July 1986, Item 8, p. 4.
Bisgay, Louis and Susan Jayson, "Ralph Walters on Harmonization," *Management Accounting*, August 1989, pp. 22-24.
Choi, Frederick D. S., *Handbook of International Accounting*. (New York: John Wiley & Sons, Inc.), 1991.
Choi, Frederick D. S. and Richard M. Levich, "Behavioral Effects of International Accounting Diversity," *Accounting Horizons*, June 1991, pp. 1-13.
Ernst and Whinney, "Doing Business in West Germany," 1988a.
Ernst and Whinney, "Doing Business in the Netherlands," 1988b.
Foust, Dean, "The SEC is Relaxing–So Investors Should Be Nervous," *Business Week*, July 2, 1990, p. 32.

SUGGESTED READINGS

Bisgay, Louis and Susan Jayson, "Ralph Walters on Harmonization," *Management Accounting*, August 1989, p. 22-24.
Choi, Frederick D. S. and Richard M. Levich, "Behavioral Effects of International Accounting Diversity," *Accounting Horizons*, Vol. 5, No. 2, June 1991, p. 1-13.
Hadder, James E., "Evaluation of Manufacturing Investments: A Comparison of U.S. and Japanese Practices," *Financial Management*, Spring 1986, p. 17-23.

Peavey, Dennis E. and Stuart K. Webster, "Is GAAP the Gap to International Markets," *Management Accounting*, August 1990, p. 31-35.

Ragan, Paul, "Foreign Financials: Reading Between the Lines," *Export Today*, Vol. 8, No. 5, June 1992, p. 48-50.

Schweikart, James A., "The Relevance of Managerial Accounting Information: A Multinational Analysis," *Accounting Organizations and Society*, Vol. 11, No.6, 1986, p. 541-554.

Tang, Robert Y. W., "Transfer Pricing In The 1990s," *Management Accounting*, February 1992, p. 22-26.

Chapter 11

International Financial Databases and the Practice of Accounting

Abdel M. Agami

INTERNATIONAL FINANCIAL DATABASES

Several international financial databases are available and can be accessed by multinational enterprises as well as researchers and educators. These financial databases vary significantly as to the countries they cover. Some are international, i.e., include databases from many countries; others are regional, i.e., include corporations from Europe, Asia, Latin America, etc.; still others include only a national coverage, i.e., U.S. corporations, U.K. corporations, etc. They also vary as to the type of information they make available, i.e., complete financial statements, selected items from the financial statements, market prices, financial ratios, etc. They also vary as to the frequency of updating the information; some update information annually, others quarterly, monthly, weekly, or daily. They also vary as to media in which the information is provided; some of the services provide the information in hard copies, others provide it in the form of datadisk, some provide on-line services, etc. Table 1 provides a list of selected international financial database services, Table 2 provides a list of selected regional financial database services, and Table 3 provides a list of selected national financial database services that provide financial statement information in English (Choi, 1988).

USING INTERNATIONAL FINANCIAL DATABASES

Many business schools are providing business students an opportunity to do part of their study abroad. The purpose of these pro-

TABLE 1. Selected *International* Financial Database Services that Provide Financial Statements Information

NAME OF THE SERVICE	PUBLISHER	NO. OF CORP.	MEDIUM
CAPITAL INTERNATIONAL	CAPITAL INTERNATIONAL PERSPECTIVE, SA	1,600	HARD COPY
FINANCIAL LEADERS	JAPAN EXPORT MAGAZINE	250	HARD COPY
EXSTAT	EXTEL FINANCIAL	3,500	ON-LINE
FINANCIAL TIMES	INSTITUTE OF OIL & GAS	3,500	HARD COPY
FORTUNE WORLD	FORTUNE INC.	500	HARD COPY
GLOBAL VANTAGE	STANDARD & POORS	3,000	DATADISK
DATASTREAM	DATASTREAM INTERNATIONAL	8,000	ON-LINE
ICAP FINANCIAL	ICAP HELLAS, SA	16,700	HARD COPY
INTERN. CORP. SCOREBOARD	BUSINESS WEEK	1,000	HARD COPY
INVESTEXT	BUSINESS RESEARCH CORP.	5,000	ON-LINE
TIMES 1000	TIMES BOOK	1,000	HARD COPY
WORLDSCOPE	WRIGHT INVESTORS SERVICES	3,000	DATADISK

grams is to expose students to the cultural, economic, and business practices in other countries and to give them an early start in adapting to and appreciating diversity in the global economy that they are soon to become part of. One problem with these programs is that they are, in spite of some financial support by federal, state, and private organizations, expensive and consequently beyond the reach of many students, especially under present economic conditions and with the increase in the cost of college education. Not as a substitute for study abroad programs, but as a second alternative, the author requires students in his international accounting course to do a research project comparing the cultural, economic, business, and ac-

TABLE 2. Selected *Regional* Financial Database Services that Provide Financial Statements Information

NAME OF THE SERVICE	PUBLISHER	NO. OF CORP.	MEDIUM
ASIA MEASURES & MAGNITUDES	ASIAN FINANCIAL PUBLICATIONS	1,000	HARD COPY
BUSINESS ASIA	BUSINESS INTERNATIONAL	NA*	HARD COPY
FINANCIAL LEADERS	BUSINESS COMMISSION –HONG KONG	NA*	HARD COPY
NIKKIE TELECOM	NATIONAL KEIZAI SHIMBUN	5,200	DATATAPE
DISCLOSURE EUROPE	DISCLOSURE INFORMATION GROUP	2,000	ON-LINE
EUROPE'S 5000 LARGEST COMPANIES	GOWER PRESS LTD.	5,000	HARD COPY
EUROPE'S TOP 15,000	DUN & BRADSTREET	15,000	HARD COPY
VISION–EUROPE'S TOP 500 COMPANIES	SEPEG, SA	500	HARD COPY
BUSINESS LATIN AMERICA	BUSINESS INTERNATIONAL	NA*	HARD COPY
MAJOR COMPANIES OF BRAZIL	GRAHAM & TROTMAN	NA*	HARD COPY

* Number not available

counting standards and financial reporting practices of global business in the U.S. with that of a foreign country of the student's choice.

In past years, the author has required students to do the financial part of the project using hard copy financial sources such as Annual Reports, 10-K, Moody's Industrial, etc. Recently, electronic financial databases are used in gathering the data needed for this project. The author has found that the use of computerized financial databases reduces the time the student spends on collecting and processing data and computing certain ratios, gives students more time for analysis, interpretation, and inference without increasing the total time spent on the project. It also encourages students to increase the horizon over which they analyze the performance of the company,

TABLE 3. Selected *National* Financial Database Services that Provide Financial Statements Information

NAME OF THE SERVICE	PUBLISHER	NO. OF CORP.	MEDIUM
AUSTRALIA ASSETS, LIABILITIES, INCOME & EXPENSES: AUSTRALIA	AUSTRALIA BUREAU OF STATISTICS	4,000	HARD COPY
CANADA ICC CANADIAN CORP. DATABASE	ICC CANADA, LTD.	5,000	ON-LINE
CHINA THE LARGEST IND. CORP. IN ROC	CHINA CREDIT INFORMATION SERVICE, LTD.	1,500	HARD COPY
DENMARK GREEN'S DANISH STOCK & BUND	AS FORLAGET BORSEN	3,000	HARD COPY
FINLAND THE 2000 LARGEST COS. IN FINLAND	YRITYSTIETO	2,000	HARD COPY
GERMANY HOPPENSTEDT	HOPPENSTEDT WIRSCHAFTS– DATENBANK	36,000	ON-LINE
GREECE YEARBOOK OF THE ATHENS STOCK EXCHANGE	ATHENS STOCK EXCHANGE	NA	HARD COPY
HONG KONG HK STOCK EXCHANGE YEARBOOK	HK STOCK EXCHANGE	NA	HARD COPY
INDIA CALCUTTA STOCK EXCHANGE YEARBOOK	CALCUTTA STOCK EXCHANGE	NA	HARD COPY
IRAN MAJOR COMPANIES OF IRAN	GRAHAM & TROTMAN	2,000	HARD COPY
IRELAND IRELAND: A DIRECTORY AND YEARBOOK	INSTITUTE OF PUBLIC ADM.	NA	HARD COPY

NAME OF THE SERVICE	PUBLISHER	NO. OF CORP.	MEDIUM
ISRAEL TEL AVIV STOCK EXCHANGE INFO.	HALEVI & CO. ECONOMIC COUNSELING SERVICE, LTD.	NA	HARD COPY
ITALY ITALY'S LEADING COMPANIES	DUN & BRADSTREET S.P.A.	2,000	HARD COPY
JAPAN ANALYSTS GUIDE	DAIWA SECURITIES CO., LTD.	900	HARD COPY
KENYA NAIROBI STOCK EXCHANGE YEARBOOK	AFRICA REGISTRAT, LTD.	53	HARD COPY
KOREA FINANCIAL STATEMENTS	BANK OF KOREA	1,857	HARD COPY
LEBANON YEARBOOK: THE LEBANON JOINT STOCK COS.	MIDDLE EAST COMMERCIAL INFO. CENTER	NA	HARD COPY
LUXEMBOURG THE 30 MOST IMPORTANT LUXEMBOURG COS.	LUXEMBOURG EMBASSY	30	HARD COPY
MALAYSIA KUALA LUMPUR STOCK EXCHANGE: ANNUAL COMPANIES HANDBOOK	KUALA LUMPUR STOCK EXCHANGE	281	HARD COPY
MEXICO MEXICO: BUSINESS OPPORTUNITIES	METRA CONSULTING GROUP, LTD.	500	HARD COPY
NEW ZEALAND MINES STATEMENTS FOR THE YEAR	GOVERNMENT BOOKSHOP	NA	HARD COPY
NIGERIA MAJOR COMPANIES IN NIGERIA	GRAHAM & TROTMAN	2,000	HARD COPY
NORWAY COMMERCIAL BANKS– YEARBOOKS	A.S. OKONOMISK LITERATUR	8,500	HARD COPY

TABLE 3. (continued)

NAME OF THE SERVICE	PUBLISHER	NO. OF CORP.	MEDIUM
PAKISTAN			
KARACHI STOCK EXCHANGE	KARACHI STOCK EXCHANGE, LTD.	30	HARD COPY
PHILIPPINES			
BUSINESS DAY'S 1000 TOP COS.	BUSINESS DAY CORP.	2,000	ON-LINE/ HARD COPY
SCOTLAND			
SCOTLAND'S TOP 500 COMPANIES	JORDAN DATAQUEST, LTD.	500	HARD COPY
SINGAPORE			
STOCK EXCHANGE OF SINGAPORE HANDBOOK	STOCK EXCHANGE OF SINGAPORE LTD.	400	HARD COPY
SOUTH AFRICA			
JOHANNESBURG STOCK EXCHANGE HANDBOOK	JOHANNESBURG STOCK EXCHANGE	600	ON-LINE/ HARD COPY
SRI LANKA			
HANDBOOK OF RUPEE COMPANIES	COLOMBO BROKERS ASSOC.	250	HARD COPY
SWEDEN			
SVENSKA AKTIEBOLAG	PA NORSTEDT & SONER	3,500	HARD COPY
SWITZERLAND			
LES PRINCIPALES ENTERPRISES DES SUISSE	UNION BANK OF SWITZERLAND	667	HARD COPY
TANZANIA			
NATIONAL DEV. CORP. ANNUAL REPORT	NATIONAL DEV. CORP.	NA	HARD COPY
THAILAND			
DIR. OF THAILAND'S 100 TOP COS.	BANGKOK BUSINESS	100	HARD COPY
TRINIDAD & TOBAGO			
FINANCIAL OFFICE	CENTRAL STATISTICS	NA	HARD COPY
UNITED KINGDOM			
EXTEL UK LISTED COMPANIES SERVICES	EXTEL	3,000	HARD COPY
YUGOSLAVIA			
EKONOMSKA POLITIKA	EKONOMSKA POLITIKA	200	HARD COPY

and gives students more self-confidence in use of the computer and state-of-the-art information technology.

USING FINANCIAL DATABASES
IN INTERNATIONAL ACCOUNTING

There has been a steady increase in the number of business schools offering international accounting courses at the undergraduate and/or graduate level in the last 20 years (Mueller 1965; Seidler 1967; Bomeli 1969; Rueschhoff 1972; Kubin 1973; Dascher, Smith, and Strawser 1973; Ameiss 1974; Schoenfeld 1974; Brummet 1975; Foutz 1975; Clay 1975; Burns 1979; Pearson, Ryan, and Hicks 1980; Mintz 1980; Agami 1983; Foroughi and Reed 1987; Sherman 1987; Stout and Schweikart 1989). A typical international accounting course covers the accounting problems that face multinational enterprises as well as accounting standards and practices in selected countries.

The first part of the course includes topics such as accounting for the translation of foreign transactions and financial statements from foreign currencies to domestic currencies, and considers the conceptual basis for choosing a particular method of translation. Also contained in this section are accounting for inflation in various countries, and the issue of whether MNEs should translate the financial statements of their foreign subsidiaries and branches from foreign currencies first and then restate these translated financial statements for the domestic inflation, or whether they should restate the financial statements of those subsidiaries and branches for local foreign inflation and then translate them from foreign currencies to domestic currencies. Some other topics referred to include consolidation of foreign subsidiaries; segmental disclosure of foreign operations; social responsibility disclosure of multinational enterprises; evaluation of foreign investment proposals; determining the most economic financial outlets; minimizing financial risk associated with investments in different parts of the world and in different currencies; evaluating the performance of foreign branches, subsidiaries, and their respective managers; establishing equitable transfer prices for goods or services exchanged among affiliates; and principles of foreign and domestic taxation of international operations.

The second part of the course deals with the study of accounting and auditing standards and corporate financial reporting practices in selected foreign countries and regions such as Europe, Canada, Central and South America, Australia and New Zealand, socialist countries, and developing countries. The purpose for studying these countries is to identify similarities and differences between accounting standards and practices of those countries and those of the U.S.A., and the need for harmonizing accounting standards among countries.

Lecture, class discussion, oral presentation by students, and the case method are frequently used in teaching the course. Many instructors also assign independent projects to students in order to give them the opportunity to research an area of particular interest to them such as the accounting and auditing standards and/or corporate financial reporting practices in a specific country or region of the world.

The international accounting course which the author teaches includes a survey of the accounting standards and corporate financial reporting practices in selected foreign countries. The objective of this part of the course is to give students an opportunity to identify similarities and differences in cultural, economic, business, and accounting standards and practices of the U.S. and other countries (see Table 4).

Each student chooses a foreign country that he or she is interested in. The student also chooses a corporation that is domiciled in the foreign country and a similar U.S. corporation. The student researches the cultural, economic, business, and accounting standards of this country and the accounting practices of the corporation. The student then compares the cultural, economic, business, and accounting standards of this foreign country and the accounting practices of the corporation with those of the U.S. and the U.S. corporation. The student is required to state whether the differences in accounting standards and practices between the two countries have hindered the student's analysis in any respect and what the student's views are as to how to overcome those national barriers.

The computerized financial database that the author uses is DIS-CLOSURE/WORLDSCOPE. The most recent edition of this software provides access to the financial data of about 7,000 companies

TABLE 4. The Project

I. Objective
To familiarize students with cultural, economic, business, accounting, auditing, and financial reporting practices of corporations in foreign countries

II. Information Needed
1. Literature dealing with the cultural, economic, business, accounting, auditing, and financial reporting practices of corporations in foreign countries

2. Financial information of:
a foreign corporation(s)
a US corporation(s)

III. Report's Contents
1. Similarities and differences between the foreign country's and US's:
a. Culture
b. Economy
c. Business practices
d. Accounting standards
e. Auditing standards
f. Financial reporting practices of companies

2. Decision as to which company is financially stronger and identifying problems encountered in making the decision and methods used to overcome these problems

IV. Advantages of Computerized Financial Databases
1. Saves students time in collecting and processing data and consequently encourages them to increase the horizon of their study

2. Gives students more time for analysis and interpretation

3. Gives students self confidence in use of the computer

4. Makes students aware of differences between countries

---

in over 25 countries and over 24 industries (see Table 5). The data for each company are presented in standardized format. The financial data are available for ten years (five years of displayable data). The record of each company contains 500 data fields (see Table 6). The data are updated monthly. Retrieved data can be displayed, printed, or transferred to disk. This is a very important feature; it allows students to transfer whatever data they need onto their own disk for whatever analysis they want to do on another computer. This way they do not tie up the computer on which the DISCLOSURE/WORLDSCOPE disk is stored so that other students can use it. It is also a very useful feature for the instructor to use for grading purposes. The author requires the students to submit a copy of the disk where they saved the data and their analysis along with the final written report. Generally the final report consists of four sections. The first section provides general information about the country chosen by the student such as geographical information about the country, the political system, the population, the language, culture, economy, etc. The second section contains information about the business environment, accounting and auditing standards and practices of the country, and status of the accounting profession in the country. The third section includes a study of financial reporting practices and the financial performance of a corporation domiciled in the country. The fourth section presents the student's observations and remarks as to similarities and differences in cultural, economic, business, and accounting standards and practices of the U.S. and other countries.

AN ILLUSTRATION OF A STUDENT PROJECT–AUSTRALIA

General Overview

Australia, known to many Americans as "the land down-under," is a country of 2,972,000 square miles and about 15.3 million people. Australia's most noted attributes include the koala bear, the kangaroo, the pop group Men At Work, and comedian Paul Hogan, and is temporary home of yachting's greatest trophy, the America's Cup. The country is located in the Southern Hemisphere, and consists of the mainland continent and several outlying islands. The population tends to be concentrated in the cities along the coastline, as the inland parts of the country are primarily arid desert.

Politically, the country is a Commonwealth made up of six States (New South Wales, Queensland, South Australia, Tasmania, Victoria, and Western Australia), and two territories (Australian Capital Territory and Northern Territory), plus the non-self-governing territories offshore. Australia is a member of the British Commonwealth of Nations, and the Queen of England is the titular head of government. Legislative power is vested in a parliamentary system, with the Legislature of the Commonwealth and the various States being

TABLE 5. Countries Included in Disclosure/Worldscope

1. Australia	14. Malaysia
2. Austria	15. Mexico
3. Belgium	16. Netherlands
4. Canada	17. New Zealand
5. Denmark	18. Norway
6. Finland	19. Singapore
7. France	20. South Africa
8. Germany	21. Spain
9. Hong Kong	22. Sweden
10. Ireland	23. Switzerland
11. Italy	24. United Kingdom
12. Japan	25. United States
13. South Korea	

bicameral, and being elected by universal suffrage. The division of powers between the States and the Commonwealth is similar to that of the United States, with the Commonwealth legislating in the area of defence, foreign affairs, income and sales taxes, customs and excise, tariffs, social services, overseas trade, postal services and communications, banking and currency, and copyrights, patents, and trademarks. The residual powers are delegated to the States, with a greater tendency towards overlap in recent years.

The legal system is based on the English common law system, and while much of the law has been codified, some still remains in case law. The language is English, and there are no restrictions on religion.

The economy has historically been based on the rural sector, with significant levels of the Western world's supply of wool, wheat, and sugar being produced there, as well as large quantities of meat. In recent years, Australia has developed its mineral production, including bauxite, beach sand minerals, iron ore, lead, zinc, and coal. It has ample supplies of energy resources, including oil, natural gas, and coal, and a potential for nuclear fuel. Its only resource limita-

TABLE 6. Summary of Data Included in Disclosure/Worldscope

RESUME DATA:

Name	Stock Exchange(s)
Address	Stock Indices
Telephone	Ticker Symbol
Business Description	CUSIP Number
SIC Codes	SEDOL Number
Number of Employees	VALOR Number
Currency	ISIN Number
Exchange Rates	Current Outstanding Shares
Auditor	Number of Shareholders
Auditor's Opinion	

FINANCIAL DATA: Unless otherwise noted, all data is available from 1980 to the present.

Annual Income Statements
Annual Balance Sheets (Assets/Liabilities)
Supplementary Financials including loan, debt and other line items
Sources of Funds
Uses of Funds
Proceeds from Sale/Issuance of stock
Ratios – Annual
Ratios – Five Year Averages: 1984 to the present
Annual Growth Rates
Five Year Growth Rates: 1984 to the present

STOCK DATA: Unless otherwise noted, all data is available from 1980 to the present.

U.S. and Non-U.S. Stock Price/Trading Data
Stock Performance Data
U.S. Interim Share Data
Non-U.S. Interim Share Data: 1989 to the present
U.S. Month End Market Prices: 1985 to the present
Non-U.S. Month End Market Prices: 1987 to the present
Annual Stock Statistics
Five Year Stock Averages

TEXTUAL DATA:

Accounting Practices Abstracts
Financial Footnote Abstracts
Key Officers and Titles

tion is water, which is being increased with dams and irrigation systems.

The wholesale and retail industry is the largest employer in Australia, with manufacturing the major contributor to the GDP. Other strong industries include construction, mining, and agriculture. Potential growth areas include oil and gas extraction, and uranium extraction, along with some growth of the manufacturing sector. Agricultural industries are dependent on exports, and will be affected greatly by world economic activity.

Foreign investment has been encouraged in the past, and still is, but the government is taking a closer look at the costs to Australia, and the benefits that the country will gain from the investment. Certain activities are presently closed to foreign investment, including: banking (both savings and trading), radio and television broadcasting, daily newspapers, and some sectors of the civil aviation industry. Foreign banks are permitted through representative offices, however.

Business Entities

In 1981, a uniform Companies Act was created by the Commonwealth and the six States, so as to provide a cooperative scheme for a uniform system of law and administration, regarding company law and the regulation of the securities industry in the six States and the Australian Capital Territory. The Northern Territory was not a party to the agreement, but may become so in the future. A key feature in the Act is that companies incorporating in a participating State are given "recognized" or domestic status in other participating States, thus the company does not have to incorporate in each State in which it intends to do business.

The most common form of incorporation is a limited liability company having a share capital, although there are other forms that are less frequently used. A company limited by shares is a company formed on the principle of having the liability of its shareholders limited by the memorandum of association (charter) to the amount unpaid (if any) on the shares respectively held by them.

The limited liability company may be incorporated as a public company or a proprietary (private) company. A proprietary company restricts the right to transfer its shares, limits the number of stockholders to not more than 50 (excluding employees), and prohibits any invitation to the public to subscribe for any shares in or debentures of the company, or to deposit money with the company; all other limited companies are public companies.

Limited liability companies in Australia face very similar regulations to corporations in the United States. There are a few noteworthy differences, however: no-par stock is not permitted; dividends may not be declared except out of profits; a company may not deal in its own shares, nor hold shares in a company that is its holding company; and a director of a public company incorporated in Australia must retire at the age of 72.

Accounting Profession

Australia has two main professional bodies, the Institute of Chartered Accountants in Australia, and the Australian Society of Accountants. Each is governed separately by its own council, and each has its own code of ethics. Together, the two bodies sponsor the Australian Accounting Research Foundation, which, through its committees, formulates accounting standards. When approved, the councils of the parent organizations jointly issue statements containing the standards to be observed by their members.

There are approximately 13,400 members of the Institute of Chartered Accountants in Australia, and about 47,000 in the Australian Society of Accountants, the latter consisting in large part of persons in industry, commerce, and government service.

Sources of Standards

Accounting and auditing standards are strongly influenced by the United States and United Kingdom standards, and are comparable with the standards of these two countries. No other sources of possible accounting standards, for example IASC, exhibits any real influence on their standards, however.

Statements of auditing and accounting standards are promulgated in the members' handbook issued by the Institute of Chartered Accountants in Australia. Statements of accounting standards have been issued on 18 topics thus far. The standards are set through the

Australian Accounting Research Foundation, which is formed jointly by the Institute and the Australian Society of Accountants. Standards are researched by the appropriate committees, which formulates the principles. When the principles are approved, the Councils of the respective bodies jointly issue the Statements, which then become professional Standards.

A minor influence on accounting practice is the Australian Associated Stock Exchanges Limited, through its requirements for listing on the Australian stock exchanges. Its primary influence is through its disclosure requirements.

The Ministerial Council, made up of the Ministers of the Commonwealth and the six States, has established the Accounting Standards Review Board, with the powers to approve accounting standards to be applied in preparation of company accounts. This acts as a government review of any accounting standards the profession might introduce.

Statutory Requirements

Every company is required to keep in the English language and in Australian currency such accounting and other records as will sufficiently explain the transactions and financial position of the company and enable true and fair profit and loss accounts (income statements) and balance sheets (and any documents required to be attached thereto, such as the directors' report to shareholders) to be prepared from time to time.

Other records are also required:

1. Minute books of the meetings of shareholders and meetings of directors
2. Register of shareholders containing the names and addresses of all shareholders, details of shares held by them, date in which entered into the register, date in which a person ceases to be a shareholder, and the date and number of shares of every allotment
3. Register of directors, secretaries, and principal executive officer containing the name, address, other occupation (if any), particulars of other directorships in other public companies,

date of appointment or change, and written consent of appointment

4. Register of directors' shareholdings particulars in stock, debentures, participatory interests, rights or options, or contracts relating to the directors' interest in the company or related corporation

5. Register of charges (security agreements) specifically affecting property of the company and any floating charges, with a short description of the liability secured by the charge, a description of the property, the amount of the charge, the persons entitled to those charges, and a copy of the charge

6. Register of substantial shareholders, mandatory for listed public companies but may be required for others, with substantial being generally defined as ten percent or more of voting shares, or ten percent or more of a particular class of shares

7. Register of debenture holders including the name and address of the holder, and the debentures held by them.

Information required by Statute and usually published in the Directors' Report includes: the list of directors; the scheme of arrangement, principal activities of the company; the subsidiaries acquired or disposed of during the year; the reserves accounts and changes to them during the year; provisions accounts changes; share issues for the year; share options issued; debenture issues from the year; dividends declared or paid; and other matters, which includes any additional information.

Financial Statements

Statement prepared for filings under the various Company Acts normally include:

Directors' report
Auditors' report
Balance sheet
Statement of profit and loss (income statement)
Notes to the financial statements

Statement of source and application of funds (for
companies listed on stock exchanges only)
Directors' statement

These requirements are set out under the Company Acts, and are
supplemented by the statements of accounting standards issued by
the Institute of Chartered Accountants in Australia, and the Australian Society of Accountants, and the Australian Associated Stock
Exchanges' listing requirements.

Both the auditors and the directors must insure that the statements of accounts are made up in accordance with approved accounting standards, except where the standards would not present a
"true and fair view" of the accounts. Where the accounts are not
drawn up in accord with the standards, the auditor is required to
send a copy of the audit report to the Ministerial Council of the
Commonwealth for review.

Australian financial statements and principles are very similar to
the standards found in the United States. Several of the more important points have been selected for examination here.

Income Statement

All items of income and expense that arise during that period are
brought into the income statement as a credit or charge to net profit,
regardless of whether they apply to ordinary business operations,
prior periods, or other events.

Accounting principles are expected to be consistent from period
to period, with any changes noted in the directors' report. Significant accounting policies and methods are disclosed in the notes to
the financial statements. The quantified effect of changes in accounting principles must be disclosed in a note to the financial
statements.

The following items are given extraordinary treatment, and are
disclosed net of tax effect, if any, in a separate section titled "Extraordinary Items": disposal of a major segment of a business;
disposal of an investment not acquired for resale; and profits or
losses attributable to a major currency realignment.

Only dividends paid or payable, or transfers to or from reserves
are permitted as appropriations.

Capital Accounts

As mentioned earlier, the Companies Act gives several limitations on capital which are not found in U.S. corporate laws. A company cannot deal in its own shares (i.e., no treasury stock), nor can it hold shares in its own holding company. Australian companies cannot issue no-par stock; most companies issue stock of $A1 par value.

In addition, a company is prohibited from giving financial assistance to any person, either directly or indirectly, in connection with the purchase of shares in the company or its holding company, if one exists, except under the following conditions: if the money is loaned or a loan is guaranteed by the company in the normal course of business, on ordinary commercial terms; or if financial assistance is given to employees or officers to enable the purchase of fully paid shares, so long as the assistance is approved at the general meeting of the company and its holding company. Special regulations in the Companies Act govern the company's actions in providing financial assistance in the purchase of its own shares.

Companies may issue various classes of stock, generally ordinary (common) and preference (preferred) shares. Details of the share capital must be disclosed in the financial statements, and any premium on the issuance of shares must be recorded in a share premium account, and disclosed as such under Capital Reserves.

Valuation of Assets

Marketable securities–for securities listed on the stock exchange, the value is at lower of cost or market value. Lowest price is the lowest of the last sale price, selling offer, and bid offer. If the market value is lower than the book value and the asset is current, the directors will generally make a provision for a dimunition in value; long-term investments, if the decline is temporary, will generally not need a provision.

Inventories–stock (inventories) is valued at the lower of cost and net realizable value, usually on the actual, average, or FIFO basis. LIFO is prohibited for either tax or accounting purposes. Costs include the cost of purchase, and costs of conversion, including direct labor and other production costs, production costs being in accordance with direct-costing or absorption-costing, but does not include sales or general administrative expenses. Any stock may be valued with any of the three alternatives.

Real property–The value of real property depends on the reason for which the property is held. When held for other than resale, the property is generally valued at cost, with the cost of the buildings segregated and depreciated. Unlike U.S. financial statements that are based on historical cost, when there is an upward trend in the value of the property, the market value of the property *may* be taken into account by revaluation of the property, and the increment being taken directly to an assets revaluation reserve. When land and buildings are owned by property investment companies, they are sometimes taken as composite assets, and depreciation is considered inappropriate, so long as the market value is above cost, and any decline below cost is temporary.

Machinery and equipment–termed "plant and equipment," it is normally shown at cost less depreciation, or like real property mentioned above and unlike U.S. practices, it may be included at "directors" or "independent" valuation in excess of cost, with the increase or decrease taken to an asset revaluation reserve. Depreciation is charged off over the estimated useful life of the property. Factory buildings are not included in plant and equipment.

Depletion (natural resources)–exploration and evaluation costs are written off directly to income, unless costs are expected to be recovered through successful development or sale, or if the activities have not yet lead to estimates of recoverable reserves, in which case they are capitalized. In the production phase, costs are amortized over time, or (preferably) by output.

Investment incentives–incentives are usually given in the form of tax benefits, and are credited on the income statement as a reduction in the tax expense in the period in which the incentive arises.

Purchase of Another Business

In the purchase of another business, the usual treatment is the acquisition method. Beginning in 1985, any excess of the purchase consideration over the fair value of the identifiable assets acquired is purchased goodwill. It is to be recognized as a noncurrent asset at acquisition, and be amortized over the period of time that benefits are expected to arise, not to exceed 20 years.

Discounts on acquisition are to be accounted for by reducing proportionately the fair value of the nonmonetary assets until the discount is eliminated. Where there remains a discount balance after the nonmonetary assets are reduced to zero, it should be classified as a gain, and taken to the profit and loss account.

Consolidation

Consolidated statements are prepared by combining the assets, liabilities, and results of the parent and the subsidiaries, with all intercompany profits and losses and transactions eliminated. Subsidiary companies should be accounted for by the equity method in equity supplementary financial statements, if the parent holds more than half of the issued ordinary shares, or if the parent controls the composition of the Board of Directors.

Provisions

Provisions is used to denote amounts set aside for known liabilities, the amount of which cannot be determined with reasonable accuracy, such as employee and retirement benefits, major repairs and rehabilitation of assets, and for taxes. Provisions are carried as current liabilities, and are not deducted from assets. Estimates for future liabilities are added to the provisions account; when the liability becomes due, it is removed from the provisions account.

Reserves

Reserve accounts are appropriations of profits (or retained earnings) rather than charges against profits. These accounts are not found in U.S. financial statements, and consist of two types, capital reserves and revenue reserves.

Capital reserves are those funds, which for statutory or other legal reasons, not available for distribution through the profit and loss account. This includes such things as premiums on the sale of stock, which is accounted for in the "share premium account."

Other capital reserves include reserves for increased cost of replacement of assets, and capital asset reserves, which arises from a surplus on the revaluation of fixed assets. Also included in this group is goodwill.

Revenue reserves are retentions of distributable profit available for general use in the business that have not been created in accordance with statutory or other legal requirements or policies. Often included in this group is reserves for fluctuations in stock (inventory) value.

Exchange rate variations are included in each of these accounts, depending on which account is affected.

Funds may also be moved between capital reserves and revenue reserves, owing to changing circumstances.

Footnote Disclosure

All footnotes are considered part of the financial statements, and are covered in the auditor's report. Australian accounting policies require a summary of accounting policies to be included in financial statements, and are included in the footnotes. Often, disclosures required by Company Acts are more conveniently put into footnotes, rather than on the main body of the accounts. Such matters usually include the list of subsidiaries and their related information, estimated contingent liabilities of the group, and the aggregate amount of capital expenditures contracted for, but for which no provision is yet required to be made.

Recording of Income

Financial statements are usually prepared annually at June 30, the most common fiscal end-of-year in Australia. All income and expense that arise during that period, regardless of whether they relate to current year activities or prior period activities, are usually included in the current year's profit and loss statement. In general, costs are matched with income.

Differences between taxable and financial income are usual, and are either permanent or timing differences. Permanent differences include investment allowances for expenditures on specified plant and equipment, exempt income, and expenses not deductible for tax purposes. Timing differences would include income and expense items recognized at different times from recognition for tax purposes. Deferred taxes are included under noncurrent liabilities.

Auditors' Report

The Auditors' Report includes the Statement of Financial Position, the Statement of Profit and Notes, the Statement of Sources and Applications of Funds, and the Statement by Directors, plus the additional items listed in the section, *Financial Statements*, above. The auditor must indicate compliance with not only the accounting principles of the profession, but also with the Companies Code for the State in which it is chartered (incorporated).

The accounts for the company and its subsidiaries must be "drawn up in accordance with the provisions of the Companies (name of State} Code," and "properly kept in accordance with the provisions of that Code," and the auditors must so state. The auditors' report must also state that he has examined the accounts, or the reports of other auditors who did examine the accounts (which must be noted in the subsidiaries' information in the footnotes).

The key paragraph in the report states,

> In our opinion, the accounts and Group accounts are properly drawn up in accordance with the provisions of the Companies Code [name of State] Code and so as to give a true and fair view of–
> (i) the state of affairs of the Company and of the Group as at [date] and of the profit/(loss) of the Company and the Group for the year ending on that date so far as they concern the members of the holding company; and
> (ii) the other matters required by Section 269 of that Code to be dealt with in the accounts and in the Group accounts. [emphasis added]

The auditor is required to give a qualified opinion in certain circumstances where approved standards have not been applied.

SUMMARY

In summary, Australian accounting and auditing practices and standards parallel those of the United States, with some significant differences. Statutory requirements are somewhat greater than those of the U.S., while the stock exchange requirements are somewhat less than their U.S. counterparts. The details of the footnotes to the financial statements are much greater, in all probability due to the smaller size of the companies, for if the same detail of information was required in the reports of some U.S. companies, the annual report would fill several volumes.

All in all, someone familiar with U.S. accounting practices and standards would not feel ill at ease with Australian principles and practices.

END OF CHAPTER QUESTIONS

1. Distinguish between hard copy and electronic sources of international financial information. What are some of the advantages of electronic sources of financial information?
2. Describe some of the data included in electronic sources of international financial information.
3. Why is it important to expose U.S. students to cultural, economic, and business practices in other countries?
4. What are the advantages and disadvantages of study-abroad programs?
5. How could electronic sources of databases be used in internationalizing business curricula?
6. Describe the contents of an international accounting course.
7. Why do international accounting courses include a study of accounting and auditing standards and corporate financial reporting practices in selected foreign countries and regions?
8. What is the educational value of assigning to students an independent project that requires research, class presentation, and submission of a written report?
9. Describe the political, legal, economic, business, accounting and auditing systems and practices in Australia. Compare them

with those of the U.S. Identify similarities and differences between Australia and the U.S.

10. Choose a country you have a special interest in. Identify sources of cultural, economic, political, business, and accounting information about this country that are available in the library. Extract financial information about two companies in this country from DISCLOSURE/WORLDSCOPE. Study the information you collected. Compare them with similar information and companies in the U.S. Prepare a presentation outline and written report that summarizes your findings as to similarities and differences between the country you chose and the U.S.

REFERENCES

Agami, A.M. (1983). The International Accounting Course: State of the Art, *Journal of Accounting Education* (Fall), 67-77.

Ameiss, A.P. (1974). International Accounting at the Senior Student Level, *International Journal of Accounting* (Fall), 107-121.

Bomeli, E.C. (1969). Curricular Recognition of International Accounting–An Appraisal, *International Journal of Accounting* (Fall), 85-96.

Brummet, R.L. (1975). Internationalism and the Future of Accounting Education, *International Journal of Accounting* (Fall), 161-165.

Burns, J.O. (1979). A Study of International Accounting Education in the United States, *International Journal of Accounting* (Fall), 135-145.

Choi, F.D.S. (1988). International Data Sources for Empirical Research in Financial Management, *Financial Management* (Summer), 80-98.

Clay, A.A. (1975). Undergraduate International Accounting Education, *International Journal of Accounting* (Fall), 187-192.

Dascher, P., C.H. Smith, and R.H. Strawser. (1973). Accounting Curriculum Implications of the MNC, *International Journal of Accounting* (Fall), 81-97.

Foroughi, T. and B. Reed. (1987). A Survey of the Present and Desirable International Accounting Topics in Accounting Education, *International Journal of Accounting* (Fall), 69-82.

Foutz, P.B. (1975). The Teaching of International Accounting, *Management Accounting* (June), 31-33.

Kubin, K.W. (1973). The Changing Nature of International Accounting Courses, *International Journal of Accounting* (Fall), 99-111.

Mintz, S.M. (1980). Internationalization of the Accounting Curriculum, *International Journal of Accounting* (Fall), 137-151.

Mueller, G.G. (1965). Whys and Hows of International Accounting, *Accounting Review* (April), 386-394.

Pearson, M.A., J.K. Ryan, and L.J. Hicks. (1980). Internationalizing the Accounting Curriculum, *Massachusetts CPA Review* (Nov.-Dec.), 29-30.

Rueschhoff, N.G. (1972). The Undergraduate International Accounting Course, *Accounting Review* (October), 833-836.

Schoenfeld, H. (1974). International Influences On the Contemporary Accounting Curriculum: International Accounting Instruction at the University of Illinois at Urbana-Champaign, *International Journal of Accounting* (Fall), 71-85.

Seidler, L.J. (1967). International Accounting–The Ultimate Theory Course, *Accounting Review* (October), 775-781.

Sherman, W.R. (1987). Internationalizing the Accounting Curriculum, *Journal of Accounting Education* (Fall), 259-275.

Stout, D.E., and J.A. Schweikart. (1989). The Relevance of International Accounting to the Accounting Curriculum: A Comparison of Practitioner and Educator Opinion, *Issues in Accounting Education* (Spring), 126-143.

Index